Border Life

Experience and Memory

in the Revolutionary

Ohio Valley

Border Life

ELIZABETH A. PERKINS

The University of North Carolina Press

Chapel Hill and London

© 1998 The University of North Carolina Press
All rights reserved
Designed by April Leidig-Higgins
Set in Aldus by Keystone Typesetting, Inc.
Manufactured in the United States of America

The paper in this book meets the guidelines for
permanence and durability of the Committee on
Production Guidelines for Book Longevity of the
Council on Library Resources.

Library of Congress Cataloging-in-Publication Data
Perkins, Elizabeth A., 1952–
Border life: experience and memory in the Revolutionary Ohio Valley / Elizabeth A. Perkins.
p. cm.   Contains interviews conducted by the Rev.
John Dabney Shane in the 1840s and 1850s. Based on
the author's dissertation. Includes bibliographical
references and index.
ISBN 0-8078-2400-3 (cloth: alk. paper).
ISBN 0-8078-4703-8 (pbk.: alk. paper)
1. Frontier and pioneer life—Ohio River Valley.
2. Pioneers—Ohio River Valley—Interviews. 3. Ohio
River Valley—History—Revolution, 1775– 1783.
4. Ohio River Valley—Biography. 5. Land settlement—Ohio River Valley—History—18th century.
I. Shane, John Dabney, 1812–1864. II. Title.
F517.P46 1998 977—dc21 97-30009 CIP

02 01 00 99 98   5 4 3 2 1

A large portion of Chapter 3, "Distinctions and Partitions amongst Us," will appear in *Contact Points: North
American Frontiers, 1750–1830*, edited by Fredrika J.
Teute and Andrew R. L. Cayton (Chapel Hill: University
of North Carolina Press for the Omohundro Institute
of Early American History and Culture, 1998).

To the memory of
John Dabney Shane

Contents

Illustrations

Tables

Acknowledgments

A friend whose opinion I value once told me that I was on a fishing expedition in John Shane's settler interviews. Of course he was right. The lure of ordinary women and men attempting to make sense of their own lives within the stream of history was more than I—or perhaps any cultural analyst—could resist. In the process of examining these slippery and often elusive documents I have ranged widely into the preserves of disciplines other than history, and have accrued many debts—both intellectual and personal.

Northwestern University provided generous support for the dissertation research from which this book grew. I would particularly like to thank the Alumnae of Northwestern for naming me a Dissertation Fellow for the academic year 1990–91. The Fort Dearborn Chapter of the National Society of the Daughters of the American Revolution awarded me their American History Award for that same year and I would like to acknowledge their support as well. Timothy H. Breen has been an exemplary adviser. His high standards and unfailing support have earned my deepest respect and gratitude. Robert H. Wiebe has both challenged me and cheered me with his trenchant critiques and continuing friendship. Karen Halttunen, Michael Sherry, Nancy Mac-Lean, and others have also given generously of their time and advice; I have been immensely fortunate to have had such inspiring teachers and history mentors.

Centre College has supported the latter stages of my writing with a Summer Research Grant and a Teagle Faculty Development Grant. I am particularly grateful to the Teagle Foundation for its generous support for junior faculty research. I also thank Dean John Ward for a timely rearranging of my winter term schedule in 1996, which greatly assisted me in the process of revision.

Over the past few years I have presented parts of my research to a number of intellectual communities. John Mack Faragher, Andrew Cayton, James C. Klotter, Stephen Aron, and David Zimand have all read versions of the entire manuscript and have offered many shrewd criticisms and helpful suggestions. Peter Onuf, James Merrell, Fredrika Teute, Daniel Blake Smith, and others have challenged my ideas and encouraged me to persevere. At the University of North Carolina Press, Lewis Bateman, Mary Laur, Katherine Malin, Pamela Upton, Suzanne Comer Bell, and others have handled my manuscript with the highest standards of professional care.

Family and friends have buoyed my spirits and provided material support for my enterprise. In particular, I will never forget the Christmas I received both a microfilm reader and additional memory chips for my computer! In addition to my parents, Betty Perkins and the late Harley T. Perkins, I would like to thank Lucille Severance for her many kindnesses. My husband, Ralph Schiefferle, has been a most caring and supportive companion throughout this long process of research, writing, and revision. I hope that all these supporters of my intellectual odyssey will concur that I have caught sufficient insights from Shane's pioneering effort at oral history to make our expedition worthwhile.

A Note on Editorial Policy

In transcribing his oral interviews into notebooks, John Shane characteristically used a number of abbreviations which I have silently expanded—along with modernizing his punctuation and capitalization—for the sake of clarity. In order to retain clues to contemporary pronunciation, I have in almost all cases retained Shane's spelling and have used the editorial notation [*sic*] only sparingly. In a few instances I have added editorial insertions in square brackets as a convenience to modern readers. Otherwise, I have made every effort to retain John Shane's original phrasing.

John Shane dated very few of his interviews. In the notes, I have estimated the probable decade in which each took place (e.g., 1840s) based on the evidence of surrounding interviews. Where specific years are cited, I have put brackets around dates of interviews that are my estimates. (This follows the system of using brackets in the item list in Appendix A.) Otherwise, the dates are those given by Shane.

Border Life

But to return to our back settlers. I must tell you, that there is something in the proximity of the woods, which is very singular. It is with men as it is with the plants and animals that grow and live in the forests; they are entirely different from those that live in the plains.

CRÈVECOEUR, *Letters from an American Farmer*

Introduction

Since the first eighteenth-century traveler put pen to paper, observers have disagreed about the character of life in the American backcountry. As land seekers pushed west through the Virginia and Pennsylvania uplands into the mountains and rich lands beyond, they became in their critics' eyes a distinctive race, "back-woods men" or "back settlers," a "mongrel breed, half-civilized, half savage," living in squalid huts, and known more for whiskey drinking and eye-gouging than for signs of honest toil. Yet to more sympathetic observers these same settlers were the advance agents of an expanding "republican empire," sturdy yeomen transforming the wooded wastes of Kentucky and Ohio into neat farms and homesteads while struggling to re-create the social and cultural standards of the East.[1]

Two hundred years has not resolved this debate. Recent scholarship continues to oscillate between contested realities, paradigms of regression or progression, ennoblement or ensavagement. For historian Bernard Bailyn, the border was a marchland, "a periphery, a ragged outer margin of metropolitan accomplishment." Peter Onuf's West, on the other hand, was a successful testing ground for the republican experiment, a place toward which American policymakers looked "with mingled expectation and anxiety." To other scholars the frontier has represented variously the cutting edge of capitalism, the last bastion of a precapitalist *mentalité*, and of course, most famously, the birthplace of democracy. Yet by viewing the border primarily as an arena for large historical forces, modern observers have risked looking past the backcountry inhabitants themselves.[2]

This study takes a different approach, one less metropolitan in perspective, but with a more acute angle of vision. My purpose is to view the backcountry not from the perspective of distant elites but instead up close—"from the native's point of view"—through the eyes of common settlers as they reflected upon their own experiences. How did border women and men define their own world? What were the categories—situational, masked, or veiled—through which they bounded their own social spaces? How did they conceptualize their actions or describe themselves in relationship to others? What, to paraphrase anthropologist Clifford Geertz, did backcountry settlers think that they were up to?[3]

Reconstructing the mental world of a border population would at first seem to be an intractable problem. As one historian has recently observed, "common settlers left comparatively little to tell us about their expectations and experiences."[4] But in the case of the Ohio Valley, an extraordinary collection of more than three hundred transcribed oral interviews with surviving early inhabitants suggested a research strategy. The pioneer interviews recorded by the Reverend John Dabney Shane over two decades in Kentucky, Ohio, Pennsylvania, and Illinois (now housed in the Draper Collection of the State Historical Society of Wisconsin) provide not only a vividly detailed picture of everyday life on an American frontier, but also a window into the intimate perceptive universe of ordinary settlers. By employing ethnographic methods and insights in their analysis, this study examines from a plurality of perspectives how border residents made sense of what has often been depicted as an inchoate wilderness environment.

Other historical actors saw things differently, of course, and I have also consulted eighteenth- and early-nineteenth-century manuscripts that document additional or divergent interpretations of border life.

Outside observers, for example, offer a useful point of reference for activities in the backcountry. More than one hundred travelers recorded their journeys in the Ohio Valley between 1740 and 1809; as representatives of metropolitan culture, their impressions provide alternative eyewitness accounts of aboriginal and settler life in an evolving landscape. Native American perceptions of this cultural encounter are more difficult, yet not impossible, to recover in diplomatic proceedings and in the writings of captives, traders, and missionaries to the western country.[5]

Interactions between Euroamerican settlers and native inhabitants lie at the heart of this story. After an opening chapter probing the strengths and limitations of John Shane's interviews as records of cultural perception, succeeding chapters focus on the complex intermingling of peoples and cultures in the late-eighteenth-century Ohio Valley. While the vantage point from which I view this encounter is most often that of the white Europeans, Indian peoples emerge as surprisingly complex and human characters in the minds of pioneer informants. They also stand revealed, I argue, as significant influences in the shaping of trans-Appalachian cultural patterns. Chapter 2 reconstructs the "mental maps" that migrants imposed on their new environment, revealing that it was contact with this other culture, and not just distance from their own, that structured their landscape perceptions and worldview.

Yet Indians and Euroamericans were not the only strangers to encounter one another in the western country. Migrants from a variety of regions and ethnic backgrounds converged on the Ohio Valley in the second half of the eighteenth century, seeking new lands and fresh opportunities. Rather than constituting a monolithic backwoods population, these newcomers often found each other's cultural practices and intimate habits nearly as exotic as those of the Indian peoples they encountered. Chapter 3, on identity, explores how residents—new and old—sorted themselves out, made decisions about each other, and interacted with one another in a dynamic multicultural environment.

Encounters among strangers on the American border also took place under particular historical constraints. Euroamerican occupation of the Ohio Valley was concurrent with, indeed facilitated by, war for independence from Great Britain. As the widening revolutionary conflict engulfed sensitive local arrangements in trade and diplomacy, virtually all cultural categories became subsumed under the larger political division that traced the fault line of border war: immigrant and native. Chapter 4 focuses on the "micro-politics" of the Euroamerican society that took shape in the Kentucky country during the 1770s and 1780s, tracing connections forged by this war between the traditionally separate realms of military and civilian life. Contests among immigrant males for authority and status, staged in fortified stations and on militia campaigns, resulted in a new style of political persuasion (later associated with the democratization of public life), even as the region's economic conditions came to reflect the disparity of wealth found in longer-settled areas to the east.

While the first four chapters are more topical than chronological, Chapter 5 examines the efforts of border residents to give temporal shape and narrative coherence to their lives. Here again, as at many points, contact and conflict with native inhabitants shaped migrants' perceptions. By reference to the lengthy struggle for control of the Ohio Valley, white colonizers created personal and public chronologies based on their wartime experiences. As time passed and wartime hatreds dimmed, a few Native Americans even traveled back to the area to join white borderers in the recollection of a mutual past. Sadly, in the heyday of American expansionism and a prickly "neocolonial" nationalism, history writing did not serve as a healing force. This chapter concludes by sketching the work of early historians and popular authors in reshaping participants' complex oral traditions into a shared national mythology about the character of what one settler suggestively called "Indian times."[6]

In retelling settlers' stories about their westering experiences, I seek not only to make a contribution to the history of a region too long characterized by crude cultural stereotypes, but also to explore the local construction of knowledge and the fashioning and refashioning of historical narratives. By consulting the border residents themselves, as well as their critics, supporters, and adversaries, I hope to shed light on the interpretive process by which experience, filtered through layers of perception, eventually came to be molded into divergent—and radically simplified—historical texts.

Finally, a word about what this study does *not* attempt. In seeking to understand the perceptions and aspirations of ordinary settlers, I offer no apology for their actions. Taking the long view of American history, Anglo-American occupation of the Ohio Valley—like the entire course of European expansion across the continent of North America—came at the expense of Native Americans whose historical voices are just now beginning to be heard. Understanding the tragic consequences of this dispossession from an indigenous perspective has permanently transformed our narratives of western history. There is no going back now to staging the play with only a portion of the actors.[7]

Yet it would be ironic if this new sensitivity to Native American perspectives simply turned the old heroic narrative on its head, if Euroamerican settlers went from being cardboard heroes to cardboard villains without a stop in between. Here, as at many points, I will follow the lead of John Shane's informants: few made any effort to justify their actions beyond the messy complexity of individual or family motivations. It would be left to later (or more distant) authors to craft heroic nationalistic explanations hinging on such themes as "civilization versus savagery" or the "taming of a virgin land." Old settlers, it seems, knew too much about their native opponents—and themselves—to be entirely comfortable with the new world they had brought into being.

Through recollection we recover consciousness of former events.

DAVID LOWENTHAL

My aim has been to get of them, what they themselves know.
And they may not know I will ever see another person.

JOHN DABNEY SHANE

What They Themselves Know

An old farmer living between the ferry turnpike and the mill road was in his field when the young Presbyterian minister came to call. John Dabney Shane recorded the man's reaction to his inquiries about early times: "Wouldn't stop from his corn to talk longer. Unimportant." Yet as Ben Guthrie warmed to his tale—an account of moving to Kentucky in 1783 to settle a frontier outpost—his words filled five closely written pages of the young minister's notebook. On another day, Mrs. Stagg, with "a lively tongue, and a minute recollection," was anxious to speak of her experiences—especially of her memories of an Indian attack on Wheeling in 1777, when "women ran bullits in frying pans . . . and one Scotchman prayed all day." In fact, Shane noted of this overwhelming interview, "the old lady talked so fast, so much of it, so little that I was conversant with," that he determined "to prepare myself, and at some time have a regular siege." But the day never came to return to her. In the early 1840s the pioneer generation of trans-Appalachian settlers was rapidly dying off.[1]

Even as Ben Guthrie and Mrs. Stagg recounted stories of their west-ering experiences, authors were writing the history of Euroamerican settlement in the transmontane West. In crafting their accounts, early chroniclers took scant notice of such ordinary settlers, emphasizing instead dramatic occurrences and the exploits of notable men. Par-tisans boosted or defended the reputations of their chosen favorites among political leaders; armchair adventurers collected old Indian sto-ries and created frontier military heroes of mythic stature.[2] Later his-torians would analyze what they called the "process of frontier expan-sion" and debate its impact on the character of American political institutions. Raised (or reduced) to representative types—hunters, yeomen, or entrepreneurs—backcountry settlers became stock histor-ical figures, roles from which today they still struggle to emerge.[3]

A recent surge of historical interest in the back settlements of early America follows in the wake of several decades of intensive and inno-vative research on the coastal colonies. Heirs more to an eighteenth-century colonial world than a Turnerian vision of an endlessly repli-cating frontier, backcountry historians have explored the relationship of the American periphery to a larger Anglo-American world. In par-ticular, the political negotiation of "revolutionary settlements" in rapidly growing frontier regions has engaged historians of the early republic. Although ethnohistorians continue to emphasize that the American backcountry was an area of cultural interaction between Indians and whites, as well as a zone of ecological transformation, their works have had less impact on what one historian has called the pre-vailing themes of "independence and integration"—the relationship of metropolitan culture to an emerging frontier subculture. Because most of the surviving written evidence comes from elite observers, this historical discourse has tended to privilege elite over nonelite voices; the motivations and aspirations of ordinary settlers remain largely hidden from view.[4]

Reading John Shane's interviews a century and a half later, one is struck by the wealth of detail he recorded about the lives of these largely anonymous backcountry inhabitants. In contrast to his con-temporary Lyman Draper, perhaps the best-known western antiquar-ian, Shane displayed as deep an interest in routine explanation as in the elucidation of particular dramatic events. He betrayed neither a preoccupation with border heroes nor an obvious interpretive agenda. Rather, in more than three hundred interviews and conversations recorded over two decades in Kentucky, Ohio, Pennsylvania, and Illinois, John Shane seemed most interested in "what they themselves know," the historical perceptions of ordinary women and men. His research process might be compared to that of the ethnographer, an anthropologist who "closely observes, records, and engages in the daily life of another culture . . . and then writes accounts of this culture, emphasizing descriptive detail."[5]

John Shane remained a collector, however, never organizing his materials into the history of western settlement and the early Presbyterian Church that he proposed to write. But his interviews survive, an extraordinary ethnographic resource for those attempting to understand cultural patterns of meaning and perception shared by thousands of Americans who poured into the backcountry in the revolutionary era. Although long familiar to western historians, and mined selectively for descriptive or biographical detail, Shane's interviews have yet to be considered as a whole, as texts for cultural analysis—a window into what one author has aptly termed the "alien mentalities of a past people."[6] As the testimony of backcountry settlers, rather than metropolitan travelers or distant elites, Shane's interviews are of exceptional interest—offering rare insight into a perceptual world left largely unexplored by a number of recent studies.

Yet for this source, as for any other, we must consider whose imagined frontier is represented here. In the battle for a mythic past, how is it that these particular voices still may be heard? Whose voices are not heard? Who was not consulted, or did not live long enough to tell her story? Researchers in the past have tended to use Shane's materials uncritically, without reflecting at much length about the hidden assumptions and interpretive underpinnings of these rich, but admittedly problematic, retrospective accounts.[7] Memory is fallible, and many years passed between event and recollection; the impact of intervening experience or external interpretation may be an important consideration in evaluating settlers' observations. In dealing with a "second generation" primary source—one step removed from the informants themselves—we must also ask of these transcribed interviews: under what circumstances were they acquired? Shane, his methods, and his critical judgments play a crucial role here, as a sort of ethnographic alter ego, the anthropologist on the scene whose field notebook by some quirk of fate has entered the archives. What motivated John Shane and how did his expectations help shape the responses he received? This chapter addresses these questions by taking a closer look at Shane, his informants, the subject and scope of his investigations, as well as the strengths and limitations of his materials as artifacts of the alien cultural world of border inhabitants. It also begins an exploration, continued in succeeding chapters, of the complex interaction of perception, memory, oral tradition, and printed accounts in the process of historical interpretation.

The Western Country

The crafting of western history and imagery began with the region's first promoters. "The Ohio is the grand artery of this ultramontane part of America," proclaimed French essayist Hector St. John de Crèvecoeur on a trip west in 1784. "It is the center where meet all the waters which, on the one hand, start from the Allegheny mountains, and which, on the other hand come from the elevated regions in the neighborhood of lakes Erie and Michigan." Although few people living in the Ohio Valley today share a sense of common identity, the watershed of this great western river remained an important regional concept well into the nineteenth century. At the close of the eighteenth century, it comprised nearly three-quarters of the western lands controlled by the new American nation. On the east, long chains of mountains separated the "western waters" from those that drained into the Atlantic Ocean. To the north lay the Great Lakes region, dominated by the powerful Iroquois confederation and the British fur trade; to the south and west resided other populous tribes on lands nominally controlled by Spain. Also to the west lay the Mississippi River, the acknowledged key to the future of western commerce, although closed by Spain to American trade in 1784. Divided from the coastal settlements by a significant geographic barrier, and bounded on three other sides by sovereign interests suspicious of American territorial intentions, the Ohio Valley in the early republican era maintained a distinct regional identity as America's "western country."[8]

The tributaries and waterways draining into the Ohio River define the region's geographic boundaries (Fig. 1). Formed by the confluence of the Allegheny and Monongahela Rivers in western Pennsylvania, the Ohio flows almost a thousand miles in a southwesterly direction before emptying into the Mississippi River at Cairo, Illinois. Geographers divide the lands encompassed by the Ohio River basin—an area

WHAT THEY THEMSELVES KNOW

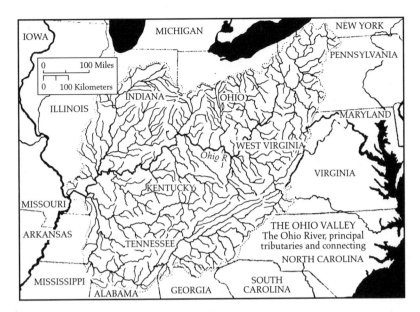

FIGURE 1. The Ohio River Basin.
(Adapted from Jakle, *Images of the Ohio Valley*, 5)

covering most of the present states of Kentucky, West Virginia, Ohio, and Indiana, as well as parts of Maryland, New York, North Carolina, Virginia, Pennsylvania, Illinois, and Tennessee—into three parts. In the upper valley the river rises in the Appalachian Plateau and traverses a rugged topography characterized by foothills, narrow valleys, extensive forest cover, and poor-quality soils. About a third of the way downstream, between the confluence of the Scioto and Licking Rivers, the terrain begins to level out; the river channel bisects the lower valley into two further physiographic provinces. North of the river, Ice Age glaciers deposited deep rich soils on flat to slightly rolling lands; to the south, limestone bedrock underlies a mostly rolling terrain interspersed with forested areas of rugged topography and thin soils. The many tributaries that join the Ohio River during its thousand-mile course define further geographic subregions—known as "countries" in the eighteenth century—within the river basin.

Eighteenth-century inhabitants of the Ohio Valley lived in a dynamic multicultural environment. Contested by European colonial powers and ultimately seized by Anglo-Americans with force, the region was also the territory of numerous Indian tribes, including the Shawnees, Cherokees, Chickasaws, Miamis, Mingos (Ohio Iroquois),

Delawares, and Senecas. A cockpit of competing international interests, the valley also witnessed the convergence of internal migrants from a variety of areas east of the Appalachians. As disparate peoples met and interacted, they shared at least one common interest: the land. The rich soils, the abundant wildlife, "La Belle Rivière" connecting the Great Lakes region with the Mississippi River and the Gulf of Mexico, constituted a coveted strategic and economic prize; contests over its control punctuated the course of the eighteenth century. If the thrust of these events now suggests a certain linearity, an American "manifest destiny," this perception is largely an artifact of later historical understanding. In the complex intermingling of peoples and cultures in the Anglo-Indian border country, fortunes shifted quickly and identities of interest often blurred. What would be the outcome of events in the Ohio Valley was by no means clear at the time.[9]

In the broadest terms, over the course of the eighteenth century the Ohio Valley witnessed a shift from a Native American to an Anglo-American cultural regime. Disease, war, and migration transformed a multicultural frontier environment into a neo-European society. Prior to European contact, areas of the river basin supported dense aboriginal populations, but by the end of the seventeenth century so-called virgin soil epidemics and dispersal of resident Indians by the Iroquois Wars (1641–1701) left the region sparsely inhabited. When the burgeoning population of British America placed pressure on Indians living in the Susquehanna Valley, Shawnee and Delaware villagers—under the nominal control of the Iroquois confederation—gradually repopulated the Ohio country in the 1720s and 1730s. Great Britain and France both claimed sovereignty over the lands along the Ohio River, but so long as the Iroquois were able to "play off" one European power against the other, the Indian confederation maintained an illusion of control. Adding to political and imperial complications were differing cultural conceptions of what it meant to occupy the land. While European diplomats debated territorial sovereignty and negotiated for the sale of Indian lands, Iroquois leaders in New York attempted to speak for semi-independent tribes along the Ohio who had no concept of permanently alienable property. White squatters and resident Indians alike ignored the pronouncements of outside authorities.[10]

By the third quarter of the eighteenth century, treaties and proclamations formally divided the Ohio Valley into Indian and Euroamerican settlement areas. Yet areas of effective control remained, in reality, ambiguous as settlers streamed into the backcountries of Virginia, Maryland, Pennsylvania, and the Carolinas; native inhabitants continued to pursue their seasonal hunting and gathering activities across much of the same geographic expanse. At the conclusion of the Seven Years' War (1756–63), the French ceded sovereignty of their Indian lands to the British, who responded with a "Proclamation Line"—almost immediately breached—restricting Anglo-American settlement west of the crest of the Appalachians. With the Treaty of Fort Stanwix in 1768, British and Iroquois negotiators attempted once again to establish a permanent boundary between Indian and white settlement, this time at the Ohio River. When the Cherokees ceded their claims to lands south of the river by the Treaty of Lochaber (1770), these two agreements effectively opened a large area known as "Kentake," the Iroquois word for prairie land, to British settlement.[11] Disgruntled Shawnee, Delaware, and Iroquois villagers refused to recognize the cession of their valuable hunting territory, and continued to assert their claims with customary subsistence activities and forays against white settlements. Frontiersmen retaliated with raids of their own, taking captives and destroying Indian villages north of the Ohio River.

Anglo-American expansion beyond the Appalachians reached the Kentucky country in the 1770s. White hunters scouted the area as early as 1769, and in 1773 Virginia surveyors mapped out land claims in central Kentucky and at the Falls of the Ohio. Settlers constructed the first frontier outposts, called stations, in the following year, but the outbreak of Dunmore's War delayed their occupation until the spring of 1775. Native Americans watched the invasion of their hunting lands with dismay. A Shawnee man explained to the British Indian agent at Pittsburgh that when the Indians "are disappointed in their hunting, and find the woods covered with the White People, and their horses, where they used to find their Game, they are foolish enough to make reprisals." Virginia surveyor John Floyd also expressed qualms about the numbers of land claimants flowing into the area: "When I consider that the settlement of that land will ruin the hunting ground of the Tawas, Kickapoos, and some other nations, I a little dread the consequences." At treaty negotiations with Virginia's Indian commissioners in 1775, Shawnee diplomats blamed the widening conflict on hot-headed young warriors from both sides: "Your young men coming so near to us and destroying our Deer and other Game may have occasioned some of our foolish people to have stole your horses and other Effects[,] which far from being unresented by you[,] your young Men have for doing it killed our people." In a letter signed by six of their most respected leaders, the Shawnees called for a return to a lasting friendship and a mutually beneficial trade.[12]

The forces of peace did not prevail. Dunmore's War marked the beginning of a lengthy border war (1774–94) over the permanence of the Ohio River as a boundary between Indian and Anglo-American settlement. Partially concurrent with and fueled by the American Revolution, the war for the western country burned hottest during the years 1774, 1777–82, and 1786–94. As white settlers and their black slaves poured into Kentucky and squatted on Indian lands in southern Ohio, the primary military theater shifted north of the river boundary. Armies of U.S. regulars and Kentucky militiamen marched deep into the Indian country, destroying towns of the Miami, Delaware, Shawnee, Wea, Piankeshaw, and other western tribes. Native Americans continued their forays against Kentucky and Ohio settlements throughout the period as well. After suffering two disastrous defeats in 1790 and 1791, U.S. forces finally achieved victory over a confederacy of western Indians at the Battle of Fallen Timbers, near the shores of Lake Erie, in 1794. With the Treaty of Greenville in the following year, the Indian confederacy formally abandoned its struggle to maintain the Fort Stanwix treaty line of 1768, and ceded most of the Ohio country to the U.S. government.[13]

Forty-five years later John Shane began interviewing surviving white settlers of the revolutionary-era Ohio Valley. Although his fieldwork took place primarily in central Kentucky and southern Ohio, Shane's effective area of interest filled a much broader canvas, stretching east to the Blue Ridge Mountains and west to the Illinois country and Missouri, as the migrants he interviewed recalled the breadth of their geographic horizons: all had come from somewhere else, many had family and friends who had moved farther on. Following Shane's lead then, this study is primarily an account of the settlement of Kentucky and southern Ohio, or perhaps more accurately, of the settlement of the "western country": an area of soft geographic focus, but distinctive cultural identity, which only partially conformed to the later boundaries of the states of Kentucky and Ohio. It is also a story about how people perceive and communicate their own history.

The Reverend John Dabney Shane remains a relatively obscure member of a large fraternity of nineteenth-century American collectors who attempted to salvage the papers and memories of the revolutionary generation. Driven by filiopietistic enthusiasms, the imperatives of a new "scientific" history based on documentary research, as well as a keen sense of personal competition, historians and antiquarians of this era scoured attics, clipped autographs, and pursued old settlers. By the 1830s, the frenzied hunt for original manuscripts on both sides of the Atlantic was termed "bibliomania," a "crazed fixation" on documents which seemingly had to be possessed at all costs. While the obsessions of these early collectors now seem quaint to those of us living in an age of microforms, copiers, and on-line data banks, their acquisitions form the genesis of some of the most important manuscript collections in the country, including the Library of Congress and the American Antiquarian Society. Patient men who lived longer acquired the collections of their competitors: upon his death the bulk of Shane's pioneer interviews fell into the hands of Lyman Copeland Draper and, thus, to the State Historical Society of Wisconsin where they were later read by, among others, Frederick Jackson Turner.[14]

As a historical figure, John Dabney Shane remains elusive. Ironically, for the researcher interested in Shane himself, his massive manuscript collection contains few personal papers which shed light on his motivations and inspirations to become a western collector. He was born in Cincinnati, Ohio, in 1812, the second of five children of John Shane (1785–1850) and Mary Cosby Shane (1782–1844). A biographical sketch written shortly after his death claimed that from his earliest years, Shane "revealed a passion for collecting and hoarding" materials on the early West. His first contact with border stories may have come from family accounts he heard as a child: Shane's maternal grandfather, Zacharias Cosby, served in the Revolutionary War from Louisa County, Virginia; his paternal grandfather, Henry Shane, kept a tavern in Hagarstown, on the frontier of western Maryland. John Shane's interest in religious and moral concerns shared familial roots: his older brother, physician Charles Grandison Shane (b. 1809), traveled to Liberia in 1832 with twenty-one Kentucky blacks under the auspices of the American Colonization Society.[15]

Shane's Presbyterian education was his most significant intellectual influence, however. Church tradition stressed the ideal of a learned ministry and an educated laity; during the revolutionary era, Presbyterians actively participated in the founding of colleges to train new citizens for republican society. In developing a revised "republican curriculum" to meet the needs of an informed citizenry, Presbyterian educators expanded the traditional course of classical subjects to include an increased emphasis on the study of history, natural sciences, and mathematics. They vigorously defended free inquiry and the empiricist tradition of Scottish "common sense" philosophy against charges that it led to skepticism and atheism. In the early years of the nineteenth century, Presbyterians turned their attention to denominational education. Shocked by two major schisms in the wake of the Great Revival of 1800, and a new evangelical style of preaching which depended more on emotional appeals than on erudition, Presbyterians established theological seminaries in New Jersey and Virginia to offer rigorous training to their own clergy; candidates sometimes spent more than a decade in fulfilling their educational requirements. Although critics have viewed Presbyterian schools of this era as stagnating centers of orthodoxy, Presbyterians perceived that they battled skeptic and enthusiast alike. Educators struggled to implement the social ideal of both a learned and a pious ministry.[16]

Combining breadth of interest with critical scholarly inquiry, John Shane's training at two of these Presbyterian institutions left him well prepared for undertaking empirical research. As an undergraduate he attended Hampden-Sydney College, founded in 1776 and named self-consciously for two heroes of the English Civil War; in the nineteenth century, the south-side Virginia school stressed a traditional belief in a well-rounded education with an emphasis on languages. In 1831, at the age of nineteen, Shane entered Union Theological Seminary at Hampden-Sydney. There he read the Old and New Testaments and related texts in their original languages of Hebrew, Greek, and "Chaldean," and studied the new "higher" biblical criticism and the principles of exegesis, including inquiries concerning the genuine, or original text. He also attended lectures on theology, church and civil history, and biblical antiquities (archaeology), and regularly practiced the composition and delivery of sermons. After completing his studies at Union, Shane received a license from the Cincinnati Presbytery in May 1842. Moving to the West Lexington Presbytery in Kentucky, he received ordination there in 1845.[17]

Despite his religious schooling, John Shane remained essentially secular in his intellectual orientation. He declined permanent pastoral office and served instead as a "domestic missionary," traveling to a variety of Kentucky and southern Ohio congregations until his death in 1864. Shane's missionary activities, which might be compared to those of a Methodist circuit rider, gave him ample opportunity to conduct his own research. After preaching to a local congregation, he visited in the neighborhood interviewing older residents and seeking references to others. A few of Shane's manuscript sermons from these journeys survive. On each he carefully noted the multiple locations, often eight or nine, where he delivered an address; the sites correspond closely with the locations of many settlers' interviews.

Evidence suggests that John Shane performed his ministerial duties conscientiously, but that his passion lay in historical collecting. He apparently perceived no conflict between these two avocations. In a sermon on the duties of the clergy, Shane observed that "a minister, as a citizen, may be a warrior, a statesman, a philosopher, but as a minister, clothed with spirit functions, he is to render to Caesar the things that are Caesar's, and to God, the things that are God's." In notes for a prayer meeting, Shane posed the question of how one might grow in personal piety. His answer: "We must *know* more." In order to grow in grace, he explained, individuals should grow in knowledge. In a sermon on education, Shane similarly observed that "Presbyterians always have been the promoters of a sound, thorough education. So literally true is this," he added, "that whenever you find one that is not to the highest notch on this point, you may set it down, he departs from his system." At a time when the study of history was just emerging as a discrete academic discipline, the generous intellectual vision of the Presbyterian Church easily encompassed Shane's research activities within his larger ministerial role.[18]

Shane lived a scholar's life, surrounded by his books, notes, and manuscripts. A visitor to his rooms in Cincinnati observed that they were "shelved all around from floor to ceiling, divided and subdivided by partitions" for his historical collections. Pamphlets (arranged by subjects and then by years), newspapers, magazines, and reviews all had their proper location and identification. Shane stored his most precious primary materials near his bed: "*this* one he got from an old lady whose grandchild he had been off some fifteen or twenty miles into the country to baptize; *that* one was secured from the wreck of some fam-

FIGURE 2. John Dabney Shane (1812–1864), ca. 1850s.
Albumen print, stamped on back with an internal revenue stamp, 1865;
probably an enlargement from a daguerreotype. (Courtesy of the Department
of History, Presbyterian Church [U.S.A.], Philadelphia)

ily that 'had seen better days'; and *that* he obtained at a funeral, hunting with the zeal of a trapper through the garrets and cocklofts of the disconsolate mansion." A correspondent of Lyman Draper's met Shane in the 1840s and wrote that he appeared "in delicate health and of very feeble constitution"; yet a photograph, probably taken in the early

1850s, shows him in apparently robust form, with glossy dark hair, a medium build, and a piercing expression (Fig. 2). Although John Shane never married, friends described him as a genial companion and an engaging conversationalist. He died in Cincinnati in 1864 at the age of fifty-one. His death in midwinter from an "inflammation of the lungs" suggests a modern diagnosis of influenza or pneumonia, or possibly tuberculosis, the greatest killer of nineteenth-century Americans.[19]

Perhaps the best index of John Shane's intellectual interests can be found in his extensive personal library. Auctioned after his death for about $3,000, the library's sale catalog ran to forty-eight pages and more than sixteen hundred listings; several thousand pamphlets and a large collection of unbound newspapers were too numerous to detail. Comparable in size then to a small college library, Shane's personal holdings combined a generalist's interest in comprehensive knowledge with specialists' collections in religion and history. A brief review of its titles suggests a man with a lively curiosity about the totality of human experience. In addition to his large collection of historical manuscripts, Shane owned more than four hundred works on American history and politics, three hundred volumes of theology and church history, and numerous works on science and natural history, medicine, biography, travel, geography, poetry, and fiction. An avid bibliophile, he possessed 336 library and trade sale catalogs, as well as a number of dictionaries and technical aids. Mirroring one of the popular obsessions of his day, Shane owned thirty works on Freemasonry and other secret societies.[20]

Mass communications media attracted Shane's attention as well. The auctioneer's sale catalog advertised a large collection of reviews, magazines, and newspapers which included "samples of most of the Religious, Literary, Scientific and Political . . . periodicals that have been published in this country during the present century." Such ephemeral publications proliferated in the years after the Revolution, as a sharp rise in basic literacy and a dramatic increase in the availability of printed goods brought public communications to an ever-wider audience. Shane kept himself thoroughly acquainted with contemporary events; he spent many hours clipping newspapers and pasting broadsides into scrapbooks. At least six of his scrapbooks survive, purchased by Lyman Draper at auction in September 1864. While four contain news or household hints of general interest, two suggest a more coherent collecting theme, and a possible clue to the immediate inspiration for Shane's settler interviews.[21]

Accounts of the passing of the revolutionary generation filled American print media in the 1830s and 1840s. "Another Patriot of the Revolution Gone," read one newspaper headline, as a broadside reported the death of yet another of Washington's men (Fig. 3). In western newspapers, a palpable sense of declension greeted the demise of early settlers, many of whom had fought as soldiers in the Revolutionary War. Comparing the former era with his own, one writer confessed that "the moral of this age . . . has to the eye of an older time . . . something of a dandy look." The tombs of the heroes did not speak to the rising generation, he feared, as he quoted an imaginary exchange with a "stripling which the yell of a Shawanee would annihilate." "Heroes indeed," exclaimed the youth. "Yes! youth, Heroes. . . . The lives of these men were devoted to drive towards the setting sun the savages and prepare your rich heritage. They were the men of your heroic age."[22]

Contemporary political events fueled public nostalgia. As early as 1822, Ralph Waldo Emerson feared that the best days of the Republic were over. The country had moved from "strength, to honour, . . . & at last to ennui," he lamented. Still suffering from the lingering financial effects of the Panic of 1837, Americans cast their ballots in record numbers in the presidential election of 1840, which pitted frontier military hero and Whig William Henry Harrison against New York Democrat Martin Van Buren. With songs, slogans, pageants, and printed media, Whig Party managers skillfully manipulated popular frontier images of log cabins and plain living to suggest that their candidate would never betray the accomplishments of the Revolution as had his opponent, the incumbent Van Buren. Yet Harrison, elected by a wide margin of both popular and electoral votes, served only one month in office, dying of pneumonia on April 4, 1841. Another patriot was gone.[23]

Press accounts of this pervasive historical nostalgia made a deep impression on John Shane, as he filled two large scrapbooks with more than three hundred such articles published between 1835 and 1849. Shane's clippings included the obituaries of revolutionary soldiers and border heroes, recollections of "frontier scenes," and reports of a variety of historical activities including the semi-centennial celebrations of western towns, the publication of written histories, and the forma-

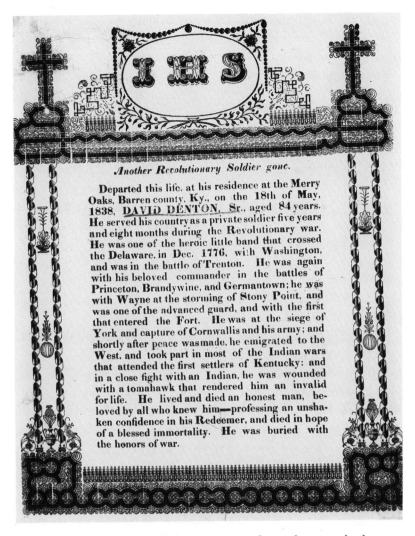

Another Revolutionary Soldier gone.

Departed this life, at his residence at the Merry Oaks, Barren county, Ky., on the 18th of May, 1838, DAVID DENTON, Sr., aged 84 years. He served his country as a private soldier five years and eight months during the Revolutionary war. He was one of the heroic little band that crossed the Delaware, in Dec. 1776, with Washington, and was in the battle of Trenton. He was again with his beloved commander in the battles of Princeton, Brandywine, and Germantown; he was with Wayne at the storming of Stony Point, and was one of the advanced guard, and with the first that entered the Fort. He was at the siege of York and capture of Cornwallis and his army; and shortly after peace was made, he emigrated to the West. and took part in most of the Indian wars that attended the first settlers of Kentucky: and in a close fight with an Indian, he was wounded with a tomahawk that rendered him an invalid for life. He lived and died an honest man, beloved by all who knew him—professing an unshaken confidence in his Redeemer, and died in hope of a blessed immortality. He was buried with the honors of war.

FIGURE 3. Printed broadside, 1838. (From John D. Shane scrapbook, ca. 1835–45, Draper Mss., 27 CC 84, neg. WHi [x3] 51221, State Historical Society of Wisconsin)

tion of state and local historical societies. A theme running through many of these accounts was that time was drawing short to preserve the memories of the founding generation. In an article recalling the deeds of General Charles Scott—revolutionary soldier, Indian fighter, and former Kentucky governor—one writer warned: "We have had remarkable men in almost every State, whose sayings and doings deserve to be remembered, and transmitted to future times; but which now only exist in the memory of their acquaintances." Another author reported that General John Armstrong, in his eighty-fourth year, was "still in the full possession of his uncommon faculties. . . . one of the few remaining links that connect us with the men of other days, with the heroic race of the Revolution." A similar article described a final visit to Simon Kenton, "The Last of the Pioneers."[24]

Perhaps inspired by the urgency of these accounts, John Shane set out in December 1840 to interview surviving Ohio Valley settlers. Writing home about six weeks later, he reported to his brother that he had thought to be in Kentucky long before, but was having such success that he would winter in Ohio. "Since I saw you, I have written in the book you sent me near 6,000 lines, besides rode some 150 miles, and made many visits. . . . You can form no idea of how absorbing & enthusiastic a nature my present pursuit is, especially as is sped on by uninterrupted success." Admitting to some homesickness, the twenty-eight-year-old Shane sent greetings to other family members and added that he had collected "a considerable box of books."[25]

Over the next twenty years, John Shane crisscrossed the Ohio Valley countryside, recording interviews and conversations with more than three hundred informants on backcountry life. As his interview notes mounted, Shane organized his materials into twenty-nine notebooks which he divided into seventeen volumes of "Historical Collections" and twelve volumes of "Collections in Church History" (see Appendix A). Each notebook contained a variety of research materials: interviews, memoranda, copies of manuscripts, lists of books, and information gleaned from publications. He also collected numerous original manuscripts including letters, diaries, church records, and court documents. The first three volumes of Shane's historical collections date principally from the early 1840s and contain the bulk of his settler interviews. As time passed and eyewitness informants died off, Shane filled later volumes with oral traditions supplied by the sons and daughters of pioneers, or by those who had taken an interest in local history. He also increasingly turned his attention to the history of the Presbyterian Church and to the events and controversies surrounding the Great Revival at Cane Ridge, Kentucky, in 1800.[26]

Nostalgia alone cannot fully explain John Shane's extraordinary enterprise. While his initial inspiration may have come from the filiopietistic appeals of the antebellum press, Shane's research methodology suggests the more deliberate undertaking of the natural scientist:

the systematic gathering of data by a man of academic training. What intrigues the modern researcher about Shane's archival project is that he went beyond the acquisition of already-existing documents—so fashionable in his time—to record his own oral histories. Even more remarkable, in light of the nineteenth-century fashion for the grand narratives of national and imperial history, was his interest in the activities of ordinary people. Recognizing that most ordinary settlers would leave behind few written records, Shane labored to save their humble stories for posterity at a time when Founding Fathers and Revolutionary War heroes strode more confidently across the pages of history.[27]

Classic ethnographic accounts written in the early twentieth century painted a similar picture of a vanishing world threatened by the forces of modernism. Anthropologist Bronislaw Malinowski lamented in 1921 that just as "men fully trained for the work have begun to travel into savage countries and study their inhabitants—these die away under our very eyes." It perhaps strains analogy to view John Shane—working decades before the emergence of professional ethnography—as a sort of salvage anthropologist, but his methods do bear some connection to an earlier generation of fieldworkers—missionaries, travelers, and traders—who also gathered and transmitted information about other cultures. Yet John Shane was more than just a traveler or an outside observer: he viewed border life with both an insider's and an outsider's eye. Shane immersed himself in the vanishing cultural world of Ohio Valley settlers through two decades of intensive research, yet retained by and large the more neutral observational stance of a cultural relativist. Moving between the very different worlds of the eighteenth-century backcountry settler and nineteenth-century midwestern cleric, his approach was instinctively ethnographic, even if his training was not.[28]

The subtle interplay of romanticism and empiricism which guided Shane's fieldwork is evident in his record of an 1856 research trip to southwestern Kentucky. The ostensible purpose of this journey was to identify the grave of David Rice (1733–1816), the "Father" of Kentucky Presbyterianism, an outspoken advocate of the abolition of slavery and a delegate to the state constitutional convention of 1792. As the trip progressed, Shane amassed information on an astonishing variety of topics. He scrutinized the cultural and physical landscape, describing in detail roads and landmarks such as "Bear Wallow" in

Barren County where early hunters came to kill bear at the "little ponds of water that the bear loved to play in." He collected artifacts as well, prodding a host for the gift of an Indian axe, querying a road crew about fossil remains, and collecting mineral samples as his buggy paused at a creek ford. His energy and enthusiasm seemed boundless. Upon locating David Rice's gravesite, Shane recorded the inscriptions of all the surrounding tombstones. He also copied local church records, Rice's will, and the early court records in three county courthouses. Along the way, Shane interviewed over a dozen people about local history and the details of Rice's burial, and found one "pioneer, of whom I found I could get information, and I promised to call upon him."[29]

Historical Conversations

Recorded over a span of two decades, Shane's pioneer interviews vary considerably in form and content. They range from a few lines documenting a brief conversation to more than thirty-one pages of notes taken down over several days' time. Most are several pages in length, however, and usually contain a brief introductory comment about the informant and the location where the interview took place. Not all accounts are dated, although some missing dates can be construed from internal evidence. Shane organized the first two volumes of his "Historical Collections" by county in Kentucky; his third volume contains interviews from both Kentucky and Ohio and may actually represent his earliest work. The transcripts which appear in Shane's bound notebooks are probably fair copies, written out at some time after the actual interview took place.

Except for the brief memoranda, most interviews took the form of verbal autobiographies dictated to Shane. As with any oral history enterprise, however, they actually represented a dialogue between interviewer and informant, a "shared authority" between the researcher and his source.[30] Shane left some clues about how this dialectic took place. After taking notes and transcribing an interview into his notebook, Shane revisited the informant to read the interview back and record any corrections or additions that he or she might have to offer (Fig. 4). Some elderly settlers, like the bedridden Jane Stevenson (see Appendix B), obviously died before Shane could make a return trip. Others, like Andrew Thompson, heartily approved of what they heard. Shane noted in his interview with Thompson that the "old man,

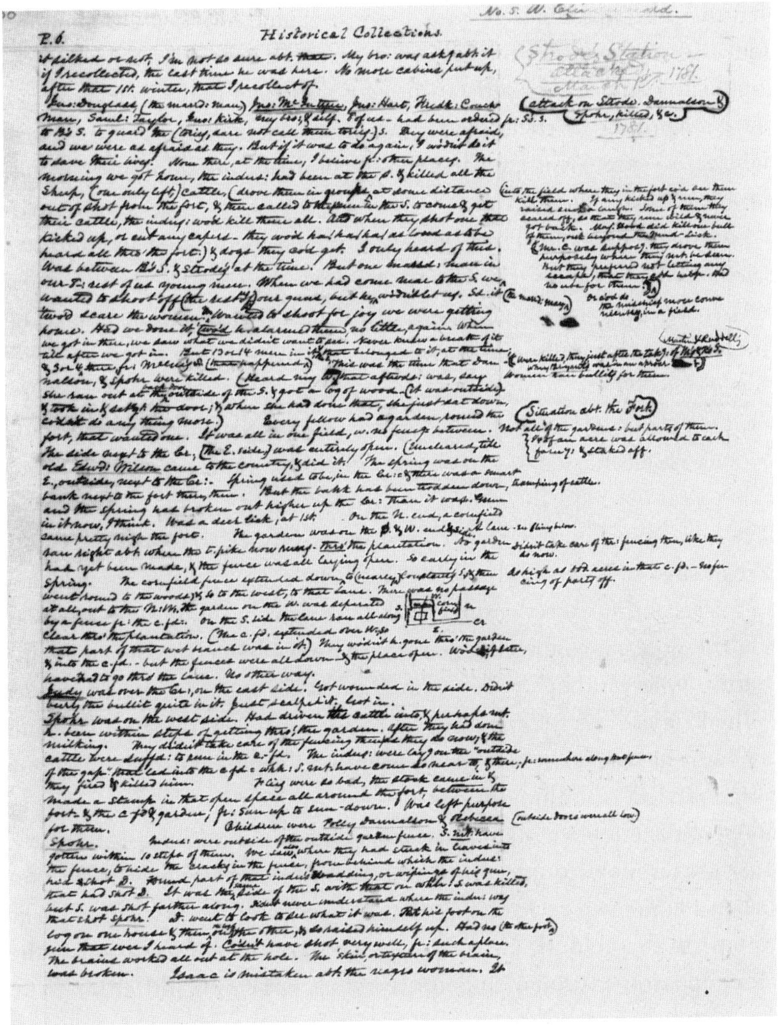

FIGURE 4. Page from John D. Shane's interview with William Clinkenbeard (1760?–1843), ca. 1841–43. Note Shane's record of Clinkenbeard's amplifications and corrections in the right-hand margin. (Draper Mss., 11 CC 56, neg. WHi [x3] 51222, State Historical Society of Wisconsin)

just married to a young girl," was "quite certain of his statement, when I had read it to him, and very enthusiastic." However, on another occasion Shane failed to repeat a story to suit its narrator. "Rankins being a swearing man, he noticed my leaving out the swearing part of McMullen's story," Shane noted. "I read it over to him, after it was written out, and wouldn't repeat that. He thought I ought to have put that in." But Shane *had* recorded "by J—s" and "by G-d" in his note-book. Reflecting later on what had occurred, he observed that "as men supply the smaller circumstances of a narrative" they often recite a story according to their own conceptions of how it should be; "so habitual swearers think no sentence smooth and euphonious, which is not filled up in their style."[31]

Some material that John Shane recorded obviously made him un-comfortable. What seems even more remarkable than his willingness to write it down, however, was his informants' equanimity in sharing the often earthy humor of backwoods raconteurs with a Presbyterian clergyman. When Shane interviewed Josiah Collins in 1841, for exam-ple, the settler related old gossip about the paternity of one of Daniel Boone's children. As the story went, when Boone returned home after a two-year absence, there was a new child in the cradle. " 'Oh well!' says he, 'whose is it?' 'Why, it's Brother Squire's,' replied his wife. 'Well,' says he, 'one of the name is all the same'; and so hushed her up." A second story concerned Boone's daughter Susan. The details of this anecdote are slightly hazy, because Shane left a blank in the man-uscript, where probably the word "cuckold" should have appeared. "When Hays came to Boone for his daughter, Boone told him it would not suit, she would — him. Hays wavered all apprehensions, and they were married. The thing was realized. Hays came and complained to Boone. Boone replied, didn't I tell you she would — you. Trot father, trot mother, how could you expect a pacing colt." Shane noted that "when I expressed to Mr. Collins my surprise at Boone's injustice to himself in this remark, he reminded me that Boone was raised in the backwoods of Carolina, that those times were very different from these, and that such things then were not what they now would be." Collins added that he had met Boone's daughter Susan at Boones-borough and found her "a clever, pretty, well-behaved woman. These were stories that were in circulation, and not anything that I saw." Shane concluded of this exchange, "And yet Mr. Collins would not deny but he believed them true."[32]

Besides a gritty determination to persevere, Shane brought to his interviews critical scholarly skills. Training in languages, for exam-ple, helped him to appreciate—and attempt to capture—the provincial idiom of local speakers. As he noted in his interview with Josiah Col-lins: "The above is taken in very near verbatim, Mr. Collins' own language; he being able to dictate very deliberately, and at the same time correctly." Written down one hundred years before the use of magnetic tape recordings, Shane's interview notes, of course, are not direct transcriptions. But they do preserve patterns of speech and usage which suggest Shane's sensitivity to the form as well as the content of settlers' recollections.[33]

In recording Mrs. John Arnold's statement, for example, Shane retained colloquial expressions which lent great immediacy to her account. Arnold arrived in Kentucky in 1781 from Fauquier County, Virginia. A time of relative peace, "there was not a stick amiss then" between Lexington and Gilbert's Creek Station, where her party rested for a time. But "Jimmy Arnold, my brother in law, told us we could get no meat on Gilbert's Creek, and we would be just exposed to the Indians," she said, relating that they soon moved on to Bryan's Station where Arnold had "raised bread" the year before. Buffalo came into the cornfield, she recalled, and they collected their wool: "We had hemp seed . . . and if I would sow up a sheet and give them, my two boys would bring me in some wool. It was right fine. Wove coverlids." Arnold also remembered an Indian attack: "Huky Lay went out to carry the horse out to grass for a while. . . . The grass was fine out a piece from the fort and the horse could easily fill himself. As he came back, he was shot in the calf of the leg—the ball went through the heart of his horse, which ran about 60 yards, and fell dead." Shane used punctuation marks and phonetic spellings to help reproduce Arnold's pronunciation and verbal emphasis: "The first moonlight night in March, you would hear the men hollowing out, boys! put up your horses, if you don't the Indians will get them." Although Shane's notes are clearly a complex mixture of abridgement and direct quotation, they nevertheless offer tantalizing glimpses of the oral storytelling culture of his backcountry informants.[34]

Shane's training in textual criticism led him to reflect at length upon the quality of his historical evidence. Recognizing that "there is an open contest, here, between truth and fancy: history and fiction," in the oral accounts that he collected, Shane often noted the circumstances surrounding an interview and any mitigating circumstances which might have influenced its outcome. He recorded, for example, that Mrs. Shanklin, a widow with a failing memory, "was assisted to converse by her son, a lawyer in Nicholasville." Josiah Collins used "a book, with Boone's piece in it, *Filson's*—to assist him in dates." Shane "might have had another sitting" with a Cincinnati woman, "but she seemed of so lively an imagination, my confidence flagged." A careful scholar, Shane took pains not to influence his sources' information, explaining at one point, "Seldom have mentioned names or alluded to the knowledge of the persons I was talking with to what any other person had been telling me. My aim has been to get of them, what they themselves know. And they may not know I will ever see another person." On rare occasions Shane did intervene with a question or a prompting remark, as when he noted that he had visited Collins "after I had seen Schull and Sudduth, and some remarks are in allusion to my conversation about their statements."[35]

The most salient quality that John Shane brought to his work was an open mind. Schooled in the empiricist tradition of Scottish "common sense" philosophy, Shane based his research principally on observation and the gathering of data rather than on any preconceived theory of history—including providential explanations of historical causation. "The patient acquisition of the simple facts is the clue to the true spirit of the times: they are that spirit itself," he reflected at one point. Shane's interviews are rich sources of ethnographic data precisely because he was willing to listen to the commonplace and the everyday as well as the dramatic event, because he sought information from the illiterate farmer as well as the local magnate. In contrast to Lyman Draper, who often plied his informants with long lists of questions about specific battles or border heroes, John Shane allowed his narrators to construct their own stories. He may have doubted some of their embellishments or details, but the historical agenda was, by and large, theirs and not his. Thus Shane's interviews are doubly significant, not only for the wealth of cultural detail that they record, but also because they document the efforts of ordinary women and men to make sense of their own lives within the stream of history.[36]

Back Settlers

From Shane's notes a portrait of his backcountry informants gradually emerges. Its lineaments are perhaps not as clear, nor as representative, as one could wish: Shane was by no means a modern quantitative historian, and his eyewitness informants—chosen for survival, proximity, or simple willingness to converse—did not represent a scientific sample of backcountry inhabitants. Most certainly, the group he interviewed was disproportionately white and male. In 1790, for example, one in six Kentuckians was an African American, yet Shane identified none of his informants as being black. Nor did he interview any native inhabitants of the Ohio Valley, although an estimated 10,000 Shawnee, Delaware, Munsee, Mingo, Piankeshaw, Miami, and Wea lived just north of the Ohio River at the time of the Treaty of Fort Stanwix. Female settlers achieved better, although still not equal, representation in Shane's archives. Out of almost four hundred informants' names appearing in the pages of Shane's notebooks, at least fifty were those of women. These are, however, far from crippling problems in using Shane's materials. Social historians have had years of experience in reading between the lines of historical documents for traces of nonhegemonic social groups; African Americans, Indians, and women all left identifiable traces in Shane's archives as well. Although a precise statistical analysis of Shane's informants is impossible due to the irregularity of his data, some generalizations can be made about their geographic origins, age, religion, and economic standing.[37]

Between a third and a quarter of Shane's informants revealed information sufficient to identify their immediate or ultimate origins (Table 1). Of these, more than half resided west of the Blue Ridge before moving to the Ohio Valley, a third came from piedmont areas, and only 9 percent came from the tidewater or coastal plain. Located within political rather than geographic boundaries, almost half of Shane's informants migrated from Virginia, a quarter came from Pennsylvania, and one in nine had lived in two or more colonies or states, usually Virginia, Pennsylvania, or Maryland. The rest came from North Carolina, Maryland, New Jersey, New England, New York, or Ireland. Eleven settlers mentioned parents or grandparents who had migrated from Europe: Ireland (5), Scotland (2), "Scotch Irish" (1), England (2), Holland (2), and Poland (1). These figures are generally consistent with what is currently known about the geographic origins of Kentucky and southern Ohio settlers.[38]

Age is an important consideration in evaluating informants' testimony about backcountry life. By the early 1840s, many of the original Ohio Valley settlers had died; most of the survivors that Shane interviewed were either children or young adults when they migrated west. Of Shane's eyewitness informants—those who lived in the Ohio Valley before 1800—120 supplied information about their date of birth, date of arrival, age at arrival, or age at the time of their interview. Forty-two settlers mentioned their date of birth (Table 2). Slightly

TABLE 1. Geographic Origins of John Shane's Informants

Origins	Percentage
By geographic region	
Tidewater/coastal plain	9.2
Piedmont	32.2
West of Blue Ridge	55.2
Moved between two regions	3.4
Total responses (N=87)	
By political boundaries	
Virginia	45.0
Pennsylvania	22.9
Moved between two colonies/states	11.9
North Carolina	5.5
Maryland	4.6
New Jersey	3.7
Ireland	2.8
Vermont	0.9
Massachusetts	0.9
Connecticut	0.9
New York	0.9
Total responses (N=109)	

Note: Out of 389 informants counted in John Shane's surviving notebooks, 111 gave sufficient information to locate their immediate or ultimate origins. Variable response patterns account for the discrepancy between geographic and political designations.

over half of these were born before 1770, old enough to have personal memories of the early settlement era. The rest were children or even infants during the 1770s and 1780s, their accounts offering a more limited range of autobiographical information and including more oral tradition acquired from parents or other adults.

More than one hundred settlers mentioned their date of arrival (Table 3). Two-fifths reached the Ohio Valley during the first decade of settlement (1775–85), one-third came between 1785 and 1789, and one-quarter arrived during the 1790s. Cross-referencing informants' birth dates with their dates of arrival yields their ages at arrival (Table 4). Including those informants who reported in passing that they had been children, were married, or had served in the militia at the time of their arrival, we can estimate that over half of Shane's eyewitness informants were fifteen years or older when they arrived in the Ohio

TABLE 2. Dates of Birth of John Shane's Informants (N=42)

Year of Birth	Percentage
Before 1760	9.5
1760–64	14.3
1765–69	28.5
1770–74	16.7
1775–79	11.9
1780–84	14.3
After 1784	4.8

Note: Tables 2 through 5 are based on information supplied to John Shane by 120 eyewitness informants who arrived in the Ohio Valley before 1800.

Valley. This information further supports the supposition that many settlers were old enough to have personal memories of the crucial experiences of migration and initial occupation.

In a critical appraisal of John Shane's interviews, the memories of children must be considered hearsay evidence. Often an informant signaled a shift from personal observation to family tradition by using a phrase such as "my father said," or "it was believed"; fortunately, Shane's transcriptions retain many of these subtle changes in tone and language which help us to evaluate the speakers' own knowledge of a particular circumstance. Children's memories also offer valuable insights of their own. Almost sixty years after the event took place, William Niblick recalled in vivid detail the shooting of a neighbor. "I stood at the little gate, having hold of my mother's apron, and heard the women crying; and directly I saw them bring in Wymore in a sheet that was all bloody, hanging on a pole. I recollect the women had gathered, and there seemed to be trouble and confusion." To modern readers, many of Shane's informants seem strangely matter-of-fact as they narrate horrifying accounts of carnage and destruction. Perhaps it is through the eyes of a young child, confronting death for the first time, that we best grasp the emotional impact of the random brutality of border life.[39]

Another common objection to the use of retrospective interviews is that informants were simply too old to supply reliable recollections. In the 1930s, the Federal Writers' Project of the Works Progress Administration interviewed former slaves who were asked to recall events that occurred seventy or eighty years earlier; for years, doubts about

TABLE 3. Dates of Arrival of John Shane's Informants (N=110)

Year of Arrival	Percentage
1775–79	14.5
1780–84	25.5
1785–89	32.7
1790–94	22.7
1795–1800	4.5

the reliability of these sources left them virtually untapped by historians. Only in the past few decades have scholars turned to these remarkable narratives to help reconstruct slaves' perceptions of antebellum plantation life.[40] John Shane's backcountry informants were similarly advanced in age, although perhaps not quite so old as the former slaves interviewed during the 1930s (Table 5). Of thirty-eight settlers who supplied sufficient information to estimate their ages, over half were in their seventies at the time of their interviews. The rest were equally divided between those in their fifties and sixties and those who were in their eighties.

The advanced age of many of Shane's informants may not be as problematic as appearances would at first suggest. Although conventional wisdom holds that mental function decreases with age, researchers studying human memory have found that rather than dimming over time, autobiographical memories actually become increasingly well articulated and well established as elderly people rehearse past experiences in the form of reminiscences. Often these memories concern the critical period of late youth and early adulthood, which marks the passage to a mature personal identity. One researcher has discovered that "when people older than 30 years receive various cues and are asked to retrieve past experiences, they tend to retrieve more events from the ages of 10 to 30 than from after 30." Moreover, as people become older, they increasingly draw their recollections from this earlier time. "As a result, the elderly may provide much more information about a given period of life (e.g. 10 to 30) than people who are younger. They also may be able to generate this information much more quickly to the extent that they have reviewed the past more often and more recently." Daniel Drake, who accompanied his parents to Kentucky in 1788 and later recorded his memoirs for his children,

TABLE 4. Ages at Arrival of John Shane's Informants (N=60)

Age at Arrival	Percentage
1–4	1.7
5–9	5.0
"Boy" or "girl"	20.0
10–14	11.7
15–19	23.3
Young adult	23.3
20–29	15.0

suggests how this consolidation of memory took place. Describing an Indian attack a few miles from their own settlement, Drake observed: "That night made an unfading impression on my mind. . . . The alarm of my mother and aunts, communicated, of course, to all the children, was deep, and the remembrance of the scene was long kept vividly alive by talking it over and over."[41]

Generalizations about the religious affiliation and economic standing of Shane's informants must, unfortunately, be based on more impressionistic evidence. As a cleric, John Shane was naturally interested in the religious beliefs of the people he interviewed; in about twenty cases in his Historical Collections he noted an informant's church membership in his brief introductory remarks. He recorded, for example, that Mrs. Arnold and her son were both Baptists, while James Wade was a "Methodist, living on Peeled Oak, about 3 miles from where Morgan's Station was, on Slate." Because Shane traveled as a Presbyterian missionary, it should be expected that many of his informants were Presbyterians. Yet apparently he adopted an ecumenical approach in gathering data: Baptists, Methodists, Catholics, Universalists, New Lights, New Sides, and various other sectarians all appeared in his notes. Even a manifest lack of religious belief did not deter Shane's interest in an informant. "Ephraim Sowdusky, a great infidel," merited a five-page interview. James McConnell, who lived "in a pretty little cottage one mile from Lexington," informed Shane that "he had destroyed his mind by intemperance." Shane further noted that McConnell "had two engravings hanging up. One an improper one, the other, of the Battle of New Orleans." Without leaving any further clues as to the nature of an "improper" engraving in the

TABLE 5. Ages of John Shane's Informants in 1843
(or at Time of Interview) (N=38)

Age	Percentage
55–59	5.3
60–64	10.5
65–69	7.9
70–74	28.9
75–79	23.7
80–84	15.8
Over 84	7.9

1840s, Shane proceeded to record two pages of notes; he also decided to inquire in town if McConnell was "the man seen sometimes in Lexington with buckskin pants and hunting shirt."[42]

Estimating the economic standing of Shane's informants is a far thornier problem. Good tax lists for Kentucky begin only in the 1790s and even later for Ohio. Moreover, the technical difficulties in undertaking a quantitative analysis of informants' property ownership would probably vitiate the value of any such exercise. If the economic standing of Shane's informants cannot be stated with precision, then at least a few tentative generalizations can be offered.[43]

Many of Shane's informants arrived in the Ohio Valley with few financial resources. John Crawford made an indenture of his time for nine months upon his arrival in 1790; in exchange, Enoch Smith gave him a bond for one hundred acres of land. "Land was then a dollar an acre," Crawford recalled. "So that the hundred acres were just equivalent to $100." At a rate of approximately forty-two cents per day, Crawford earned the same pay as the work crew hired about this time to cut the Wilderness Road. Other propertyless young men also gambled that a move west would improve their personal fortunes; in the midst of a border war, many risked their lives to acquire even a modest competency. George Yocum, for example, recalled: "I waggoned at Bullit's Lick for six or seven years after I came out with my family. . . . Waggoned at the Licks every fall till I got a load of salt. Sometimes they would give me two bushels for going out three miles in the night, for one load of wood. I gave two dollars down there, and would get four dollars a bushel up here." Traveling at night was a hazardous under-

WHAT THEY THEMSELVES KNOW

taking; most settlers barred their doors and stayed inside from sunset to sunrise. Indeed, Yocum recalled that one of his fellow salt packers "was caught by the Indians and tied and whipped, on top of the knob, right in sight of the Licks"; fortunately, "the first or second night he got away, without being taken over the river." As another man observed, "the Indians got a great many salt packers in early times."[44]

Other informants spoke of apprenticeships, fur-trapping expeditions, military service, or tenant-lease arrangements which suggested that they, too, initially commanded few economic resources beyond their own physical labor. William Clinkenbeard described the paucity of his household goods when he arrived at Strode's Station in 1779. "My wife and I had neither spoon, dish, knife, or anything to do with, when we began life. Only I had a butcher knife," he recalled, explaining that their first dishes came from a local turner in exchange for meat and tallow; their landlord sold them a cooking pot for "four dollars and a French crown." Sixty years later Clinkenbeard still recalled his pride in their new domestic possessions. "A parcel of those dishes out of buckeye, new and shining, and set on some clapboards in the corner of the cabin, I felt prouder of in those times, than I could be of any dishes to be had now."[45]

Not all migrants achieved even a modest success. When John Shane visited the surveyor Samuel McDowell in the early 1840s he noted that he "lived in a miserably open house. It was a cold time and they were just filling in mud [chinking] to make it more comfortable. Bed clothing not enough. Neither table cloth, nor table ware." Others, like Abel Morgan, had lost what property their families once possessed. The son of the former proprietor of Morgan's Station, Morgan was "without a house" when Shane interviewed him in the early 1840s.[46]

A few of Shane's informants came from families of some property or standing. John Graves traveled down the Ohio River in 1786 with his father, mother, and thirty slaves; his brother had come out the year before to purchase land in Fayette County, commonly considered the site of the richest and most productive agricultural land in Kentucky. George Stocton's father first visited the area in 1776 and journeyed there repeatedly after that to make surveys and cover land entries. His son George, born while his father was out in 1776, was ten years old when his family finally moved west to found their frontier settlement. Stocton recalled the leasing arrangements that his father offered to the landless settlers who came to reside at their station. "A portion of land was separated from the station, and divided into parts. The residents of the station were allowed the use of this land . . . seven years, for clearing it."[47]

Other families commanded at least a few modest resources. They might be termed the "middling sort"—people who owned livestock or a few domestic possessions, or knew a valuable skill, such as carpentry. Often, however, their economic standing remained precarious. Jesse Kennedy's father was a carpenter, but when he came out to Kentucky along the wilderness trace in 1776, rumors of an impending Indian attack forced him to abandon his tools "along the road, hid in the woods." His son recalled that "he got out nothing but our featherbed, on William Moore's old bull. They never got any of the tools. Their horses tired and gave out, and had to be left, and were never gotten." A few educated men taught school in frontier stations, such as the famous "Wildcat" McKinney who fought with a native bobcat that invaded his classroom. "The cat had torn his buckskin dress, and fastened its claws so deeply in him, that it took the two or three men to extricate him," his widow and son later told Shane. School teaching was neither a lucrative nor a particularly honored profession in the backwoods, however. Martin Wymore attended McKinney's school at the time of the wildcat incident, and recalled that "many of the boys were sent merely to keep them from wandering about where the Indians would catch them." Taken as a whole, these and other impressionistic accounts of economic behavior suggest that John Shane drew insights and observations from an unusually broad spectrum of the early modern population.[48]

Memory and History

In the end, John Shane's quest for comprehensive knowledge sabotaged the great written work that he planned. In an 1858 letter to Lyman Draper, thanking his fellow antiquarian for his recent election as a corresponding member of the Wisconsin Historical Society, Shane voiced concerns about the possibility of ever completing his task. "Between 15 and 20 years earnest devotion to historical studies, has thrown into my possession a vast mass of historical matter. . . . And now as the scenes of life are passing rapidly by me, I begin to feel some solicitude that I should do—what if I try, I can do—and not let my life be spent *simply* in accumulating materials." Yet Shane expressed continued doubts about his preparation. "I am fully satisfied that ten years will not enable me to digest and mature, as I ought, what I have in view. . . . As for compassing the whole *material*, or disposing finally of any one topic—we may as well attempt the finishing and perfecting of one of the natural sciences."[49]

The modern researcher approaches Shane's notebooks with much the same sense of awe. Thousands of pages of notes and transcribed interviews, complex braided narratives of eyewitness testimony, oral tradition, folk culture, and simple gossip, threaten to overwhelm the unwary historian caught up in Shane's heroic effort to document the vanishing cultural world of backcountry settlers. Shane's materials are problematic, but then, upon reflection, so are all historical sources full of traps for the unwary. From the moment that a legislator sat down to write a letter, a traveler penned an entry in her diary, or a government functionary noted his estimate of a family's taxable wealth, an act of translation took place in the past. Some details were highlighted, others lost entirely, a few reshaped to serve immediate interests. Surviving in modern archives and repositories, these more familiar historians' resources are no more transparent representations of reality than are John Shane's settler interviews: they all transmit perceptions of the past, albeit some through more layers of interpretation than others. The task, then, is to approach Shane's materials critically, but without abandoning the extraordinary insights that they contain. Two strategies—inspired, in part, by recent work in anthropology and psychology—suggest a means of grappling with the rich complexity of these retrospective oral interviews.

Retaining the voices of individual speakers is a simple approach to the problem of narrative complexity. In recent years, an ongoing debate about the nature of representation in anthropology has raised serious questions about the tension between indigenous perception and externally based interpretation. Ethnographers have responded, writes one analyst, with "a *specification of discourses* in ethnography: who speaks? who writes? when and where? with or to whom? under what institutional and historical constraints?" John Shane recorded many different types of evidence—ranging from eyewitness accounts to public rumor; but he also left clues of voice, tone, tense, and context which registered these different points of view. Adding contemporary

accounts and eighteenth-century documents to this story will compli-
cate, but also further enrich this historical discourse. By not smooth-
ing out these clamorous voices into a seamless narrative—by paying
close attention to the bumpy texture of opinion, discussion, and interpretation which surrounded events in the western country—modern
readers can reflect upon the efforts of people in the past to make sense
of their own history.[50]

Those who use Shane's materials, however, must also be candid
about their strengths and weaknesses. In short, there are both "good"
and "bad" questions to ask of his interviews. Time doubtlessly altered
some settlers' recollections. Shane himself was sensitive to the problem of accuracy, observing at one point that "dates are, of all statements, most likely to be confused." Lyman Draper, obsessed by chronology yet confronted with conflicting testimony, doubtlessly went to
his grave still attempting to discover if the Indians had captured the
Boone and Callaway girls on July 7 or July 14, 1776. Current studies in
the psychology of memory suggest that rather than the mind acting as
a sort of camera, freezing memories in their original form, over a
period of years "people conflate details from similar experiences into a
generalized recollection that can stand for a class of experiences." A
fetishism for hard data—the trap of positivism—is one that must be
avoided in using Shane's materials.[51]

Yet some "mistakes" and distortions may also offer important clues
to systems of meaning only barely articulated in ordinary conversation. John Shane collected variable accounts of a number of stories,
including descriptions of a man called "Ready Money Jack" who was
either "a black man set free by Colonel Lyle," or "an Irishman" who
lived in a double log cabin "this side of Maysville."[52] This difference of
opinion may at first seem only a minor point, a tiny irritation in the
quest for perfect historical truth, but, considered from another angle,
it may actually offer insight into indigenous perceptions of identity: to
be either a "black man" or an "Irishman" was to be a stranger in this
remembered cultural universe. In another time and at another place,
this conflation of ethnic and racial identities would not have been quite
as easy to make. The objective "truth" about Ready Money Jack will
probably never be known, but the subjective systems of meaning
which swirled about his debated identity can be recovered from the
recollections of Shane's informants. These categories of kinship or
"otherness" point to other avenues of inquiry: the cognitive mapping

of remembered landscapes, conceptions of power and authority, and efforts to organize the passage of time. These are an anthropologist's questions for Shane's notebooks, less commonly those of the social historian. But they seek a common goal: the meaning of social life for those who enact it.

We entered the wilderness in high spirits. . . . Every thing looked new to me. Traveling along in Powls Valley where the Indians had broak up some people, seeing wast[e] [and] Desolate Cabbins I began to feel strange.

DANIEL TRABUE

Views of the Western Country

Like many young men in the back settlements of revolutionary America, John Dyal first viewed the Ohio Valley as a soldier. Raised near Pittsburgh, he joined a company of dragoons in 1781 and traveled down the Ohio River to guard the new Kentucky settlements against British and Indian attack. Years later Dyal recounted his early impressions, describing a countryside chiefly notable for its lack of human habitation. "There was then not a stick cut at Maysville," he recalled; "from Wheeling down to the falls, no settlement at all." Louisville was "a fort, and a few cabins around it." Several miles east of the falls, a number of small fortified settlements called stations stood on various branches of Beargrass Creek: Floyd's Station, Hoagland's, the Dutch Station, Sturgus's, Sullivan's, and Spring Station. Dyal's western landscape suddenly bloomed with detail as he named and precisely situated each frontier station that he had helped to guard, and eventually had joined to settle.[1]

Only three years after John Dyal's dragoons floated down the Ohio

41

River, the French essayist Crèvecoeur made a similar voyage. Securing passage on a flatboat loaded with cattle, tools, and supplies, Crèvecoeur's thoughts, like Dyal's, turned to the land passing before him. Yet the scene he described was strikingly different: where Dyal had passed over areas uninhabited by Euroamericans, Crèvecoeur filled them in with visionary predictions of the future greatness of the Ohio Valley. "I foresaw these splendid banks adorned with neat houses, covered with harvests and well cultivated fields," he wrote; "to the north I saw well arranged orchards, and to the south vineyards, plantations of mulberry trees and acacia." Instead of the huts, the tents, and the primitive cabins that he expected at Louisville, Crèvecoeur found many "elegant and well painted" houses of two stories, and (as far as the stumps of trees would permit) spacious and well-laid-out streets. Wherever he turned, the Frenchman discovered new evidence of social progress and evolution; particularly suggestive was the gradation of houses stretching inland from the river's edge, ranging from those finished, incomplete, or just commenced, to cabins built against the trees. For a student of the Scottish Enlightenment, this gradation of houses would have suggested the four stages of social development from primitivism to civilization thought to be common to the history of all human societies. Rich with symbolic significance, Crèvecoeur's visionary landscape evoked the promise of the western country and the future greatness of the young American nation.[2]

Landscape

Landscape is an ambiguous term, connoting not so much an objective measurable reality as a personal geographic perspective. The perception of landscape is selective: it is the singular view of "the mind's eye," picking and choosing among external stimuli to create what geographers intuitively call a "cognitive map"—a mental image of the physical world. The ways in which people perceive and evaluate their surroundings, the mental maps that they draw, are highly varied. Some may be broad ranging while others reveal only a narrow geographic experience. How eighteenth-century women and men perceived the landscape of the western country depended upon what might be termed the "visual angle" of the observer: station in life, mobility, education, and place of residence were all important variables.[3]

Consider for a moment the landscape perceptions of the two western travelers. Although Dyal and Crèvecoeur arguably viewed the same western landscape (allowing for the dramatic growth of a border town in three years' time), they did so from radically different points of view. Crèvecoeur's perspective was the fleeting glimpse of the tourist: expansive, visionary, the confident view from above of a citizen of the world reporting back on the progress of the newest member nation. Modern observers most often have seen the western country through the eyes of such travelers. Armed with the rudiments of a classical education, a sharp eye for dramatic detail, and a romantic appreciation for the beauties of nature, scores of travelers swarmed over the mountains and down the Ohio River at the end of the eighteenth century. Many recorded what they saw. Some viewed rough cabins and ragged clearings and questioned whether European civilization would survive the trip over the mountains; others of a more visionary bent blithely predicted future greatness for towns as yet little more than collections of log huts. As outside observers and representatives of metropolitan culture, travelers have offered important eyewitness accounts of aboriginal and settler life in an evolving landscape. Their perspective has informed, and at times misled, historians ever since.[4]

John Dyal's perspective is less familiar. His brief comments about the absence or presence of a few frontier stations might not conventionally be considered landscape description at all. His was the oblique, barely articulated view of the inhabitant expressed, in the words of geographer Yi-Fu Tuan, "only with difficulty and indirectly through behavior, local tradition, lore, and myth"—the angle of vision of a figure standing *in* the landscape rather than one soaring conceptually above.[5] Dyal's experience of place is by no means readily apparent; in order to capture a sense of his cognitive landscape, we must first unravel the significance of the geographic information that he recalled and thought sufficiently important to communicate. That Dyal paid such close attention to the relative locations of fortified settlements is a significant clue: by delineating spaces of security and enclosure he also, by default, suggested a surrounding and potentially dangerous aboriginal landscape rendered culturally invisible by Crèvecoeur's vision of an endlessly replicating European spatial order.

We still know relatively little about the landscape perceptions of such ordinary settlers. As land seekers pushed west through the Appalachian uplands into the mountains and rich lands beyond, how did they experience space? What were the "maps of meaning" that they imposed upon a wilderness environment? Fortunately we do have access to their cognitive landscapes, through John Shane's interviews and other autobiographical accounts left by the women and men who migrated to the Ohio Valley at the end of the eighteenth century. These historical resources provide a view of the western landscape from two different vantage points: first, quickly from above in the travelers' fleeting glimpse, and then, more slowly, on the ground with border inhabitants as they recalled their mental maps of the revolutionary-era Ohio Valley.

Travelers

"In casting your eyes over the map of America, you will discover that its western (or middle) country is divided from the Atlantic country by a chain of mountains," observed Gilbert Imlay in his 1792 *Topographical Description of the Western Territory of North America.* "The western country is those parts which are watered by the streams running into the Mississippi," he further explained to his European readers, citing the two great geographic features—mountains and westward-flowing rivers—which distinguished the "western continent" from Atlantic America.[6] In Europe such natural demarcations in the landscape traditionally implied linguistic and cultural divisions as well: changes in elevation separated Spaniards from French, Italians from Germans, and in Britain, a Celtic highland from a Norman plain. In North America, the long chains of mountains that separated coast from interior represented a more ambiguous frontier: the crest of the Appalachians officially divided Indian and British North America for a time, but the boundary was ineffective in practice and rapidly breached by settlers who cared little for royal proclamations. With the rising tide of immigration, another sort of boundary materialized—a hazy cultural frontier between Americans who lived east and those who resided west of the mountains. Indeed, whether the Atlantic country and the western country would remain united as one American nation loomed as a serious geopolitical problem in the final decades of the eighteenth century.[7]

Mountains and gaps, rivers and valleys, delineated the basic outlines of the traveler's western landscape. Of the numerous separate ranges that made up the Appalachian Mountains, the Blue Ridge stretching from southern Pennsylvania to northern Georgia was surely the most striking. Swelling abruptly above the piedmont plateau like a long azure wave, it was the first landmark encountered by travelers from the east. One such migrant was a young Massachusetts native who set out in 1784 from Orange County, Virginia, to practice law in Kentucky. "A man must be insensible not to be charmed with the beauties of that mountain," he wrote of the Blue Ridge to a friend in Massachusetts; "a thousand nameless beauties peculiar to such places almost made me imagine myself on enchanted ground." A decade later an itinerant Baptist preacher similarly recorded aspects of a changing landscape: "I find the face of the country, even here, wears a different appearance to what it does with us," he noted. "The land is very red, and here lie the south-west mountains, and the blue Ledge, perfectly in view." West of the Blue Ridge lay the great valley of the Appalachians and then more mountains, stretching in long chains and broken jumbled masses for almost 250 miles to the more level open lands of Kentucky. At the close of the eighteenth century, the Blue Ridge marked the beginnings of the western country.[8]

Travelers from the tidewater perceived this easternmost mountain chain as a significant cultural as well as a physical boundary. Inhabitants on the western side of the mountain appeared "altogether different from what they call the lowlanders, i.e. the people of the east side," observed the young lawyer from Massachusetts. "They have but few slaves, are much more industrious, and instead of raising tobacco, turn their whole attention to corn and grain." Farther west in the Allegheny Mountains, however, he found "all sorts of indolent ignorant people, who raise a little corn, but depend chiefly on hunting for their support." Living in "little log huts, destitute of every convenience of life," their only wants were apparently salt and whiskey. After boarding overnight in one such cabin, a Philadelphia woman reported that she had barely escaped "being fleaced alive." Granting that her hosts were very kind, she nevertheless observed that they were "Amazing dirty."[9]

Beyond these primitive settlements lay an even more daunting prospect for the western traveler: the wilderness. Although the term "wilderness" has commonly referred to the entire western country, at the end of the eighteenth century it carried a more specific meaning for migrants to the West. "The wilderness is 195 miles from the block house to the first settlement in Kentucky," explained the young lawyer to his correspondent in Massachusetts, noting the region's most salient characteristic: an absence of European habitation. Like its biblical namesake, the broken, mountainous region which divided the Virginia and Kentucky settlements was a place of trial and testing, a "landscape of fear," where travelers might easily lose their way or be attacked by Indians. "Scarce a day but we found the marks of a defeated company," recalled the young man of his passage along the wilderness trace.[10] For protection, parties going west collected in large companies at the Block House, the last station on the road to Kentucky, to wind their way through the "high, rugged, and barren hills" which Gilbert Imlay predicted would not be inhabited for centuries to come. A Virginian invoked a similar image when he wrote that his large traveling company put him in mind "of the Caravans crossing the Deserts of Arabia." The wilderness remained, in other words, an aboriginal landscape: viewed by Euroamericans as a place of desolation and potential danger, it belonged to what one author has aptly termed "the realm of cultural darkness."[11]

Rivers and their associated valleys divided, named, and made comprehensible the large body of sparsely settled land which lay west of the Blue Ridge. If mountains most readily distinguished the "western continent" from Atlantic America, it was the Ohio River and its tributary streams that formed the basic map of cognitive orientation within that region. Crèvecoeur recognized the importance of the Ohio River as an organizing feature of western geography. He suggested that "the anatomy of this great artery, that of the veins which convey their water to it, and of the branches whose union forms its course, presents a feature in American geography which it is very important to investigate at this present time."[12]

The many tributaries that joined the Ohio River during its thousand-mile course lent their names to the indistinct geographic regions that they watered. Thus the mountainous "Monongahela country" lay along the river of the same name, while the more level open lands of the "Kentucky country" lay roughly west of the Kanawha and south of the Ohio River in a region drained by the Kentucky River. As Anglo-American settlement stretched across the North American continent, such parochial identities often preceded political ones: Virginia and Pennsylvania disputed ownership of an area known as the "Redstone country" until the two seaboard governments agreed on an extension of the Mason and Dixon Line in 1779. "When we say 'this country,' we do not mean North America, nor the United States, nor any state, but a particular section of country, frequently of indefinite extent," explained one resident of Illinois in the early part of the next century. "It is applied to a large region, when that region is unsettled, or has not yet been divided into districts or counties, or when those divisions are little known, and the names of them not in familiar use."[13]

Western rivers also, upon occasion, defined distinct frontiers. For a quarter century after the Treaty of Fort Stanwix in 1768, the Ohio River divided the western country into separate Indian and Anglo-American provinces; travelers journeying downstream wrote of an "Indian coast" or a "Virginia shore" as if an ocean's expanse rather than a few hundred yards separated the north and south banks of the river. Such cultural boundaries often persisted despite a flow of personnel across them; even after white settlers occupied both banks of the Ohio River, a Cincinnati woman recalled that residents customarily rowed miscreants across to the other shore. During the early years of the new Republic, federal administration of the Northwest Territory and restriction of slavery north of the river reinforced this cultural divide. In one historian's evocative image, to "see the glare of northern lights reflected on the white mansions lining the southern bank of the river is to understand that the Ohio flows symbolically as well as literally through the world of everyone who lives in its valley."[14]

Eighteenth-century maps illustrate the cognitive structure lent by mountains and water courses to perceptions of the western landscape. Maps are useful in an investigation of spatial perception because they are culturally mediated images, not the passive reflections of reality that we usually assume them to be. Maps carry hidden structures of perception and cognition which help to shape their geographic information; they can be "read" or interpreted like paintings for cultural clues that they transmit. In particular, distortions and irregularities, often dismissed as the result of imprecise surveying or problems of geographical control, may reveal what one analyst has called the "subtle process by which the content of maps is influenced by the values of the map-producing society."[15]

In Thomas Hutchins's 1778 "Map of the Western Parts of Virginia, Pennsylvania, Maryland, and North Carolina" (Fig. 5), long chains of

Following page: FIGURE 5. "A New Map of the Western Parts of Virginia, Pennsylvania, Maryland, and North Carolina, Comprehending the River Ohio and All the Rivers Which Fall into It," by Thomas Hutchins (London, 1778). (Courtesy of the Library of Congress)

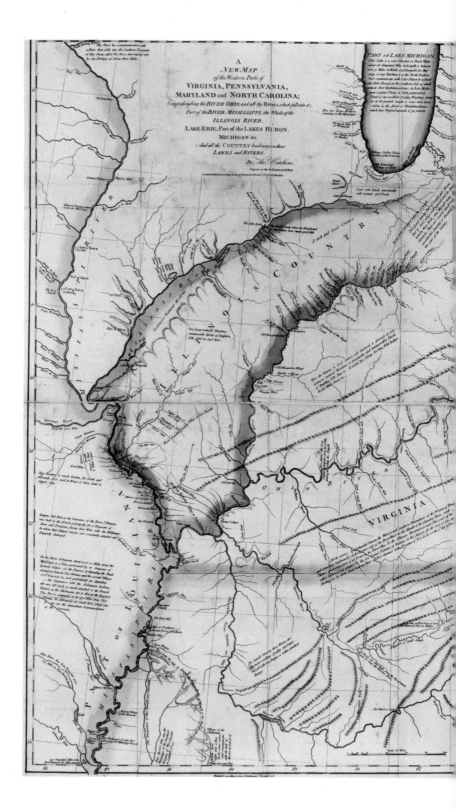

A
NEW MAP
of the Western Parts of
VIRGINIA, PENNSYLVANIA,
MARYLAND and NORTH CAROLINA;
Comprehending the RIVER OHIO, and all the Rivers, which fall into it;
Part of the RIVER MISSISSIPPI, the Whole of the
ILLINOIS RIVER,
LAKE ERIE, Part of the LAKES HURON,
MICHIGAN &c.
And all the COUNTRY bordering on those
LAKES and RIVERS.
By Tho. Hutchins.
Captain in the 60 Regiment of Foot.

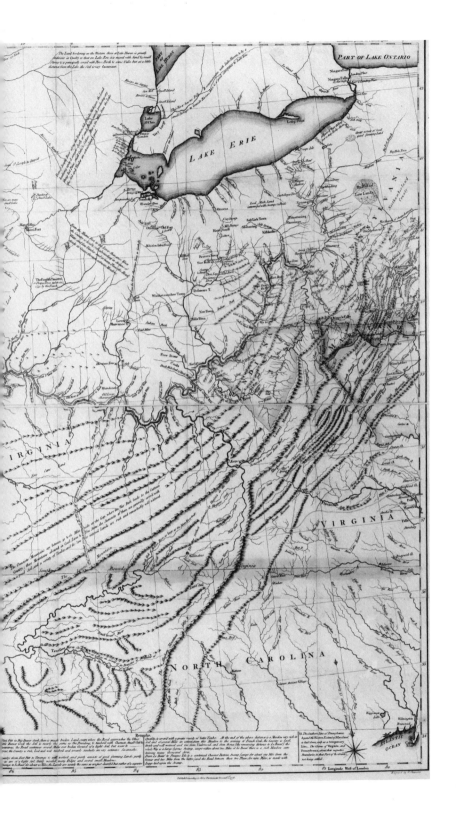

mountains reinforced with written legends fall in parallel waves across the surface of the map. Their strong diagonal lines (extending much farther west than the mountains actually reached) graphically emphasized—indeed exaggerated—the magnitude of the physical barrier separating the western country from the coastal settlements. Their powerful visual impact suggests that the geographic distinction between east and west—between the Atlantic country and the western country—dominated this mapmaker's perceptions of the North American landscape. Hutchins's map made a subtle geopolitical statement as well. In early-modern geographical discourse, mountain ranges formed the "natural frontiers" of adjoining polities. Perhaps unintentionally, Hutchins's exaggerated continental divide lent dramatic visual support to the widespread contemporary concern that no single republican sovereignty could ever unite the divergent interests of seaboard and interior regions.[16]

In contrast, the most important graphic elements in John Filson's famous 1784 "Map of Kentucke" (Fig. 6) are the sinuous arms of rivers framing and dividing the cartographic image. The long arc of the Ohio River defines the upper and left-hand margins of the page, while the undulating lines of the Green and Cumberland Rivers form its base. Rivers define but they also distort Filson's map. In crowding all of the significant waterways onto the rectangular page, the mapmaker compressed the east-west axis of the lower Ohio Valley land mass, creating a general outline of the region that was much less accurate than Hutchins's map of six years earlier. Paradoxically, in a map meant for settlers and land claimants, Filson's detailed representation of water courses took primacy over the accurate depiction of land.[17]

The distortions in Filson's map were not mere technicalities. They were purposive statements woven into the cartographic design. As a surveyor, Filson was familiar with the customary English system of "metes and bounds" land measurement which Virginia bequeathed to its western province. Depending on visible topographical markers rather than an abstract grid for orientation, claimants under this system often used the meandering lines of creeks and streams to anchor one side of a land survey. The record book of surveyor Enoch Smith, for example, contains many surveys of this type. In the early 1780s, Smith located a 2,000-acre claim for James Hickman "on a small branch Emptying into Licking about 4 miles above the upper Blue Lick. Beginning where a Buffalo Road crosses the Said Branch & Run-

FIGURE 6. "This Map of Kentucke Drawn from Actual Observations," by John Filson (Philadelphia, 1784). (Courtesy of the Kentucky Historical Society)

ning up the Same for Quantity on both sides there of." Smith's subsequent claim for John Lewis depended on both fluvial and cultural landmarks: "Beginning at a Black walnut marked S.E. on the middle fork of Miller's Creek about 1¼ of a mile below John South's and Felt Sterns Hunting camp that was burnt with their Bear meat in the year 1780." The enumeration of Kentucky's water courses, formalized for the first time in Filson's widely reproduced map, was thus an important cognitive step in the transformation of a seemingly undifferentiated aboriginal landscape into Europeanized private property.[18]

Strip away the romantic landscape descriptions and tidbits of local color, and ultimately it was this transformation of the Ohio Valley into a neo-European society that characterized most travelers' images of the western country. Metropolitan visitors compared frontier settlements with their own homes and measured migrants' progress on a scale from primitivism to civilization. The metropolis—be it Europe, London, or Philadelphia—was always the civilized norm. While some travelers dwelt on what was yet missing in the western landscape, others, like Crèvecoeur, filled in the blank spaces with their own visionary pastoral scenes. By focusing their attention on Europe's replication, however, many visitors remained largely blind to other maps of meaning. The testimony of backcountry settlers suggests that a quite different cosmology structured their landscape perceptions.

Interior Settlements

Patterns of human habitation and use also defined settlers' cognitive landscapes. Yet having a longer familiarity with the land, the men and women interviewed by John Shane actually perceived multiple landscapes—nuanced, layered patterns of geographic activity traced by Indians, hunters, settlers, and surveyors. While from a historical perspective these landscapes usually have been seen as archaeological—that is, succeeding one another in time—in the experience of Shane's informants they were interactive, coexisting and intersecting as arenas of contest in the shaping of the western landscape.

Migrants' mental maps began in what they called the "interior settlements." Their earliest geographical references formed a patchwork of personal recollection and family oral tradition. "My father was from [New] Jersey," one settler told Shane; "[then] lived in Culpepper [County, Virginia], where my first recollections were." While a number of Shane's informants traced their origins to the piedmont or tidewater regions of the Chesapeake and Middle Colonies, almost half named family homes located west of the Blue Ridge.[19] "I was said to have been the first white child born in Greenbriar," explained James Wade, who was born in 1770 on Indian Creek in the neighborhood of the "Sinks" in western Virginia. George Yocum also knew his birth date but was less certain about the location of his nativity: "I think mamma said at Harness' fort, or close by." Mrs. Crouch was from the South Branch of the Potomac River, where her family had migrated from the eastern shore of Maryland. "My mother said I was 4 years

old when I left the South Branch," she recalled, in words that suggested a sense of longing even after so many years. "It is the earliest
thing I recollect—crying for a little toy my cousin Ashby had. I told
him he might as well give it to me, for I was going away, and he might
never see me again, and it has been so."[20]

David Crouch and his wife, both blind and in their seventies when
Shane interviewed them in 1843, retained particularly vivid recollections of their early homes. Crouch was born on the "heads" of the
Monongahela; his family moved to Tygart's Valley when he was three
years old and then on to Kentucky seventeen years later. "We were
forted there almost till I was a man grown. In fact the Indians did
mischief in the neighborhood after I left. I came to Kentucky with
my father in 1787." His father "wanted to live on the gun and the
range," Crouch explained; "as soon as the range was gone, he wanted
to move." Tygart's Valley, where the couple met (and eventually married at the age of nineteen), was an isolated settlement on one of the
headwaters of the Monongahela River. Only thirty miles in length and
hemmed in by mountains "so steep, a horse could hardly carry a man
over them," the valley held some ten or twelve stockaded forts "with
bast ends [bastions], for sentry to stand in of nights." Crouch recalled
infrequent contact with the outside world: his father, he claimed, sent
in to the South Branch only once a year for the two bushels of salt they
needed for food preservation and seasoning.[21]

Although isolated, Tygart's Valley was rich in wild fruits and game;
the couple remembered living largely on nature's bounty. "It was the
beautifullest country for wild fruit I ever saw," one said. "Sarviceber-
ries growing on a tree as thick as your leg, and high as the joice of a
common log house. . . . Spread a sheet under the tree and shake down a
half bushel." Crouch speculated that had it not been for the fruit and
the game, the valley could not have been settled. "Indeed, too, we did
not know how to make a living," he added, "but mostly as our fathers
taught us, we lived by hunting." Quickly challenging her husband's
act of mythic formation, Mrs. Crouch interrupted to remind him of
their livestock; but apart from grazing their domestic animals, the first
white settlers of Tygart's Valley apparently engaged in little agriculture. After Indians killed several of their neighbors, the Crouches and
a number of other families left for Kentucky. New arrivals drained and
planted the swamps which "brought, it was said, fine corn."[22]

Other images of the homes left behind were less romantically hued.

John Crawford recited a suggestive list of place names in the Redstone country: Devil's Alley, Shades of Death, Sideling Hill, and Big Grave Creek. "A rocky, mountainous, laurelly country for 60 miles across the mountains," he said; "over which they had to pack their alum salt, bar-iron, pot-metal, and sometimes grain." Jacob Lawson lived for a time "in a place called the Barrens of York: a poor place." Perhaps recalling the agricultural assessment of those who had attempted to farm the land, James Wade observed of the "Sinks" in Greenbriar that the land was rich but full of sink holes. Jane Stevenson grew up on the Calfpas-ture River in western Virginia, where Indians killed her mother and captured her aunt and three cousins. "I was forted from the time I was seven years old," she recalled, "and was never rid of the Indians till I moved to this place."[23]

Many informants' families had migrated several times, following the courses of westward-flowing rivers in search of richer land, better grazing, or security from Indian attack. "My father moved thirteen times in one year—the year before he moved down here from the Red Stone Country," Patrick Scott recalled. "Moved up and up, untill [sic] he moved and lived near to a place called the Standing Stone." James Wade's family migrated several times during his childhood. When peaceful relations with local Indians broke down along the Greenbriar River, his family returned to the relative security of the Blue Ridge for eight years, then out to the Greenbriar settlements once again ("the Indians then being all quiet") before traveling to Kentucky in the fall of 1784. Long-distance relocations were thus often accomplished in stages. A North Carolina woman recalled that her family moved first to Moore's fort on the Clinch River (in present-day Tennessee) then to another settlement on the nearby Holston River "to get rid of the Indi-ans." There they spent a year preparing for their ultimate destination, the new Kentucky settlements across the Cumberland Mountain.[24]

Migrants

At the end of the eighteenth century thousands of Americans imag-ined new geographic horizons. Many eventually settled in the Ohio Valley. By 1790, only fifteen years after settlers built the first log forts in Kentucky, the first American census estimated the territory's popu-lation at almost 73,677 people, including some 12,430 enslaved Afri-can Americans and 114 free blacks. Two years later, a German traveler calculated that several thousand settlers lived north of the Ohio River on lands still claimed by a confederacy of western Indians, but vigorously contested by the newly appointed military government of the Northwest Territory.[25] Evidence of this mass migration astonished contemporary observers; its magnitude remains equally impressive today, prompting the question of how so many families learned about the western country. Upon what geographic information did they act?

The letters of a few elite families survive to suggest that wealthier settlers made considered decisions to relocate, based on the calculus of economic advantage and good information about western lands. John Breckinridge of Albemarle, Virginia, for example, corresponded for almost a decade with family members and friends about conditions in Kentucky before selling his Virginia plantation and moving west in 1793. Breckinridge's correspondents interspersed reports of fine rich lands (to be had for little money) with predictions that his law practice would flourish in the growing confusion over Kentucky land titles: "I am well convinced there is no Part of this State that you can so soon make a fortune," claimed his brother in 1784. Not entirely relying on such reports, Breckinridge made his own inspection of Kentucky in 1789 and eventually settled his household, including some twenty slaves, on six hundred acres of rolling land on the North Fork of Elkhorn Creek, comprising some of the best agricultural lands in Kentucky.[26]

Letter-writing supplies and the leisure to exchange geographic insights by mail, however, were luxuries of a well-to-do minority. The landscape perceptions and decision-making processes of poorer migrants like the Wades, the Crouches, and the Stevensons have remained largely hidden from view. Lacking equivalent testimony about their preconceptions of the western country, scholars generally have fallen back on the venerable myth of the West as a "promised land" to explain why poorer migrants left their backcountry homes and headed for the Kentucky country. The evidence most frequently cited for this Edenic myth as a motivation for migration is the traveler Moses Austin's widely quoted 1797 account: "Ask these Pilgrims what they expect when they git to Kentuckey the Answer is Land. have you any. No, but I expect I can git it. have you any thing to pay for land, No. did you Ever see the Country. No but Every Body says its good land." Austin then commented sourly: "can any thing be more Absurd than the Conduct of man, here is hundreds Travelling hundreds of Miles, they Know not for what Nor Whither, except its to Kentucky, passing land almost as good and easy obtain.d . . . but it will not do its not Kentuckey its not the Promis.d land its not the goodly inheratence the Land of Milk and Honey." Austin concluded with the gloomy prediction that these improvident migrants would become "hewers of wood and Drawers of water" in their new homes.[27]

As the owner of an extensive (and undoubtedly toxic) lead-mining operation in southwestern Virginia, Austin observed the out-migration of so many potential laborers with understandable alarm. Indeed, as his son later recalled, Austin eventually transported English miners to America to work at his New River excavations. Yet scholars have taken his interested observations—like those of many other metropolitan travelers—largely at face value, accepting his claims that western migrants knew "not for what Nor Whither" they journeyed to Kentucky. Reading over the entire journal of Austin's trip suggests that a more cautious approach to his observations may be in order. On the whole, Austin found few positive things to say about the West. Louisville, praised sixteen years earlier by Crèvecoeur for its progress, was now in Austin's eyes "an inconsiderable V[i]llage . . . not an Elegant Hous . . . a detestable place." The "Town of Shelby is small and like all the Towns in Kentuckey badly built."[28]

Westerners, it seems, were equally unimpressed with Austin. At one frontier house when Austin "demand.d or rather request.d leave to stay," the family suggested that he travel farther on. "Finding moderate words would not answer," Austin recalled, "I plainly told Mr. Yancy that I should not go any further, and that stay I would. Old Mrs. Yancy had much to say about the liberties some Men take, and I replied by observing the Humanity of Others, and so end.d our dispute." As these comments suggest, Austin was hardly an unbiased, nor a particularly empathetic observer of western life, yet his portrait of the ignorance and irrationality of poorer migrants in search of a chimera has become narrative convention.[29]

Pushing beyond vague notions of an "Edenic quest" still leaves the problem of what geographic information motivated middling and indigent settlers to migrate to Kentucky. Flattering promotional materials such as Filson's narrative of *The Discovery, Settlement, and Present State of Kentucke* (1784) and Imlay's *Topographical Description of the Western Territory of North America* (1792) circulated along the eastern seaboard and in Europe, yet it is unlikely that these works enjoyed wide distribution in isolated back settlements, where a printed book was often a rarity.[30] Travelers wrote of their experiences and a few of these accounts found their way into eastern newspapers as "letters from the western country"; again, few copies passed into the hands of the herders and farmers who had settled along the folds and crevasses of the Appalachian divide. Even with access to an occasional newspaper, a prospective western migrant might not have found much encouragement in the almost constant reports of Indian hostilities. Virginia newspapers in 1782, for example, predicted an imminent Indian war: "We are sorry to inform the public, that all our accounts from the frontiers . . . afford a gloomy prospect; scarcely one of the Counties along the Alleghany, that has not had some of its inhabitants massacred by the Savages." After surveying newspaper accounts of the Kentucky country during this period, one scholar has concluded that "the scant and overwhelmingly negative newspaper content . . . supports the supposition that people did not use newspaper information for making such decisions."[31]

John Shane was also curious about how people had come to hear of the West. A number of his informants (perhaps in reply to his direct question on the matter) recalled how they or their families learned about the lands along the Ohio River. From their responses, it is evident that even as a proliferation of printed materials transformed the diffusion of information in port towns and cities during the second half of the eighteenth century, many rural Americans continued to rely upon word-of-mouth transmission as their primary means of communication. Although tantalizingly brief, the available record of these exchanges illustrates how individuals in a predominantly oral culture shared geographic information and landscape perceptions.[32]

Personal observation informed many decisions to migrate. Hunters and explorers, often in the pay of eastern land companies, visited Kentucky as early as 1750; by the early 1770s, backcountry entrepreneurs like Daniel Boone and John Floyd were making cabin improvements for themselves as well as for absentee investors who stayed safely on the eastern side of the mountains. "Having been informed by the report of some hunters and Indians that there was a rich and delightful tract of country to the west, on the waters of the Ohio River, which at that time opened a wide field for enterprising individuals," Robert McAfee set out to explore the area in May 1773, accompanied by a group of men from Bottetourt County, Virginia. Two years later,

McAfee and his brothers returned to clear two acres of land on the Salt River, and eventually secured settlement rights by raising a crop of corn at Boonesborough.[33]

Militiamen recognized the area's potential when they traveled west to help secure Virginia's claims to the Kentucky country. As we saw at the opening of this chapter, Captain John Dyal settled in Kentucky after serving with Clark's troops near the falls of the Ohio; David Gass visited Kentucky eleven times on militia duty before moving there in 1777. Military service also drew coastal residents to the Ohio Valley. John Stites, originally from the Scotch Plains in New Jersey, served as captain of a company of militia rangers in the Redstone country. He first glimpsed the fertile Miami country in 1786 when he transported a boatload of military supplies to Limestone and then joined a volunteer party pursuing Indians north of the Ohio River. Within two years his brother's family occupied a Miami Valley tract acquired with the help of New Jersey speculator John Cleves Symmes.[34]

In the interior settlements, such eyewitness accounts became important sources of information about western lands. William Niblick's father sold out his lands near the Blue Ridge in North Carolina on the strength of having had "some word from Boone of the West." Levi Todd recalled that "there was a great deal of talk" about Kentucky in 1774 when Captain James Harrod and a company of men from the back parts of Pennsylvania and Virginia joined Colonel Andrew Lewis's campaign against the Scioto Indians. When their fellow soldiers learned of their recent visit to Kentucky and their plans to build a frontier settlement, "some hundreds determined, as a treaty took place between Lord Dunmore and the Shawanese, to come the ensuing Spring and take possession, not doubting but they would be deemed proprietors by occupancy of at least some valuable tracts." When Daniel Trabue returned to southside Virginia after his Revolutionary War service, his relatives and neighbors similarly plied him with questions. "They asked me a bundence of qustions about kentucky and the Indians," he recalled. "I told them all about it. My Relations and the neighbours all would come to see me and I must go to see them in return." Such firsthand accounts did not always encourage migration, however. Benjamin Allen's neighbors in northern Virginia journeyed down the Ohio River to locate land claims in the West and almost did not return to tell of their experiences. After viewing his neighbor's wounds from an Indian attack, Allen declared that "it scared me from coming to Kentucky, and I didn't want to come at all, when father came."[35]

Exaggeration, of course, also occurred as migrants waxed enthusiastic about the qualities of the lands they had seen. Some accounts resembled tall tales, obvious overstatements, yet nevertheless compelling in their exaggerated claims. Patrick Scott's father traveled down to the falls of the Ohio with Clark's troops in 1778 and planted corn on an island in the middle of the river. "Have heard my father say, as he used to set of nights in his cornfield, that he thought he could hear the corn go tick, tick, it grew so fast." General Scott's tales, "eastward in Virginia, were that the corn was so plenty, they took it in bushel baskets. If an ear fell out, it took two Negroes to put it back. Said the deer's horns spread nine and ten feet." When questioned on how the deer could get through the thick undergrowth if this were true, Scott replied, "that was none of his look out."[36]

A Virginia newspaper in the 1780s satirized such inflated accounts of western fecundity: "A GENTLEMAN, lately returning from the western country . . . was asked by a friend . . . whether he really believed all those sublime things were true, which had been spoken concerning the goodness of that promised land; whether ten penny nailes did indeed sprout up from a crow-bar, after being planted *only* twenty-four hours." The traveler replied that, of course, he did not believe in such tales, but that he *had* barely escaped from some pumpkin seeds that he had dropped to the ground and which grew so quickly into enormous vines that, by clapping his spurs to his horse, he escaped only with difficulty! That such accounts were current in the popular humor of the day suggests that most hearers were well able to separate fact from fiction in tales of the western country.[37]

Like their wealthier counterparts, middling and poorer migrants heard glowing reports of the fertility of western soils. Yet by traveling west themselves, or questioning neighbors or family members who had made such a trip, prospective migrants also gained access to reliable firsthand observations of the western landscape. Limited in their exposure to the burgeoning world of print media, back settlers continued to value the judgments and observations of their peers with a broader geographic experience. Although the great folk movement of humble settlers across the Appalachians has often been portrayed as an irrational quest for a new Eden, many backcountry families made pragmatic decisions to relocate based on multiple trips to view lands and good information about actual conditions.[38]

Coming Out

In settlers' cognitive landscapes "coming out" along the Ohio River or on the wilderness trace linked the "interior settlements" with new homes in the West. As one migrant explained, "in Indian times, there was no road through the Ohio, and the only routs to east of the mountains were up the river and through the Wilderness." Financial resources, the point of embarkation, and the likely threat of Indian attack all helped to determine the route chosen. During times of relative peace, those who could afford to hire boats or who lived near navigable streams found the Ohio River a speedier and more comfortable route. On the Monongahela River, Marcus Richardson and his brother-in-law Colonel Buck purchased a boat for $40 dollars in the spring of 1793 and took on passengers at $2 apiece to help recover their costs. Reluctant to be crowded with family parties, they refused passage to all women until one man begged that they make an exception for his sister. "We were afterwards very glad," said Richardson, "as to get our cooking properly done was a great convenience."[39]

Proximity to the Indian shore made the Ohio route a dangerous choice, however. In what would prove to be a vain attempt to stem the flow of Euroamerican immigration into the region, warrior bands of mixed tribal identity routinely harassed river parties. When John Graves floated downstream with his parents and their thirty slaves in 1786, he glimpsed the bodies of a family recently killed by the Indians. "The woman had a child in her arms, and it was taken from her when they struck her, and its entrails taken out and wrapped round a sapling before the house, which I saw myself next morning." Graves added that "we were often asked by Indians to come ashore for fresh meat, and in turn asked them to come aboard; but were not interrupted."[40]

Other river parties were not so fortunate, or perhaps, so prudent. John Thickston's family, from the South Branch of the Potomac River, traveled downstream with Captain Runnells and a number of other migrants in 1780. Just below Pittsburgh where the river narrowed, a party of Indians attacked the first two boats, killing Runnells's group and capturing two women and six children in the second boat. The third boat narrowly escaped, carrying the Thickstons. and another family downstream to safety. Even those migrants arriving without incident received unpleasant reminders that native residents opposed their occupation of the western country. One of the first sights that Vermont native Asa Farrar witnessed upon his arrival in Maysville in 1788 was another boat landing with "a dead woman, two wounded children, and a dead horse, on board." An infant still suckled at the dead woman's breast.[41]

Poorer migrants or those driving livestock usually journeyed overland on the wilderness trace. Ned Darnaby traveled with packhorses through the wilderness in the fall of 1784 and did not recall hearing of anyone coming down the river. "By land was the cheapest way to come west," explained David Crouch. "We drove our stock. It was the fall season. We had narry [a] river to ferry at all. . . . Did not cost us $5 to come." While acknowledging its economic advantages, settlers generally considered the wilderness the more perilous route. After leaving Greenbriar, Jane Stevenson's family waited on the road for over a week for another family to travel with them. Another man recalled that "some strangers, Bakers, got in company about the edge of the wilderness, not far from the Block-house. Drove a gang of hogs with bells on them, what makes me recollect." Other migrants journeyed in groups as large as two or three hundred with armed guards to accompany them. In 1781 an entire Separate Baptist congregation moved out from Virginia and prayed and sang on the road every night. "We were sometimes in a string of three miles," one member said, crediting Providence with their survival.[42]

Although a few migrants commented on the natural beauty of the wilderness, most remembered it as an eerily alien cultural space. "We entered the wilderness in high spirits," recalled Daniel Trabue. "I was truly Delighted in seeing the mountains, Rivers, hills, . . . spruce, pine, Laurril, etc. Every thing looked new to me." Trabue's optimism soon faltered, however, when his company reached Powell's Valley (about thirty miles west of the Block House) where a war party had destroyed an outlying settlement: "seeing wast[e] [and] Desolate Cabbins I began to feel strange." Other migrants noted the disturbing absence of familiar landmarks such as fences, houses, or the smoke of chimneys. "I had come 300 miles without seeing a house," said one North Carolina woman. "Saw no sign of a house, except where some men had put up a few logs, and done some cutting, as if they were going to build." On Cumberland Mountain she began to be discouraged: "thought I never should see a house again." Even more ominous were the signs that some traveling parties never made it through the wilderness at all. Daniel Deron waded ankle-deep through the feathers from the ripped-open mattresses of a defeated company; James Wade discovered a hastily dug mass grave by the side of the road. Another man suspected that his party, too, had been shadowed along the way. Before he could recapture a straying sheep, "some one had shot it, and cut a piece out of the side." The wilderness was alive with Indians, he believed.[43]

In the absence of man-made structures, a series of natural topographical features measured migrants' progress along the wilderness trace. Colloquial and possessive identifications such as Moccasin Gap, Powell's Mountain, Walden's Ridge, Little Flat Lick, Stinking Creek, and Raccoon Spring symbolically tamed the aboriginal landscape by taking possession of it; knowledge of these homely, almost humorous names may well have eased the psychological distress of migrants crossing alien terrain. Familiarity with these landmarks appeared to be widespread among migrants, suggesting that a description of the wilderness trace constituted some part of the oral lore passed on by returning travelers; in 1784 John Filson included a partial list of these traveling stages in his promotional tract, *The Discovery, Settlement, and Present State of Kentucke*. One of the most important of the landmarks along the road was a low patch of shrubby bushes called the Hazel Patch. Not far from there the wilderness formally ended with the first Kentucky settlements at Crab Orchard. Sarah Graham recalled that when her family reached Crab Orchard in 1780, Benjamin Logan came out to greet them with a loaf of pumpkin bread. "His wife did not do anything else but bake in the ashes what he ground on the hand-mill and give to the people moving out," she said. "He was so glad they were coming."[44]

Fortified Communities

Small fortified communities called stations formed the basic settlement unit of early Kentucky and southern Ohio. "Any family settling on a frontier point and strengthening themselves as they could, was called a station," explained William Boyd. "None of these was anything more than a collection of families, with sometimes a hired guard, and hunters, in dangerous times." The product of the brutal border war between Ohio Valley Indians and encroaching settlers, the frontier station provided a means of defense while securing possession of the land. The physical configuration of such settlements varied widely. Some, resembling stockaded military forts (their obvious source of inspiration), housed as many as thirty families and boasted elaborate defenses such as barred gates, corner bastions, and portholes for firing weapons. Others were simply a few cabins built closely together near a spring or other source of water. As one station resident explained, "a few hours would have picketed them in if needed—if troublesome times had come."[45]

In occupying the Ohio Valley over the objections of native inhabitants, Euroamericans blurred what had become a customary European distinction between military and civilian populations. Stations, as compact militarized settlements, helped white settlers seize and colonize the aboriginal landscape. Spencer Records, who migrated from western Pennsylvania to the Licking Valley of Kentucky in 1783, gave detailed instructions for constructing one of these stockaded settlements in his 1842 memoir, leaving little doubt of its military purpose. First, the builders cleared off the ground "the size they intend to build the fort, which was an oblong square." Then they dug a ditch three feet deep and threw the excavated dirt inside. Next, the workers cut and split logs "twelve or fifteen inches in diameter and fifteen feet long." After sharpening the tops of the logs, they set the butt ends into the ditch with the flat sides facing inside, threw dirt in around them, and rammed it in well. Portholes, he noted, "were made high enough that if a ball should be shot in, it would pass overhead," and cabins "were built far enough from the stockades to have plenty of room to load and shoot." Bastions (or bast ends) stood at opposite corners for riflemen to rake fire along the sides "should the Indians get close up." Strong gates with bars completed this type of fortification which Daniel Boone's party constructed at Boonesborough in the 1770s (Fig. 7). Although most settlers used the terms "fort" and "station" interchangeably, Spencer Records distinguished between the two types of structures. "Some forts," he continued, "sometimes called Stations, were built with cabins all set close together, half-faced or the roof all sloping one way with [the] high side out." Spring Station on Beargrass Creek, which John Dyal guarded in 1781, was an example of this type of construction (Fig. 8).[46]

Stations were significant points of communal assembly in the western landscape. Migrants arriving in the first decade of settlement fre-

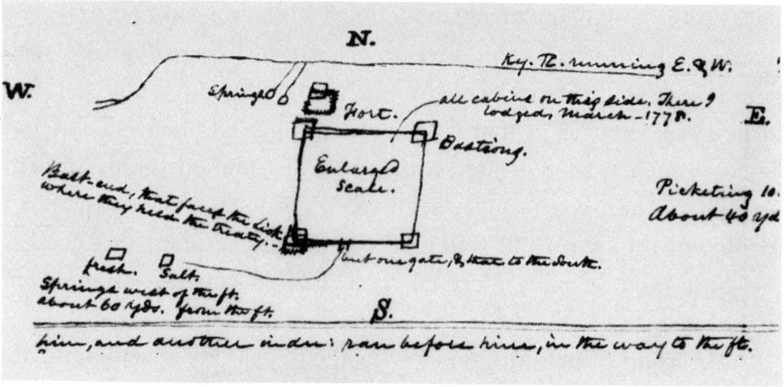

FIGURE 7. Plan of fort at Boonesborough, Kentucky, in 1778, drawn by John D. Shane during an interview with Josiah Collins, 1841. (Draper Mss., 12 CC 74, neg. WHi [x3] 51224, State Historical Society of Wisconsin)

quently recalled spending several years in one of these communities; in sparsely settled areas vulnerable to Indian attack, settlers lived in or near stations well into the 1790s. Elijah Foley helped settle John Bowman's station in the "hard winter" of 1779. Starting from Frederick County, Virginia, in the fall of that year, his family arrived at Bowman's unimproved claim on Cane Run Creek in the middle of December. "Our coming was the first settling of the station," he recalled. "There was nothing but a camp there, till some time in March, because it was too cold to work." Once they had established a few primitive shelters, Bowman (who commanded the Kentucky militia) brought his family over from the fort at Harrodsburg. Other groups continued to arrive, and by spring Foley recalled that "we had 20 families that had camped in the snow and had remained during that winter." When the weather finally cleared, work proceeded quickly. In three months more than thirty families had built cabins, "in the form of a half H," about 150 yards apart on each side of a spring, leaving just enough room for livestock to gather in between. This first group of tenants occupied Bowman's station for about four years before they began to scatter, some to their own farms and others to Tennessee. Important communal bonds formed over these four years: sixty years later Foley could still recite twenty-two of his neighbors' names.[47]

By the late 1780s, fortified settlements dotted both banks of the Ohio River. Benjamin Stites's party landed at the Kentucky port of Limestone in August 1788 and spent three months preparing to oc-

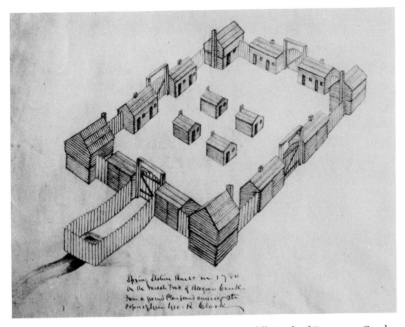

FIGURE 8. "Spring Station Built in 1780 on the Middle Fork of Beargrass Creek. [Modern rendering of] a ground plan found among the papers of Gen. Geo. R. Clark." (Reuben T. Durrett Collection, Department of Special Collections, University of Chicago Library)

cupy their Miami Valley tract purchased from New Jersey speculator John Cleves Symmes. While they camped on the Kentucky side, Stites and his father "rived out clapboards at which he [the father] was a first rate hand." They also purchased flatboats from arriving migrants ("could get them for from $1 to $2 according to their size") to use as floors and gates in their station, which eventually would boast four blockhouses and a palisaded enclosure. Arrival at their new settlement came on Sunday, November 18, 1788. After scouting ahead for Indians, the party guided a flotilla of seven or eight flatboats downstream to the north bank of the river. "We landed, cleared away paw-paw bushes, stood sentries, sung a hymn, went to prayer, and then went to work," Stites recalled. Less than two years later, when Levi Buckingham arrived at nearby Covalt's Station on the Little Miami River, he found there four blockhouses, eight to ten cabins in a square, and part of the stockade already completed. Staying long enough to help finish the picketing and to plant a patch of corn, Buckingham then returned to the Redstone country for the rest of his family.[48]

Euroamerican occupation of southern Ohio thus proceeded rapidly. On a trip down the Ohio River in 1792, the German traveler John Heckewelder noted settlements at Marietta (1788), Wolf Creek (1789–91), Belpre (1789), Gallipolis (1790), Massie's Station (1790), Columbia (1788), and Cincinnati (1788). Heckewelder recorded in his diary that at the town of Columbia he stayed overnight with a "Major [Benjamin] Stites . . . who is from New Jersey [and] has purchased a tract of 20,000 acres from Judge Symmes and has laid out a town upon it." Only four years after its founding, Stites's settlement had "many well built houses" and more than a thousand inhabitants.[49]

Ohio Indians shrewdly read the meaning of these rapidly multiplying settlements. In his travel journal, Heckewelder reported that the speculator John Symmes had shown a party of Shawnee and Delaware visitors around his North Bend settlement, and had paused at one point to explain the symbolism of the great seal of the United States, stressing the eagle's peaceful disposition. " 'Well,' said a Shawnee captain, 'now let me make my interpretation, maybe it will illustrate the picture more truthfully then thine.' " If the Americans were truly lovers of peace, the Shawnee man said, they would have expressed their sentiment more plainly on their coat of arms. "But what is the eagle? He is the largest among the birds and the enemy of all the birds. He is proud, because he is aware of this greatness and strength. Perched on a tree as well as in his flight he expressed [sic] this pride openly, by looking down with contempt upon all the other birds. His head, his eyes, his bill, and his long, brown and sharp claws make known his power and hostility." This bird was terrible enough, the man continued, but the Americans had also given him "weapons of war, a bundle of arrows in his one claw, and switches in the other," and had placed him "in horrific position, in the act of pouncing upon his prey." Symmes had to grant the validity of the man's interpretation, but remarked that only the enemies of the United States were threatened by the eagle; friends should view it as a harbinger of protection. Heckewelder recorded no response from the Shawnee to this veiled threat, but the German traveler suggestively followed this anecdote with an account of the murder of friendly Seneca villagers nearby.[50]

Although their time of occupation was often very brief, fortified stations were important conceptual nodes in settlers' cognitive landscapes. Before towns, roads, or fences inscribed other man-made refer-

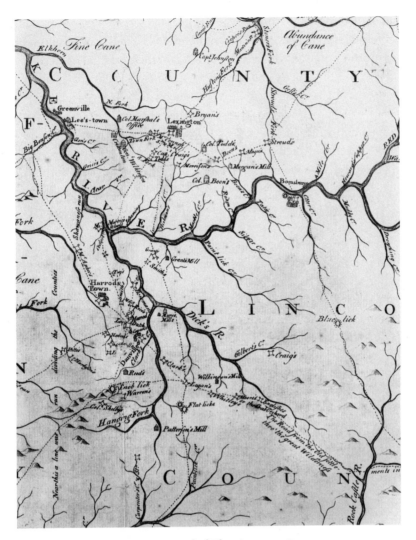

FIGURE 9. Detail of Filson's map, 1784.
(Courtesy of the Kentucky Historical Society)

ence points on the Ohio Valley landscape, a web of settlements linked
by paths or traces supplied a system of spatial orientation (Fig. 9).
Settlers reckoned distances from stations and placed events in regard
to their location; they distinguished between "inside stations" or "outside stations" based on their vulnerability to Indian attack. The influence of stations radiated beyond their stockade walls; even after the

end of "troublesome times," when residents "settled out" on individual farms, stations gave rise to neighborhoods like Bryan's Station or Masterson's Station which today still retain their original names.

As spaces of security and enclosure, stations also defined a gendered landscape of an expansive male and a narrow female geographic experience. While men ranged widely on hunting or military expeditions, women and children, for fear of Indian attack, remained largely restricted to the fortified compounds or the fields and gardens surrounding their walls. "A woman dare not go 40 yards to pick beans without a guard," John Dyal observed of the settlements along Beargrass Creek. Jane Stevenson similarly recalled that the "first summer we came out, Daddy stood sentry, while we milked." After making the long journey from the interior settlements, some women found being cooped up inside forts frustrating. Sarah Graham recalled that the women in Fisher's Station used to quarrel a great deal out of boredom. Another female settler lamented: "so many rich places to see, and the women couldn't get out to see them." When buffaloes invaded the cornfield at Bryan's Station, she remembered that the female population turned out to see them—a rare opportunity for the fort-bound women. For some women, low geographical mobility persisted well beyond the settlement era. John Shane noted that a Mrs. Pierce had lived within thirteen miles of Lexington for forty-one years after migrating with her family from the South Branch of the Potomac River. In all that time she had never visited the central Kentucky town which was, by 1800, the metropolis of the West.[51]

Paradoxically, while most women had few opportunities to venture outside the station walls, stories of captured and murdered women figured prominently in the narratives of Shane's informants. In one typical account, Indians killed Dick Scearcy's wife as she came home from visiting her nearest neighbor. Searching for his wife along the road, Scearcy "heard something groan, and found her, a little way from the path, not yet dead." In another story, Indians killed Rachel McCutchen's child and took her as a captive to the Shawnee towns north of the Ohio River. McCutchen finally escaped, but "she was crazy after she returned," a neighbor recalled. "Went about with a rake, turning over the leaves in the fence corners, looking for her son." Told and retold for decades, these and similar stories about murdered or captured women became part of the oral tradition of station life. Yet in their early existence, they may well have served a more specific purpose: as "cautionary tales" depicting the risks and dangers that women faced "outside," they discouraged other women from abandoning the safety of fortified compounds. Although the dislocations of migration challenged some received structures of patriarchal authority, cultural restraints on the mobility of women were reproduced and, indeed, strengthened in the new geographic setting.[52]

Parents similarly attempted to restrict the movement of children, although perhaps with less success. Forbidden to wander off from the station, Sarah Graham nevertheless remembered sneaking out to gather wild cherries and paw-paws. William Moseby recalled that fishing was "against orders" at Scott's station, but still a favorite pastime with the boys. He recounted their narrow escape when young Daniel Scott and the other boys agreed to set out their hooks for Buffalo fish: "old aunt Sarah would cook them, and pa wouldn't know it." When the boys went back to check their lines that evening, an owl "hallooed very pert." Having been taught that Indians "could halloo like owls, and these owls were on the ground," the boys ran back to the station and confessed their misdeed. The most famous episode of this sort was the capture of the Boone and Callaway girls while they were out "pleasuring" in a canoe in July 1776. A small war party of Shawnees and Cherokees grabbed the three girls when their canoe neared the north bank of the Kentucky River, opposite Boonesborough. Their screams alerted the settlement, and, after a dramatic pursuit and rescue led by Daniel Boone, the girls returned home tattered and exhausted. Much like the cautionary tales of captured women, the Boone and Callaway story also served as an object lesson to other venturesome children. After Betsy Callaway's son heard his mother relate the incidents of her captivity and rescue, "I thought the yard was full of Indians and I was afraid to go out of doors."[53]

We can only speculate on the psychological impact that these and similar stories had on western children—and on the generations that came after them. In a suggestive passage, Daniel Drake recalled that adult warnings about their "great enemies" the Shawnees and the Wyandots had given him nightmares as a child. At bedtime he and his brothers and sisters were told to "lie still and go to sleep, or the Shawnees will catch you," Drake remembered. Because of this, "through the period of which I have been speaking, and for several years afterward, . . . nearly all my troubled or vivid dreams included either Indians or snakes—the copper-colored man, and the copper-colored snake, then extremely common. Happily I never suffered from either, except in dread."

Did such deep fears implanted by parents contribute to lasting emotions in their offspring? Perhaps. One historian who has studied American children who grew up during World War II reports that even after fifty years, bitter anti-Japanese sentiments still characterize the homefront children of that war. On the other hand, Daniel Drake, who later became a Cincinnati physician and visited the Shawnees after their forced removal from Ohio to Kansas, seemed relatively un-marked by his childhood fears. In a sad bit of irony, he noted that the Shawnee mothers he visited in the 1840s "threatened their children at night with [stories of] the wild Indians who lived beyond them."[54]

African American slaves of both sexes occupied an uncomfortable middle ground between geographic restriction and exposure to danger. Most enslaved blacks who accompanied white settlers across the Appa-lachians probably shared the narrow domestic geographies of women and children. Grinding corn on a handmill in the station yard was a common work assignment for young black males; at John Craig's sta-tion "a negro boy . . . turned it nearly half the time, the family was so large." Sarah Graham recalled that "Barbee's black man said they ac-cused him of parching the corn, but he didn't. He put his hand in the mortar and ate the meal as he pounded it. Their supply was so limited, he became so weak, he could hardly carry a bucket of water." Female slaves performed other domestic chores: "old aunt Sarah" who cooked the boys' fish at Scott's station was most likely a black woman. Do-mestic work space extended into the area immediately outside the stockade walls; both male and female slaves routinely labored there tending gardens, planting corn, picking wild berries, gathering "sugar water" from tapped trees, or looking after livestock. We know about these latter tasks because slaves performing them were either killed or captured by Indians.[55]

In an ironic gesture to their servile status, some African Americans found themselves literally placed outside the fortified community. David Crouch recalled that "a black woman was poked thro' and told to go and alarm the nearest station" during an Indian attack in Tygart's Valley. A similarly besieged Kentucky family put out their slave Moses to give the alarm; when he returned (apparently unable—or unwilling—to find his way), they "let him in and put out Bob" who ran on to Fisher's station. Other slave owners expressed surprisingly few qualms about risking human property to secure their property in land. When John Breckinridge moved his family to Kentucky in 1793, he sent most of his slaves ahead to prepare for their arrival. A year before John Bowman moved his household to Kentucky, he planted a crop of corn at Harrodsburg and left a black man to tend it. For some blacks, life outside the station compound offered a rare chance for independence. William Hardin "wanted to save his cabin from being burned by the firing of the prairies" when he departed the Green River country for a time, so he left behind a black woman "who proposed to stay." During the three years she lived alone, Hardin and other hunters brought the woman game occasionally and, as "she had nothing to do but to dress the deer skins . . . she got to be an excellent hand."[56]

Such independence bore risks, however. A particularly grisly tale concerns the four slaves of Nathaniel and William Ewing. When the Ewing brothers returned temporarily to Maryland, they left a man named Jerry, another man named Russel, a woman named Bet, and an unnamed little girl in a cabin near Troutman's Station. Alarmed at signs of Indians about the place, Russel asked the others to go with him to the nearby settlement. When they refused—poignantly suggesting a preference for relative freedom and possible death to life in the station—Russel fled by himself. By the time a party of men returned to investigate, the three blacks remaining behind were dead. "It was believed from the sign, that the Negro man had fought, and that with an axe," said James Wade. "The wall was seen bloody (I was not there) off a little piece from where the Negro lay."[57]

Outside

With discretionary mobility over wide areas, male settlers had ample opportunity to observe the Ohio Valley landscape. "We were all minute men, ex-officio," said John Graves. "A little parched corn, kept in a little bag, and some jerked venison in another . . . and a horse standing in the stable. Whenever you saw a man coming, all you wanted was to know where you were wanting." Military, hunting, and trading expeditions brought Euroamerican males in close contact with the aboriginal landscape, and traces of former habitation or use intrigued many as they journeyed throughout the region. Old fields, flint beds, earthen mounds, and burial sites all sparked a lively debate as to their origin. Most whites considered mound building beyond the powers of the

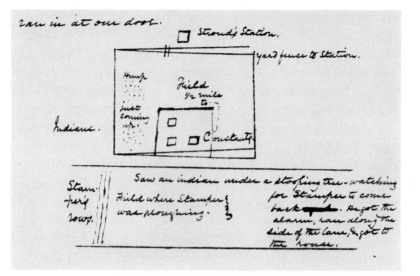

FIGURE 10. Plan of Constant's Station in 1785, drawn by John D. Shane during an interview with Henry Parvin, ca. 1840s. (Draper Mss., 11 CC 173, neg. WHi [x3] 51223, State Historical Society of Wisconsin)

Indians they knew, however. Many Euroamericans explained their presence by resorting to ethnocentric legends such as that of Madoc and the Welsh Indians, which told of a band of Welsh explorers, led by Prince Madoc, who landed at Mobile Bay in 1170 and later settled near the falls of the Ohio, intermarrying with the local Indians. Earthworks along the Mississippi River were thought by some to be Welsh-inspired fortifications, although they are now known to be prehistoric Indian constructions. But in addition to evidence of past occupation, there were also signs—if one knew where to look—of continued occupation: of Indians utilizing the land for seasonal hunting, sugar-making, and salt-making activities or traveling through the countryside for trade or for war. In occupying the Ohio Valley, white borderers learned to read this aboriginal landscape and passed on their lore to John Shane.[58]

For most settlers, the aboriginal landscape began just outside the fortified compound (Fig. 10). A variety of signs, ranging from the skittish behavior of domestic animals to the discovery of moccasin tracks, signified the presence of Native Americans. "It was a sign Indians were about, when the cows stood in the head of the lane, and wouldn't go out," John Gass told Shane. Mrs. Pierce thought (perhaps erroneously) that it was against the law for whites to wear moccasins, and that the sign of moccasin tracks was a proof of Indians. "The Indians were around every night, and round the stable," recalled John Graves. "We could see their tracks. But it was a puncheon door we had, and a good lock. They couldn't get in. We shut our door early; and in the morning, it was sun up, before we opened it." Another man similarly observed that "in those times they always shut the doors towards night, and never opened them again, till after we had peaked out at the port-holes next morning." Daniel Drake recalled that it was his duty to ascend the ladder to the loft the first thing in the morning to look through the cracks for Indians. A few settlers professed an ability to distinguish the footprints of particular Indians who visited in the night. William Clinkenbeard claimed "we could tell their tracks. Knew one Big-Foot's. He used to visit us often."[59]

Station residents termed this besiegement as being "forted." Jane Stevenson recalled that she "was forted from the time I was seven years old"; David Crouch's family was forted "almost till I was a man grown." When Joe Taylor arrived in Kentucky in 1784, he found David Tanner "forted there at the salt-works, with about 5 or 6 kettles." In outlying settlements, small raiding parties regularly came at night to steal horses or scatter livestock. Martin Wymore's family lost fourteen horses; the last was a mare wearing a bell. "When they had gotten her, in the night, they ran all round the fort, ringing the bell, and nickering." Wymore's father started out to round up the stray horse, but "my mother told him, that wasn't old Dumpsy. He went to the gate, and listened, and found it wasn't her." The next morning they found moccasin tracks all around the fort, suggesting that the Indians had mimicked the sound of the horse in order to lure out her owner, or taunt him with her theft. Mrs. Morrison recounted a similar incident when her mother "heard the Indians come and take the bells off their horses. Right back of their cabin. Never waked her husband. Knew he would be too venturesome." Most settlers described this psychological warfare as harassing but, unlike a full-scale attack, not particularly frightening. One man, however, claimed that his neighborhood "had like to have been broken up on account of their stealing so many horses. . . . The Indians said they didn't want to kill people; they wanted the whites to raise horses for them." Serving as a test of a warrior's courage and skill, horse theft was a none-too-subtle reminder of just how easily Ohio Valley Indians continued to move throughout the disputed countryside.[60]

Adding to immigrants' sense of encirclement was a dense native vegetation. William Clinkenbeard observed that it was a "monstrous place to travel through once, grape-vines, thorn-bushes, cane, and everything." Levi Todd visited Kentucky in 1776 and later wrote that "the land appeared more level than at present, as the thickness of the growth prevented one from discovering the diversities as they traveled." In addition to open woodlands and savannas that supported large herds of buffalo and elk, a native evergreen bamboo commonly called cane covered much of the region. Settlers admired but also feared the almost impenetrable colonies of twelve- to twenty-foot reeds which they called canebrakes. Sarah Graham claimed that cows fed on the cane gave the richest milk—"more milk than when now fed on the bluegrass pasture"; others remembered canebrakes mostly for providing perfect cover for Indian attackers. At Floyd's Station, "a man could be hid, at the distance of four feet," while at Louisville, "the cane was so thick, the Indians couldn't be pursued at all." Mrs. Gough remembered that her mother heard the cow in the cane "and would be afraid to go and see for fear of Indians. Would hear the bell, and see the cane shaking." Future Kentucky governor Thomas Metcalfe recalled that the cane grew very thick at Maysville when he arrived with his family in 1784, at the age of seven. He and the other children "were disposed to play about . . . till cautioned by their parents as to the danger from the Indians." Another man visited Strode's Station in 1780 and noted in his journal "a vast quantity of cane to ambush the enemy." Indeed, settlers' fears of this native vegetation may have contributed to the rapid environmental transformation of the region. Strode's resident William Clinkenbeard later recalled that the station's occupants quickly destroyed the canebrake for a half mile from the settlement.[61]

Animal and man-made trails provided a rudimentary road system through the dense vegetation, although travelers needed considerable experience to navigate these routes successfully. Benjamin Hardesty described his family's confusion upon their arrival in Kentucky in 1784 when they encountered the maze of trails and paths which crisscrossed the countryside. "We got out of our road at the Lower Blue Lick, and got lost with our wagons before we got to Bryant's Station," he said. "Followed an old Indian trace that led from Limestone to Bryant's Station." He added, with evident chagrin, "we took the wrong buffalo trace, of a good many that came in to the lick. Were two weeks getting to Bryant's Station [sic] from Maysville," a distance of approximately sixty miles. That same fall, Ben Guthrie helped blaze the road between Bryan's Station and the Blue Licks, which "had been cut out before, only to Bryan's Station." Prior to completing the road, "they followed Buffaloe traces, which were as plain as roads, after they got out of the cane."[62]

Dependent on wild game for their survival, male settlers gradually learned to navigate the complex network of salt licks, springs, and buffalo traces which spanned Kentucky's rich hunting grounds. "In those times, a road that went near a lick would go to it," recalled Josiah Collins. Saline springs, commonly called "salt licks," drew large game animals like buffalo and deer to lick the ground impregnated with salt particles; they also drew both native and immigrant hunters. John Rankins recalled that when he was fifteen, "John Taylor, Joe Berry, myself, and a black boy" went out hunting on horseback and found five or six deer in a nearby salt lick. John Taylor "had raised his gun and was just about to draw trigger, when another gun fired." To their great surprise, an Indian hunter came down to the lick to claim his kill. Upon seeing their horses' tracks, the Indian, now equally alarmed, whistled for his four companions and they "set off on a long trot." This episode was far from unique. As potentially dangerous spaces of social and military interaction, salt licks were the sites of numerous encounters between Indian and immigrant males during the first two decades of Euroamerican occupation. The most infamous was the bloody defeat of the Fayette militia by a Wyandot army at the lower Blue Licks in 1782.[63]

In traveling throughout the countryside, militiamen discovered ample evidence of continuing Indian subsistence activities. On a scouting expedition into the mountain country in April 1794, James Wade and a party of about a dozen men "came on a sugar camp where the Indians had been making sugar for about a month up to very lately. We judged from the sign, they had probably left there the day before. The bark troughs were scattered about over the camp, and the sign of horses was very fresh." Samuel Gibson similarly recalled that "the Indians had a sugar camp on the head of Red River, about thirty miles from here, and not far from Hazel-Green." Another man remembered an encampment at a salt spring near the mouth of Shawnee Run: "suppose it was a place resorted to formerly, for the purpose of getting salt."[64]

Settlers also recognized that native inhabitants used the Ohio Valley's streams and traces for an extensive—if only dimly perceived—communications network. In an 1824 land deposition, Simon Kenton explained the difference between animal and man-made traces. Indian "war roads were distinguished by the marks and blazes upon them, frequently the rough drawing of wild animals, or the sun or moon; and by their being leading roads, leading from one distant point to another," he said. "Buffalo roads," on the other hand, "were found along ridges and creeks, were much wider, and much more beaten because of the constant tramping of the buffaloes, and had no blaze or distinguishing marks." James Wade also recalled seeing the blazed Indian trails, remarking to Shane at one point that "the Indians often made pictures on trees, in that way. . . . They used powder, or red paint to spot them with." Former Indian captive Benjamin Allen recalled that his Shawnee captors made the print of a pipe tomahawk as they crossed one trail "to show they were Indians."[65]

Other settlers were able to identify specific Indian trails. John Crawford observed that "the Indians [who] came in between the Kentucky and Red Rivers to take horses at Lulbegrud . . . had paths around all the creeks." Robert Gwynn described the Shawnee Run Indian trace as so well used that it was a foot wide and a foot deep. "It passed through Clover bottom, where McClanahan made a pre-emption: called so, because the Buffalo Clover grew up there in a little space, about twice as big as this house." (Shane noted here that Gwynn lived in a stone house with three rooms on the ground floor.) William Clinkenbeard blamed "a war path [that] ran right through this place" for his difficulty in settling his farm near Winchester. "The Indians stole our horses and we were afraid to work here," he later told Shane.[66]

Several migrants revealed knowledge of the major north-south artery, commonly called the "Great Indian Warpath," which linked southern and northern tribes. Samuel Gibson recalled that when he crossed the Indian path at the Cumberland River in 1794, it "was so plain, you could hardly tell which was the plainest—it or the Wilderness road," blazed by the settlers. George Trumbo told of a Pennsylvania man whose house "stood right on the war path, where they went from about Ft. Pitt to kill Catawbas in the south, often in parties of fifty or sixty before the war broke out." Indians passing on the trace occasionally spoke with the settler. "They complained the whites were killing off their turkies, deer, and etc. That South Branch was once the garden spot of America." In a similar fashion, James Wade reflected on the rapidity of white colonization, observing that by 1796, "the settlements along the Ohio River had extended so far along its banks, as to close the ordinary rout (from north to south, so long used by the Indians) to this back country."[67]

In recalling their perceptions of the aboriginal landscape, immigrants acknowledged that their own coming had altered the face of the land. In particular, the destruction of the cane and the buffalo seemed a cause for widespread regret. "Kentucky never could have been settled in the way it was, had it not been for the cane and game," James Wade mused in hindsight. "They never could have gotten out the provision through the Wilderness in safety . . . and their stock and themselves would have starved in the winter." Yet the early settlers had wasted this resource, reflected Joshua McQueen: "Many a buffalo was killed by the whites, and only a little of the rump taken out, or a thigh bone for the marrow. . . . Many a man killed a buffalo, just for the sake of saying so." Another man agreed: "When I first came here, the Buffaloe bones covered all the ground. Said that men used to come down from Stroud's and the interior, when the Buffaloe were poor, and kill them for sport, and leave them lie. The trace that passed on to the upper and lower blue licks, led through here, and they would kill them on it." William Clinkenbeard admitted that he and three other hunters had once killed twenty-four buffalo for their wool alone. He granted (with a significant shift of personal pronouns), "They did destroy and waste them there at a mighty rate. If one wasn't young and fat, it was left, and they went on and killed another. Likewise the cane. I thought they never would get it out of this country, when I came, but now it is scarce and a curiosity." The Indians had lived differently, Joshua McQueen observed, with what sounded like grudging respect. They never shot the buffalo "but when they wanted them. This was their great natural park. Could come here and get fat bear, and buffalo, &c. Were always in order." At the time McQueen spoke these words, the last wild buffalo in Kentucky had been dead—shot by an anonymous hunter—for almost fifty years.[68]

Space

Having a long familiarity with the land, the surviving settlers interviewed by John Shane and other western collectors had much to say
about the transformation of the Ohio Valley landscape over the course
of Euroamerican occupation. This, then, perhaps is an appropriate
point to pause and return briefly to a question posed at the beginning
of this chapter. As land seekers pushed west, how did they experience
space? Soaring conceptually above the rich and cluttered detail of settlers' cognitive landscapes, what do we see?

In reading over hundreds of interviews with surviving Ohio Valley
settlers, one is struck that migrants often employed a distinctive spatial metaphor—the concept of "in and out"—to encompass their basic
arrangement of social space. Born in the *interior* settlements, settlers
came *out* to the Ohio Valley, lived *in* fortified communities called
inside stations or *outside* stations, *settled out* when it was safe, even
spoke of Kentucky as the *outside of Presbyterianism*. This is a metaphor, of course, because it understands one thing in terms of another,
in this case, space as a container with an inside and an outside. Lin-
guists observe that such orientation metaphors are not just rhetorical
flourishes, but are actually ways of organizing physical and cultural
experience: they can be important evidence of the ways in which people view their own world.[69]

On the most superficial level, settlers' references to "in and out" are
analogous to travelers' perceptions of metropolis and frontier. Both
imply movement from a homeland to an outlying colony and are
freighted with implications of dominance and subordination, independence and integration. Yet border inhabitants expanded this orientation metaphor to the western country itself, suggesting a more
nuanced reading of the western landscape than the simple dualism of
center and periphery. By paying such close attention to spaces of security and enclosure—to relationships of "in and out"—settlers defined a surrounding and potentially dangerous aboriginal landscape
rendered culturally invisible by metropolitan visions of an endlessly
replicating European spatial order. Look once again at the Indians in
the settler's map of Constant's Station, or consider John Dyal's fortified settlements along branches of Beargrass Creek: in migrants'
mental maps, contact with another culture—not just distance from
their own—structured their most basic spatial perceptions.

By pointing to the existence of an Indian landscape, both preceding and contemporary with Euroamerican occupation, Shane's informants revealed an understanding of the complexities of western cultural geography that did not survive into the next generation. Indeed, from the start, promoters and historians wrote the history of the Ohio Valley with the assumption of a particular inevitable outcome—Crèvecoeur's visionary agrarian landscape or, much later, Frederick Jackson Turner's relentlessly advancing frontier line. By depicting Kentucky as a new Eden, or even an empty "hunting ground" there for the taking, generations of authors replicated the injustice of Indian dispossession by erasing native peoples from the landscape. Over time, of course, most traces of this Native American landscape were written over by new inscriptions. All that remained were the place names—Paint Lick, Shawnee Run, and Mingo Bottom—to record an earlier consciousness of a prior occupation.

Migrants' mental maps assigned cultural meaning to the physical terrain. Yet, just as their cognitive landscapes described boundaries and enclosures in physical space, other maps of meaning structured social space. Indians and Euroamericans were not the only strangers to encounter one another in the western country.

You could tell where a man was from, on first seeing him.

JOHN HEDGE

Distinctions and Partitions amongst Us

At the beginning of Kentucky's "hard winter" of 1779–80, Daniel Trabue and a small party of young men set out to make salt at Bullit's Lick. They carried cast-iron pots and brass kettles to boil the salty spring water which produced a fine, grayish powder used for food preservation and seasoning. In a little over two weeks, Trabue's group rendered two bushels of salt per man, enough to preserve a large store of meat for the next spring, when game animals would be thin and tough after surviving on winter forage. As they prepared for their return trip, several men traveling together from the falls of the Ohio asked if they could join Trabue's party on their way to the upper forts. "As company was good in these times," Trabue observed in his 1827 memoir, they readily agreed.[1]

Their trip began auspiciously. On the first night the men camped, "one of these strangers (his name was Saullivon) . . . killed a cappital Buffelo." With plenty of salt, they "lived well that night for meet." Overnight, however, a deep snow fell and it turned quite cold; the

81

party was in no hurry to depart the next morning. As they warmed themselves around a good fire, Trabue recalled that "one of these Jentlemen, a stranger, observed, 'This morning is very sutiable to set in a good tavern and have to drink good rum and hot Tea or Coffey for breckfast.'" Sullivan, who had killed the buffalo the night before, observed that for his part, "he thought a pan of fryed hommany would suite him best." Trabue recorded a surprising outcome to this seemingly innocuous remark: "It was taken as an insult. Blows insued. They had a very smart scuffle in the snow. We parted them and our Tuckeyho boys laughed heatyly [heartily] at it." After separating the disputants, Trabue's party reached home safely with their salt.[2]

Quoted raw, in Daniel Trabue's fractured spelling, this passage at first seems baffling. What could possibly prompt two travelers gathered around a campfire on a cold winter's morning to come to blows over an imaginary breakfast? Conventional accounts of backwoods behavior might offer an environmental explanation: far from the restraints of civil society, men became in Crèvecoeur's words "ferocious, gloomy, and unsociable," ready to challenge any comers on matters of pride or opinion. "By living in or near the woods," he explained, "their actions are regulated by the wildness of the neighbourhood." Such crude explanations of frontier behavior have passed out of fashion; scholars today are more apt to suspect that the social or ethnic origins of these two men had a role to play in their disagreement. And what about the "Tuckeyho boys"? Who were they, and why did they find this exchange so humorous? The answers to these questions lie not in the proximity of the forest, but in the problem of identity in a fluid social setting.[3]

Americans migrating to the Ohio Valley in the late eighteenth century discovered not only a new physical terrain, but a new social setting as well. Although many migrants made the journey with kin or friends, they also encountered a host of strangers of different races, cultures, and social origins. In a letter home to Massachusetts, one man observed, "we have Inhabitants from almost every part of the world." John Filson explained in *The Discovery, Settlement, and Present State of Kentucke* (1784) that "being collected from different parts of the continent, they have a diversity of manners, customs and religions, which may in time perhaps be modified to one uniform." Filson's guarded prediction of eventual assimilation suggests that at the time he wrote, social diversity was still very much in evidence.[4]

Historians have been relatively slow to explore the dynamics of cultural pluralism in this early western population. Dating from Turner's famous dictum that "in the crucible of the frontier the immigrants were Americanized, liberated, and fused into a mixed race," scholars traditionally have viewed western migrants as either a homogeneous population or one divided principally by economic antagonisms between rich and poor. Recently scholars have sought to distinguish more precisely the racial, ethnic, and economic characteristics of early Kentuckians. The first federal census in 1790 estimated that 17 percent of Kentuckians, excluding Indians, were nonwhite; almost all of these inhabitants were enslaved African Americans. Historians interested in the European ancestry of white settlers have analyzed surnames on tax rolls to estimate that most migrants to Kentucky were of English or Ulster Scots origin, with smaller numbers coming from families of Irish, Welsh, or German descent (Table 6). Those interested in the economic rank of white males have calculated land and slave ownership and have found significant evidence of economic inequality (Table 7). One scholar estimates that in the years after the Revolution the "vast majority, perhaps 75 percent" of the settlers who poured into Kentucky, were "poor and without land."[5]

As valuable as this composite profile might be, statistics reveal little about real social and economic relationships. Left unanswered are important questions about how people sorted themselves out, made decisions about each other, and interacted with one another during a period of profound cultural flux. Categories of race, ethnicity, and socioeconomic status fit present concerns about the fault lines of American society, but did not necessarily possess the same explanatory power for those living two hundred years ago. Attitudes about ethnicity, for example, underwent a profound transformation in the nineteenth century as theorists of scientific racism speculated about the enduring biological characteristics of the Celtic or Teutonic "species." In the twentieth century, ethnicity became a rallying cry for political assertions of cultural differences between groups who had lived in the same country for generations. Differences in skin color, national origin, and economic standing *were* visible to eighteenth-century inhabitants of the Ohio Valley. Yet by privileging these social divisions or reducing all such differences to the simple dichotomy of rich and poor, historians overlook more subtle cultural distinctions not easily comprehended within any of these modern categories.[6]

TABLE 6. Estimates of the Racial and Ethnic Origins
of Kentucky's Population, 1790

Origins	Percentage
By race	
White	83.0
Non-white	17.0
By ethnicity	
English	42.8
Scotch-Irish and Scots	20.6
African	17.0
Irish	7.5
Welsh	5.6
German	4.1
French	1.3
Dutch	1.0
Swedish	0.2

Sources: U.S. Bureau of the Census, *Century of Population Growth*, 207; Purvis, "Ethnic Descent," 259.

Note: The 1790 census divided Kentucky's population into white and nonwhite classifications, with Indians supposedly excluded from this count. Due to the imprecision of this language, a few non-Africans may be included in my general classification "African." In the second section of the table, I have recalculated Purvis's statistics on European ethnicity to reflect the geographic origins of the entire population, not just those of European descent. Purvis's estimates are based on surname analysis and must, therefore, be considered highly speculative. It should also be emphasized that the vast majority of Kentucky's early population was native born. Ethnicity here refers to the ultimate geographic origins of migrant families.

The terms "cohee" and "tuckahoe" encompass one such distinctive structure of social identity. Originally a Powhatan Indian term for a variety of edible roots, by the late eighteenth century "tuckahoe" became a common name for an inhabitant of the lowlands of Virginia. The tuckahoe's counterpart was the "cohee," a resident living west of the Blue Ridge. Virginians migrating to the Ohio Valley carried this social distinction with them; Daniel Trabue's "Tuckeyho boys" were former residents of the tidewater or piedmont. In 1786, a Kentuckian wrote to the governor of Virginia that "we have two sorts of people in this country, one called tuckyhoes, being Generall. of the Lowland old Virginians. The other class is Called cohees, Generally made up of

TABLE 7. Estimates of Wealth-Holding, in Land and Slaves,
for Kentucky Heads of Households, 1792–1800

	Percentage Owning Land	Percentage Owning Slaves
1792	34.9	23.2
(Teute estimate)		
1797	40.6	—
(Teute estimate)		
1800	43–46	—
(Soltow estimate)		
1800	49.2	25.2
(Coward estimate)		
1802	48.2	27.2
(Teute estimate)		

Sources: Teute, "Land, Liberty, and Labor," 263, 275; Soltow, "Kentucky Wealth," 620; Coward, *Kentucky in the New Republic*, 55, 63.

Note: All estimates are based on Kentucky county tax lists, which enumerated all free males over age 21. Because each author used a slightly different sampling technique, estimates may vary for the same year.

Backwoods Virginians and Northward men, Scotch, Irish, & c., which seems, In some measure, to make Distinctions and Particions amongst us." A settler similarly explained to John Shane that "Irish mostly from Pennsylvania country and South Carolina were called Cohees. Mostly Presbyterians. Virginians were called Tuckahoes. You could tell where a man was from, on first seeing him." Braiding together a complex skein of social and cultural identities, the distinction between cohee and tuckahoe transcended wealth, ethnicity, or religion alone; depending on the circumstance, the terms implied any, or all, of these meanings.[7]

Largely unexplored as well is the *process* of cultural interaction in the Ohio Valley. Within the acknowledged constraints of the border war that convulsed the region from 1774 to 1795, Indians and whites, Germans and Ulster Scots, cohees and tuckahoes, encountered one another as individuals, not as abstracted cultures or races. Make no mistake: brutality, rather than mutual comprehension, characterized many of these meetings. Yet attitudes about others were always contingent, ready to be verified, muted, or altered by actual experience. Encounters with strangers formed a large part of the rich oral lore passed on by John Shane's informants. Many immigrants retained vivid recollections of their initial contacts with people who looked, spoke, smelled, or acted differently than they did. Along with other personal narratives and contemporary manuscripts, these accounts capture the variety and complexity of human interaction on the borders of early America in a way that statistics alone cannot. By examining the "distinctions and particions" that border inhabitants used to classify themselves and others, and then considering how these categories worked in practice, this chapter explores the negotiation—and essential ambiguity—of identity in a fluid frontier setting.[8]

First Impressions

Like many back settlers, Mrs. Morrison's family enjoyed broad geographic horizons. Her father was born in Cumberland County in the Pennsylvania backcountry; he later moved to southwestern Virginia and then north to Augusta County in the great valley where he married Morrison's mother, "a Miss Campbell." The couple departed for the settlements on the Holston River (in present-day Tennessee), and eventually traveled to Kentucky in 1779. After staying at Harrodsburg for a few weeks, they moved on to the fort in Lexington. Morrison recalled her mother's reaction to the other migrants who soon began arriving: "Told her, when they saw others coming, and asked her if she wasn't glad." Her mother said, "if they were the right kind. Said her heart sunk within her, when the first person she saw, was a rough old Dutchwoman. There were others, however, and after awhile some very respectable persons."[9]

Morrison's mother neatly defined the problem of the stranger in a fluid social setting: the need to discover if she or he is "the right kind." Sociologists describe this process of identification as the "coding" of strangers: using clues of personal appearance, language, and manner to discover other extrinsic and intrinsic characteristics such as rank, nationality, or moral character. The need to evaluate strangers is most commonly seen as an urban dilemma, yet this same decision-making process went on throughout much of early America (with the possible exception of a few closely knit New England towns), as immigrants from a variety of European countries and African regions came into contact with each other and with native inhabitants of equal, or even greater, ethnic diversity. Making accurate judgments about the character and intentions of strangers was important in small towns and port cities; it could be, quite literally, a matter of life and death in sparsely settled border regions.[10]

The evaluation of strangers in early America drew upon a rich symbolic code of cultural differentiation. Some distinctions relied on apparent referents such as skin color or language; others, like the food preferences championed by Daniel Trabue's fellow travelers, were normally invisible. All such group boundaries are largely symbolic in nature. Of the hundreds of distinguishing features that human beings can discriminate among, only a few become centrally important in the construction of social identity. Once in place, however, a single distinction like dress or religion can stand for a whole repertoire of other ascribed characteristics. The choice of a cultural marker may be quite arbitrary; what is crucial, writes one anthropologist, is "what the boundary means to people, or, more precisely, . . . the meaning they give to it." Identity, in short, is a cultural construct rather than a biological absolute.[11]

In the border country, culturally relevant attributes took a variety of forms. Personal appearance, especially clothing, played an important role in the rapid appraisal of strangers. As John Hedge informed Shane, "you could tell where a man was from, on first seeing him." The Englishman Nicholas Cresswell discovered the importance of dress when he visited the western country in the summer of 1775. After commenting freely on the ragged appearance of his traveling companions, Cresswell, the eldest son of a Derbyshire landowner, found the tables turned when he arrived at Fort Pitt in "very shabby dress" and tried to cash a personal note. Clothing was a sensitive indicator of social position in eighteenth-century Anglo-America; "a periwig and lace-ruffled cuffs," writes one analyst, "proclaimed freedom from manual work in field or workshop." To Nicholas Cresswell's dismay, even backcountry innkeepers judged a man's appearance for indications of his credit worthiness and genteel status. Those passing the test of dress and manner, on the other hand, could expect preferential treatment. In traveling to Kentucky from Philadelphia in 1788, Mary Dewees discovered that even in the roughest ordinary [tavern] on Sidling Hill, "by our dress or Adress or perhaps boath [we] were favoured with a bed." The other twenty, less-genteel guests slept on the earthen floor.[12]

Eventually befriended by an Indian trader, Nicholas Cresswell received a second lesson in the importance of dress when he proposed to accompany the trader across the Ohio River into the Indian country. "Mr. Anderson informs me that the Indians are not well pleased at anyone going into their Country dressed in a Hunting shirt," Cresswell recorded in his diary. The buckskin or linen hunting shirt, widely assumed to be an article of Indian dress, was to Cresswell's Delaware hosts the garb of the backcountry militiaman. As Sarah Graham later explained to Shane, "the militia in those times had no other shirts than buckskin hunting shirts; and [they] wore moccasins and bear-skin hats." Drawing an important lesson from his first fashion blunder, Cresswell "got a Calico shirt made in the Indian fashion, trimmed up with Silver Brooches and Armplates so that I scarcely know myself." Once properly attired for his trip, Cresswell found a hospitable welcome in the Delaware towns.[13]

As Cresswell's experience suggests, dress served as a potent symbol of identity in an exotic world of strangers. Reading the language of dress became part of the social expertise of every border inhabitant. Native Americans, for example, apparently recognized the status implications of European costume. A former Indian captive related the story of a man who lost his saddlebags on the road between Lexington and Frankfort. "The Indians found some ruffled shirts in his saddlebags. All the English they could say, when they got on the shirts, was, 'Massa,' signifying, I suppose, Gentlemen." Settlers recognized Indians' cultural competence in the symbolism of European attire and attempted to turn it to their own advantage. When an Indian army besieged the fort at Boonesborough in 1778, the badly outnumbered defenders agreed to a parley. Accompanying Daniel Boone outside the stockade was Major William Bailey Smith dressed in a British officer's uniform with "a red scarlet coat and maccaroni hat, with an ostrich feather in it." Visibly stressing the military credentials of their own side, Boone and Smith reported that there were still more commanders within the fort.[14]

Euroamericans expressed similar interest in, if less comprehension of, Indian costume and ornamentation. James Wade found "a very nice Indian cap" where a party had camped near Mount Sterling; Shane included a small sketch with his interview. "The cap was made of cloth, with two red tassels hanging down, one on each side of the head, at the corners that stuck up. Coarse, thick, white colored cloth. Two pieces." Another man recalled pursuing an Indian wearing "a coon-skin cap on his head, with a long tail hanging down." Lending scant support to modern stereotypes about frontier dress, this incident was Shane's only record of the now-ubiquitous symbol of the white frontiersman. William Clinkenbeard admired several examples of Indian ornamentation, including "a very nice Indian shot pouch . . . all beaded off" that another man brought in. And, at a prisoner exchange, he encountered the "most splendid looking squaw I ever saw. I suppose she had a thousand ornaments on her. Was all covered over with them." A few settlers attempted to interpret the symbolism of Indian bodily decoration. In one example, Mrs. Shanklin told of a white prisoner who escaped from his Indian captors and "got into Mann's Lick . . . naked, trimmed, and painted." The Indians had at first painted him black, the captive reported. "But he gave them intimations that he was a gunsmith, and could repair their guns. They then daubed him with spots of red: an indication of more pleasure."[15]

The passage of apparel across the permeable cultural boundary between native and immigrant complicated the process of visual identification. During a time of relative peace, John Hanks's mother made several "cappo-coats for them to take along and sell among the Indians—made them of blue broadcloth, with a cap or hood to draw over the head: otherwise like a match coat." Hanks added: "I recollect I sowed on them some myself." The "cappo" [capote] was an article of European attire, a long cloak or overcoat with a hood worn by soldiers and travelers. The matchcoat was its Native American analogue: a mantle, originally made of furs and skins, later made of imported British broadcloth. In the back settlements, such articles of dress were readily interchangeable among wearers. Benjamin Stites bought a broadcloth "cappo" from the Shawnee war leader Blackfish, which he "had to freeze, to get the lice out." He observed that "the Indians frequently wore handkerchiefs, cappo, etc. . . . The one that killed uncle David Jennings had a cappo and cocked hat, he must have gotten at St. Clair's defeat." One suspects that the symbolic power of this officer's cocked hat—a battlefield trophy—was not lost on its new owner.[16]

Mistakes in reading the language of dress caused endless confusion in border areas. William Clinkenbeard's militia company "killed a white man dressed fine in Indian dress. Cousin to General Clark. Had been wounded and was making his way in to our camp and was shot. Had gone to live with the Indians, when, I don't know." Spencer Records's brother once fired at a white captive by mistake: "we supposed that the prisoner was an Indian, on account of his running off from us, and because he wore a calico shirt." Another man shot and killed a white scout in Indian dress who was returning to Cassidy's Station. Adding to the confusion, Indians occasionally dressed as Europeans, although whether this was for disguise or as a matter of personal taste remains unclear. William Whitley recorded that a militia captain lost his life on an expedition north of the Ohio River when he "went out to seek his horse and saw some Indians drest after the Manner of whites." Inquiring of the strangers whether they had seen his straying mount, "McCrackin came near up to them before he discovered his Errow." Children, in particular, seemed to lack sophistication in quickly assessing a stranger's appearance. Indians captured two young boys gathering roasting ears near Short Creek when "one of their moccasins came loose, and he stooped down to tie it. As he did so, they saw two Indians coming; but they had such clean match coat blankets . . . they thought them whites." Native Americans also misjudged European attire. After Colonel Elliott's death, a witness reported that "the Indian went to scalp Elliott, and the wig which he wore came off. The Indian exclaimed a d—d lie—swearing. The servant heard him," an informant assured Shane.[17]

As a symbolic medium, dress had power to transform identity in the border country. By donning a calico shirt for his visit to the Indian towns, Nicholas Cresswell proclaimed his status as a potential friend rather than a probable enemy; he became, in the eyes of the Delaware, "the right kind." In a similar fashion, a company of Ottawas helped their captive Abel Janney to pass unmolested through the Wyandot town of Sandusky by turning him into a "white Indian." When their traveling party neared the town, which had been attacked only two months previously by the Pennsylvania militia and was still in mourning, Janney recalled that "the Chief of the [Ottawa] company turned about to me, and told me that he must cut my hair in their form, or else those Indians that lived in the town would beat me very much, and perhaps kill me." Having witnessed the torture and immolation of the militia commander defeated at Sandusky, Janney hastily agreed. "So he took a pair of scissors which they always take with them to war, and began to trim my hair, which they did according to the Indian custom[;] then they painted me and fixed me as much like themselves as they possibly could, and gave [me] my own gun, and we marched to the town with two scalps on a stick." As a symbolic Indian, Janney passed through the grieving town without incident. Similarly, Joshua McQueen visited the Spanish river port of Natchez on a trading trip in 1782 and adopted protective coloring. Noting that he was the only American in the boat—"they were all Frenchmen but one other man, and he was one of a sort of people that file their teeth [and] live in some hot country way to the west somewhere"—McQueen wore a handkerchief on his head, "the same as a Frenchman."[18]

Changes in dress could also alter identity within a culture. Daniel Trabue marveled at the social transformation that dress wrought in the hardy women who inhabited Logan's and Harrod's forts when George Rogers Clark sent out invitations for a ball to be held at the falls of the Ohio in 1779. Trabue recalled that Ann Harrod "Killed a Buffeloe as an exploit on the rout," yet "when these Fort Ladys come to be Dressed up they did not look like the same," he declared in his memoir; "every thing looked anew." Alcohol consumption may have aided in this impression. Trabue added that their transformation into "Ladys" was accompanied on his part by "a plenty of rum Toddy to Drink."[19]

Native inhabitants seemed particularly sensitive to the transformative capacity of personal apparel. When a party of Shawnees captured Benjamin Allen in 1790, they took him to their camp on the Licking River and told him to pull off his clothes. "They brought two calico hunting shirts, sort of red with half the arm worn off, and put them on me," Allen recalled. "They then tied on a blanket round me, with a buffalo tug; and then tied a piece of blanket round my head. They then patted me on the head, and said, 'Indian.'" Native Americans captured prisoners like Allen for a variety of reasons, including torture, exchange, or adoption into the community as replacements for lost family members. By transforming Allen into an "Indian," his Shawnee captors signaled that adoption was likely to be his fate.[20]

That this physical transformation had symbolic as well as practical intent is further illustrated by George Yocum's story of a young girl captured on the wilderness trace. "When they took her, each Indian gave her a broach," Yocum said. One Indian had no silver broach to give, however, "and he took a pewter plate they had dropped in the road, and made her a rude pewter broach and gave [it to] her." While they went off to attack another party along the road, the Indians left the girl behind and she wandered off; when Yocum's company found her, she was wearing eighteen broaches. "In this way we knew the number of the Indians that attacked the company that McFarlan was with," he noted of her return. Benjamin Allen reported a similar adoption ritual when one of his Shawnee captors asked him if he would go home with him. When Allen agreed, the Indian "put two silver rings on my fingers and a powder horn, with some yellow lace to it, over my head. From this I supposed he took me to be his." Allen most likely read his captor's actions correctly; in Shawnee cultural practice such gift exchanges created bonds of mutual obligation and established ties of kinship.[21]

While Euroamericans held more fixed notions of ethnic identity than did Native Americans, they also recognized the power of dress to transform or disguise. Settlers, in particular, maintained that white captives held for any length of time came to resemble Indians. William Clinkenbeard took part in Clark's campaign against the Shawnee towns on the Miami River in 1782 and recalled that "this white woman that we took had been a long time among the Indians. Didn't know her name, or her people's. Looked as much like an Indian for color and for dress as an Indian herself." John Rupard joined a small raiding party across the Ohio River in 1789 and later returned with a much larger force to bury their dead. In addition to the bodies of their own men, Rupard's party found the corpses of two Indians "with chunks [of earth] thrown over them" and "an Indian white man" with "a sort of stone wall around him." The latter's identity was not immediately apparent, as Rupard made plain: "We examined the place, stripped him, and found him a white man."[22]

In a telling account of the mutability of dress and identity, Daniel Trabue recorded the reunion of several Indian captives with their white families at the Treaty of Greenville in 1795. When introduced to his children after a lapse of fifteen years, one old man "cryed out aloud and fell Down on the floore, Crying and bewailing his condition. Said he, 'My cheldrin is Indians!'" Upon recovering from his initial shock, the settler gave each of his sons a suit of new clothes and convinced them to wash off their paint. Significantly, the former captives' reintroduction to European culture began with a change of their clothing; even more significant, within two hours the young men had dressed as Indians again.[23]

In addition to dress, other aspects of physical appearance aided in the rapid evaluation of strangers. Migrants used a combination of physical referents such as skin color, physique, and demeanor to construct rough categories of racial and ethnic identity. Sarah Graham maintained that skin color and height served as a guide to Indian ethnicity, telling Shane that "Shawnees were almost gold-yellow and small. Choctaws tall and large, six feet high and more." Some migrants first encountered individuals of a different skin color upon their arrival in the Ohio Valley; their responses ranged from simple curiosity to expressions of fear. James Stevenson told Shane that "the first negroes I recollect ever to have seen" were living with William Dickerson at McConnell's Station. John Redd met a "dark mulatto" man at Martin's Station in Powell's Valley and noted that "notwithstanding his coller he was treated with as much respect as any white man." Tidewater planter David Meade, who journeyed down the Ohio River to Kentucky in 1796, recalled his initial alarm at the sight of "three large keel Boats rowed by naked Copper colored men—of very savage appearance." Meade confided in a letter to his sister in Virginia that "I had little doubt [as to] what race of men they belonged & notwithstanding my reason assured me that there was nothing like hostility to be expected from them[,] my fears were all awakened." The planter confessed that he did not feel easy until the Indians were out of sight, "which was in a very short time for they plied their oars with a degree of agility and force unknown on James River."[24]

Skin color, like dress, was not an absolute guide to a stranger's identity, however. Interracial contact and cohabitation were common in the border country, blurring racial and ethnic distinctions. David Meade first thought that "white men" navigated the three Indian keelboats they passed on the Ohio River, but later learned that the voyagers were *métis*—"a mongrel race between French & Indian—they are said to make excellent watermen." Descriptive references to complexion often lacked racial specificity: whites routinely used the general rubric "yellow" to characterize the coloring of Indians, mulattoes, and *métis*; a fellow European, on the other hand, might be described as "a man of darke skin." Nathaniel Hart attributed the capture of the Boone and Callaway girls to their mistaking Indians for "Simon, a yellow man, who staid at the Fort." Another child described the Indians who waylaid her as "yellow men, with rings and beads." Henry Parvin recalled his own confusion as a child when Indians attacked Constant's Station in 1785. "We saw them, a parcel of swarthy, yellow looking things, with shining pieces of silver on, and we thought they had killed a snake, and thought of going to see what kind of one it was they were gathered round, taking them to be a parcel of mulattoes."[25]

Racial identities confounded adults as well. Peter Harper, variously described as a "half Indian" or "a sort of yellow man," lived in Strode's Station and served in the station's garrison before settling out in his own cabin near Mount Sterling. The youngest son of a former Indian captive, Harper "looked as much like an Indian as could be. Black hair and straight walk," according to his neighbor William Clinkenbeard. While out hunting one day, "Harper got killed and we never knew how, whether by whites or Indians." About this same time, James McMullen reported that he had shot an Indian on Lulbegrud Creek. "Everybody said it was Harper, from McMullen's description: an Indian on a horse," recalled Clinkenbeard. But McMullen continued to insist that he had shot an Indian. He "never seemed to do well after this," the old settler mused in hindsight. "Everybody believed he thought it was an Indian, but if it was a white man, through mistake, he ought to have told it."[26]

In the midst of a border war which blurred the distinction between military and civilian populations, personal appearance played a crucial role in rapidly distinguishing potential enemies from friends. Border inhabitants—native and immigrant alike—used clues of dress and skin color to make quick judgments about the loyalties and intentions of the strangers they met. Appearance was not always an accurate guide to identity, however. Peter Harper resembled his Indian father physically, yet his neighbors considered him a "white man" slain by a careless mistake. That racial identities seemed indeterminate and dress had symbolic power to transform identity hints at the contingency of these social relationships: in the Anglo-Indian borderland, identities of interest were not yet fixed in permanent racial categories but shifted with the free flow of events. Nicholas Cresswell did not become a Delaware with his adoption of Indian clothes, but he did become their friend. Baptist missionary David Jones pushed the logic of this reasoning to a prematurely hopeful conclusion: "It seemed strange to me to see the [white] captives have the exact gestures of Indians. Might we not infer from hence, that if Indians were educated as we are, they would be like us?"[27]

Words and Customs

Judging a stranger's appearance only began the process of determining if he or she was "the right kind." Customs, manners, and language also served as relevant attributes in making decisions about others. Western settlers—like many immigrant populations—were culturally conservative, carrying to their new homes memories and preconceptions which served as models or templates for conduct in a new geographic setting. Upon their arrival in the Ohio Valley, migrants encountered representatives of other races, cultures, and social groups, all with their own customs and cultural norms. A diversity of behaviors, including habits of speech, social conventions, and preferences in food and drink, served to identify like-minded fellows and distinguish outsiders. If dress or skin color separated strangers into large, crude categories of potential friendship or enmity, customs and manners revealed more subtle cultural distinctions based on perceptions of kinship or "otherness."[28]

In the realm of words and customs, intercultural contacts provoked laughter, sometimes disgust, but only rarely real violence. How border inhabitants used language and behavior to define themselves against others unfolds suggestively in another incident from Daniel Trabue's salt-making expedition of 1779. Trabue introduced this story by noting that "one of the men we had with us was a young Irishman who was constant contending and Disputeing with the other young men that was from old Virginia about words and customs." One morning on their way to Bullit's Lick, Trabue shot a buffalo bull, a native animal which some of his party had never before encountered. Although he felled the bison with his shot, Trabue soon realized that he "had shot this buffelo too high," and told one of the other men to shoot him again. "This young Irishman said, 'No'; he would kill him and Jumed at him with his tomerhock and strikeing him in the forehead." Trabue warned the man that the buffalo's mud-matted wool and thick skull would cushion his blows, but the Irishman "kept up his licks, a nocking a way." Suddenly, Trabue recalled, "the buffelo Jumped up. The man run, the buffelo after him. It was opin woods, no bushes, and the way this young Irishman run was rather Desending ground and every Jump he cryed out, 'O lard! O lard! O lard! O lard!'"

With the buffalo close on his heels, the Irishman darted behind a beech tree; the animal crashed headlong into its trunk, "the tuckeyho boys laughing, 'Ha! Ha! Ha!'" Later, Trabue wrote, when "these young men would Mimmick him, 'O lard! O l[ard]!' etc. and breack out in big laughter," the "Irishman said he would go no further with such fools . . . as these boys weare." After failing to persuade the young man to go on with the group, Trabue and his party "bid him a Due [adieu], leaveing him a butchering his buffelo."[29]

As Trabue's account suggests, verbal communication served as an important sorting device in contacts with strangers. Accent or idiom often revealed a newcomer's geographic or ethnic origins; in recalling face-to-face contacts with non-English migrants, memorialists like Trabue frequently attempted to re-create, or at least note, distinctive dialects or usages. Ulster Scots, usually called "Irishmen" in the eighteenth century, evidently spoke with a characteristic brogue or accent, which Trabue's "tuckeyho boys" were quick to mimic. In transcribing the Irishman's speech into his written text, Trabue summarized this linguistic distinction with his phonetic spelling of "O lard!" (as in *car*) for the exclamation "O lord!" Even more ambitious was Spencer Records's transcription of Highland Scots speech. In recalling the brutal massacre of friendly Moravian Indians in 1782, Records "never heard any person speak of the circumstance, without expressing his abhorrence, excepting one poor old dirty Scotchman, named James Greenlee, who said, 'owh mon ats a weel cum don thang, fur they suppurted the other Injuns as tha cum and gaad.'"[30]

John Shane's interview notes reflect a similar consciousness of linguistic distinctions. Jacob Stevens narrated the story of Hugh Cunningham and his wife, describing them as "both right Irish." After being captured by Indians, Cunningham was absent from the settlement for such a long time that "his wife had made another engagement . . . to a much younger and likelier man." When her husband returned just before her new marriage was to take place, Cunningham's wife could not conceal her disappointment. " 'Well Ugh, are you alive yet?' Hugh, picked [piqued] at this reception, crustily replied, 'Yes you dom fool! Don't you see I am?'" In recounting the capture of the Shawnee leader Blue Jacket, William Clinkenbeard underscored the linguistic distinctiveness of both the Indian and an Irishman who volunteered to kill him. Clinkenbeard's militia company agreed that the famous war leader "should be killed, but no one was willing to do it, but a little Irishman. Says he, By Jasus, I'll kill him." When "the Irishman's heart failed him to kill a man in cold blood," the militiamen offered their prisoner a drink of whiskey. Blue Jacket replied, "it was 'velly good turn.'"[31]

Informants frequently linked Ulster speech patterns with the liberal use of profanity. In a typical example, Josiah Collins characterized

Alexander McConnell as "some sort of Irishman" and added that he "swore pretty hard." Nathaniel Hart narrated another account of an Irishman who lost his way while out hunting near the Licking River. In his wanderings, the man encountered a buffalo and decided to follow it; but when the animal brought him back to his starting place, "he cursed the bull Buffalo, and swore he was as badly lost as himself." In contrast, Jane Stevenson repeated a more lyrical fragment of highlands speech in her brief account of "the death of bonie Alexander Crawford."[32]

Immigrants of German or Dutch descent also spoke with a perceptible accent. Usually lumped together as "Dutchmen" by English settlers, some German or Dutch speakers like Michael Stoner (Holsteiner) conversed in what Nathaniel Hart termed "very broken English." Other migrants spoke with only a trace of an accent or a slightly irregular syntax. Challenged for hiding during the siege of Boonesborough, Tice Brock reportedly exclaimed: "Py sure . . . I was not made for a fighter—I was not made for a fighter." Daniel Trabue also hinted at a distinctive German pronunciation in his story of the "poore Dutchman," Jacob Stucker, who wrapped a plundered Indian blanket around himself and declared: "this will keep me worm [sic] this winter." Admittedly here, though, Trabue's substitution of the written word "worm" for the spoken word "warm" may also be another example of the memorialist's erratic spelling rather than an intentional linguistic marker.[33]

Behavior, like language, helped distinguish familiars from "outlandish" outsiders. The account of the Irishman's attempt to kill the buffalo with his tomahawk is typical of a whole genre of border stories illustrating the peculiar proclivities of strangers or newcomers. Nathaniel Hart narrated a brief biographical account of Richard Burke, another Ulsterman, who had come out to Kentucky "as a waiting man to the Shelbys, and obtained a pre-emption" for his own farm. "He commonly went by the name of 'fool Burke,'" Hart recalled, "being very singular in all his ways." Josiah Collins similarly termed German settlers "fools" for working too hard. "These old Dutch fellows were such fools, they couldn't take care of themselves. Thought if they didn't go out and work, they would starve to death, and never thought of danger. Michael Stucker said, d—n the Indians, they had killed his father, and now he should have the corn to work, all by himself." Collins concluded that "most all of the old Dutchmen got killed in those days." Nathaniel Hart concurred: "the Dutch were not good soldiers. They understood nothing of Indian warfare."[34]

Unusual customs and awkward words tended to set German and Dutch settlers apart from the Anglo-American majority, even when they lived in close proximity. "The Presbyterian Dutch had a curious practice of sprinkling (christening) their children," one man recalled; another remembered the time "the old women in the station . . . were all in arms in a discussion" as to the custom's propriety. "Mrs. White was a Baptist and took ground against it," he said; "this was the first debate on baptism ever held in Kentucky." Several informants accused German Americans of loyalism during the late war with Great Britain. Daniel Trabue narrated a long account of a trick he played on a Dutch woman to force her to reveal her Tory sympathies. Although Trabue was clearly amused by his trick, the woman was deeply frightened when she realized that she had been led into revealing her family's political inclinations: such an act could have led to death or reprisals in the disorderly backcountry of Carolina. In an interview conducted in the 1850s, Joseph Ficklin confided to Shane that "we had no Irishmen in those days [referring to contemporary nativist stereotypes about Irish Catholics], and it was the amusement of the wits to make fun of the Dutch." More cold-blooded was Spencer Records's appraisal of his two German tenants, Abraham Gardner and Rudolph Fuss, who boarded for a time with his family in their log cabin. "They were both Dutchmen, and not used to guns," Records noted in his memoir, "so that I could have no dependence on them, only that they would make a show if Indians came in sight; and if we should be fired on, they might be shot in place of me."[35]

In much the same fashion, humorous stories targeted Irishmen as outsiders. William McClelland, a second-generation Ulster emigrant, related his uncle's story about "Higgany, an Irishman," who carried an obsolete blunderbuss on an expedition against the Indian towns above Fort Pitt during the Seven Years' War. Having never before fired a gun, Higgany repeatedly loaded the blunderbuss but hesitated to discharge it. In an emergency, the captain finally ordered him to fire: "the Irishman pulled his trigger, and the fire knocked him full a rod back, and broke his collar bone, and laid him flat on his back." As Higgany "came to a little, he called to those around him to stand back a little, he had put seven loads in, and but one had come out." McClelland explained that normally "the blunderbuss had to be tied to a log when they went to fire"; the captain had given the heavy gun to the big Irishman to carry because "they did not know what use they might want with it."[36]

Stories illustrating an outsider's lack of experience or "sense" also invite alternative readings. Considered from another perspective, intercultural contacts with outlandish newcomers often dramatized the efforts of immigrants to replicate familiar cultural forms in a new geographic setting. Actions which seemed inexplicable to migrants of a dissimilar background may well have made perfect sense to members of the same cultural group. Higgany's ignorance of firearms, for example, suggests that he was a recent arrival in America. In eighteenth-century Europe, warfare was the province of trained soldiers rather than the civilian population; most Anglo-American males, on the other hand, participated in some form of militia training. Similarly, in Daniel Trabue's buffalo story, what Trabue interpreted as the Irishman's impetuosity in keeping "up his licks, a nocking a way," was probably from the latter's perspective a logical inference based on his prior agricultural experience. Inexperienced in the handling of North American bison but familiar with a traditional technique for stunning domestic livestock for slaughter, the Irishman struck a rapid blow to the buffalo's forehead just as he might have cudgeled a steer. Unfortunately, the newcomer's cultural inheritance did not serve him well in this instance, much as German American traditions of intensive tillage and peaceful relations with neighboring Indians proved ill suited to an ongoing border war in a rich hunting territory. By the mid-nineteenth century, the Irishman's impetuosity and the Dutchman's obduracy would become ethnic stereotypes; on the Anglo-Indian border, their actions conformed to more generalized stereotypes about the unpredictability and "foolishness" of strangers or newcomers.[37]

Cultures of Rank and Region

Distinctive behavior was by no means limited to the non-English migrant. Class and regional divisions cut across the dominant Anglo-American population, endowing even the actions of fellow English-speakers with a degree of exoticism. Samuel Potts Pointer, originally from Loudoun County in the Virginia piedmont, helped Eli Cleveland with his harvest for ten days in 1789; fifty years later, Pointer still marveled at Cleveland's manner of living. Cleveland, who owned a mill at the mouth of Boon's Creek, "had hounds to hunt . . . [and] a place posted in to keep in deer. If any body went in to shoot, they would set the dogs on them. 'Twas said the dogs were dangerous, but they never troubled me. Cleveland was rich! rich! 'Twas said he hadn't slept with his wife, for fourteen years." From Pointer's remarks, it is difficult to ascertain which caused more comment among Cleveland's neighbors: the mill owner's wealth, his unorthodox marital relations, or his attempt to enforce game laws in what was widely considered a hunting commons. John Wilson encountered another wealthy man living on the banks of Beargrass Creek and was similarly struck by his domestic arrangements. "Captain Prince lived at the old station. A Virginian. His wealth consisted mostly in Negroes. They had scarcely any furniture. His daughters had servants to wait on them for every-thing—mean as they lived."[38]

Gentlemen were different, Joseph Ficklin explained to Shane. "There was at that time in Virginia, a wide distinction between the families of gentlemen, and common people—and the common man when he went to the gentleman's house, didn't pretend to go in, but stood at the door and took off his hat." Taking up residence in the rude settlements of the western country, gentlemen continued to manifest their distinctive-ness—what might be termed the "culture of rank"—in a variety of ways: through their more elaborate dress, their ownership of land and slaves, and frequently by their relative freedom from manual labor. A female immigrant characterized a member of her river party suc-cinctly: "Runnells was a gentleman. Didn't row any."[39]

In turn, genteel migrants anxiously scanned the countryside for signs of polite society. Mary Dewees's journal of her removal from Philadelphia to Kentucky in 1788 narrates a running commentary on the refinement (or lack thereof) of the people, houses, and towns she encountered along the way. Lancaster, she wrote, had "some Elegant Houses in it," but Abbot's town was "a trifling place." Crossing the Allegheny Mountains, she found the roads bad, the accommodations primitive, and the Scotch-Irish settlers "exceedingly Kind but Sur-prizingly dirty." Mary's spirits began to improve shortly after her party boarded their own flatboat on a tributary of the Ohio River: "our room 16 by 12 with a comfortable fireplace [is] far preferable to the Cabbins we met with after we crossed the Mountains." Reaching Pitts-burgh and discovering a few "very polite and Agreeable" families, her party decided to tie up for a few days in order to exchange visits. At

Mrs. Butler's, Mary exclaimed over that classic indicator of genteel aspiration: "a very handsome parlour, Elegently papered and well finished." Doubtlessly paying her hostess the ultimate compliment, Mary considered the receiving room "more like Philad[elphia] than any I have seen since I left that place."[40]

On board the Dewees's flatboat—indeed, in much of the western country—the rituals of genteel entertainment depended more on the suggestion of refinement than on the full deployment of its trappings. Guests and hosts conspired to read the most nuanced of gestures as a completed tableau. Mary partitioned off her sleeping quarters with blankets—just as the owners of gentry houses had once removed beds from parlors—and invited Colonel and Mrs. Butler to take "a bit of Biscuit and Cheese with a glass of wine" in her cabin. As low water continued to delay their departure from Pittsburgh, Mary and her husband hosted a series of dinner parties and served such local delicacies as pike and wild grapes. Refinement also called for restraint, however. Concerned about her ability to maintain genteel standards of personal appearance, Mary regretfully turned down an invitation to a Pittsburgh ball, "as it was out of our power to dress fit at this time." She departed for Kentucky with some trepidation, but soon after their arrival (and a visit from "the genteel people in the place") pronounced Lexington society "very agreeable and I flatter myself I shall see many happy days in this Country."[41]

Distinctions in western housing emerged more slowly, although they may have been subtly visible from the start: the first shingled-roof dwelling in Boonesborough belonged to the proprietor of the Transylvania Company, Richard Henderson. (Presumably common clapboard roofing was in use until his arrival.) Twenty years later, when the tidewater planter David Meade passed through Bourbon County, he was surprised to discover that "in these [log] Cabbins many opulent and some Genteel people live . . . even at this time & I am told that they are by the latter made more than barely comfortable." Meade soon founded his own rural seat, which he grandiosely called "Chaumière des Prairies," nine miles southwest of Lexington. By 1800, Chaumière stood as a rambling cluster of log and frame rooms arranged in a variation of the Georgian plan of architecture then popular in England and tidewater Virginia. Meade surrounded his log mansion with another hallmark of the genteel style: an English landscape garden complete with a Grecian temple, a lake, and forty acres of plantings and native woods. Largely cut off from the more elaborate refinements of tidewater life, Meade nevertheless cultivated a gentleman's reputation for largesse. According to a local informant, "Mead[e] spent a great deal in entertaining people. Never would receive pay. Every man was a gentleman, and as such stayed as long as he pleased."[42]

As emigrants from various parts of British America converged on the Ohio Valley, regional differences in cultural norms also became apparent. To a former resident of the Monongahela country, for example, the customs of the tidewater might seem unfamiliar, or even repugnant. How such parochial identities and prejudices influenced social conduct is illustrated by an episode narrated by Mrs. Ephraim January. When Indians captured her twin brothers, January's father decided to return to Pennsylvania. At that time, a company was preparing to go up the river, but its members divided into two different groups, one journeying by water and the other by land. "The company my father and mother were in, was a company from Virginia," January explained. "They had been out, I suppose, looking for land, and were on their way in. Some of them were pretty wild fellows. The land party were Pennsylvanians, and thought they wouldn't stay with the others." The Pennsylvanians paid dearly for their clannishness, however; Indians attacked their group and killed several of its members. As the two parties were not far apart at the time, one of the Pennsylvanians ran down to the river bank to ask the others for help.[43]

Differences between Virginians and Pennsylvanians formed a meaningful distinction in common culture. At the outbreak of the Revolutionary War, Virginia's Indian commissioners repeatedly insisted to skeptical Shawnee and Delaware diplomats that Virginians were not "a Distinct People," but "one Flesh and Blood" with Pennsylvanians and other English colonists. Political and wartime alliances did little to erase perceptions of cultural difference, however. When Needham Parry, a Quaker from York County, Pennsylvania, visited a farm near Danville, Kentucky, in 1794, the owner "took a great deal of pains to shew me his improvements, of every sort." Proudly displaying his orchard with fruit-bearing apple trees, the man "said he wished to improve his place like a Pennsylvanian. Although he was a Virginian, from Augusta County." Joseph Ficklin distinguished between the settlement patterns of the two immigrant groups in central Kentucky, claiming that "Lexington was settled principally by Pennsylvanians.

The south side of the river by the Craigs, Virginians." One of the most visible regional distinctions was in the matter of slaveholding. In 1780, the Pennsylvania legislature passed a law providing for the gradual emancipation of the state's slave population; Pennsylvanians moving west carried with them a reputation for holding antislavery sentiments. As an early resident of Fayette County told Shane: "there was a set of Pennsylvanians, all on one side of me, when I came here. They were all great abolitionists."[44]

Regional stereotypes were not always benign. On the road to Virginia, a Methodist exhorter fell in with "a company of Virginians, who (not at all to the honor of their state), drank freely, swore lustily and when we retired to rest, betook themselves to cards, which considerably disturbed our rest." Daniel Drake, originally from the Scotch Plains of New Jersey, ranked immigrants from Maryland even more unfavorably: "Whenever I am writing of our ignorance, the Maryland element of our population comes into my mind. . . . They were not only extremely ignorant compared with the Jersey, and most of the Virginia immigrants, in all school learning, but likewise in the domestic arts. . . . Many of them were indolent, and more than an equal number 'given to drink.' " Charges of loyalism dogged the steps of Carolina emigrants. William Clinkenbeard claimed that a "heap of Tories" settled at Strode's Station the first winter he was there. "Everybody coming to Kentucky. Could hardly get along the road for them. And all grand tories, pretty nigh. All from Carolina, tories. Had been treated so bad there, they had to run off or do worse." Numerous reports—both contemporary and retrospective—identified the Carolina founders of one of central Kentucky's most prominent stations as loyalists. In a letter written from Boonesborough in 1776, John Floyd noted that "the Bryans and other Tories to the number of 28 men" had sixty-six acres of corn growing on a tract near Elkhorn Creek—all under a good fence. Joseph Ficklin, who lived at Bryan's Station as a boy, confirmed that "the Bryans rested under the imputation of being tories—and all went back to North Carolina."[45]

Although differences between Tory and patriot never flamed into the civil war that engulfed other backcountry regions, political sympathies may well have led to scattered instances of violence in Kentucky. Recalling yet another mysterious death like that of the *métis* Peter Harper, Ficklin related that "one Williams, who was in the station, and was regarded as a tory . . . went out from the station to hunt . . . and never returned." Hinting obliquely at the possibility of foul play, Ficklin remarked that "it was never known what became of him—whether he went off and joined the Indians, or was killed by them, or killed himself, or how."[46]

Regional distinctions in customs and manners also cut across the political boundaries of states. Informants generally agreed, for example, that migrants from western districts were more sophisticated in their dealings with Indians. When John Hedge reached Kentucky in November 1791, he discovered that "Ready Money Jack" (the innkeeper with the ambiguous racial and ethnic identity discussed in Chapter 1) kept the only tavern on the road between Mayslick and the Blue Licks; there Hedge's traveling company "got some hot corn cake and milk, which ate admirable." Although other settlers hesitated to settle beyond Mayslick, apparently the innkeeper did not fear for his safety. "Ready Money Jack was from Monongahela country," Hedge explained; "was less afraid of Indians. The people in that country were more accustomed to them." In nearly identical terms, William Clinkenbeard characterized Major Hood, "a low Dutchman" from the Red-Stone country, as "a pretty good hand after Indians; expect he had been accustomed to them." Traveling from a greater distance and settling south of the Ohio River in fewer numbers, New England emigrants bore less nuanced identities in the memories of Shane's informants. One man termed Abijah Brooks "a right Yankee"; a woman described Elias Barbee as simply "a northern man."[47]

Culinary Geography

In the realm of customary behavior, preferences in food and drink serve as sensitive indicators of social belonging or distance. Immigrants and their descendants routinely seek out the remembered foods of their homelands; consumers discriminate among a wide array of edible commodities to mark social boundaries, commemorate events, and express personal values.[48] In much the same way, patterns of food and beverage consumption lent cultural meaning to the social universe of Ohio Valley settlers. Although corn and wild meat constituted the general provision for all residents during the early years of settlement, subtle culinary distinctions illuminated the complexity of the local cultural geography.

Some backcountry food traditions originated in Europe. Accustomed to plentiful supplies of meat and maize, native-born immigrants observed that those of European birth readily ate foods they normally scorned. Angus Ross, from the Highlands of Scotland, ate the marrow from buffalo shank bones and goose eggs with veins that others would not touch. In describing his former poverty, Ross "used to say he hired as a herder one year in the Highlands of Scotland for his board and a pair of shoes. Never got his shoes, at that. Had never had enough of meat to eat there." Descendants of Ulster emigrants expressed a fondness for buttermilk, the sour milk left over after churning the butter from whole milk. Here, the invention of tradition transformed the staple of the European peasant into a uniquely nourishing American beverage. Josiah Collins overheard John Todd tell his wife not to give their daughter "any sweet milk, but to feed it altogether on buttermilk, that was the most healthy." Todd's parents were both from Ireland, Collins explained in an aside. Not everyone viewed buttermilk as potable, however. Daniel Drake recalled that his mother, "tired out with a diet of bread and meat," broke into tears after a neighbor who had just finished churning failed to offer her "the delicious beverage, for which she was too proud to ask (and which the other perhaps did not *think* of giving)."[49]

Tea drinking, the bellwether of an expanding British consumer culture, linked a few frontier households with the tastes and styles of the metropolis. As in coastal areas, backcountry tea drinking was not the sole prerogative of the genteel, although it did suggest a certain level of social aspiration. Mary Dewees and David Meade both recorded tea parties as part of the polite social round in Pittsburgh and Lexington in the 1780s and 1790s. Mrs. Phillips invoked her polite antecedents for John Shane when she recalled that her mother and Mrs. John Todd took tea together in the fort at Lexington, even though "they had nothing but tea and dried buffaloe meat." In frontier Louisville, Jack, one of five slaves belonging to Rebecca Hite, declared his familiarity with the rituals of the ruling race and, perhaps, his social distance from less sophisticated bondsmen when he charged a half pound of Bohea tea to his own store account. For such a social gesture to be effective, however, its ceremonies had to be correctly performed. A Maryland family drew Daniel Drake's scorn rather than admiration by keeping "a quantity of tea boiling in a large uncovered Dutch oven . . . out of which they were dipping it with a tin cup and drinking it from the breakfast table."[50]

As Drake's account suggests, familiarity with the rituals of tea consumption was not yet universal in the back settlements. James Stevenson admitted to John Shane that "the first tea-cups and saucers I ever saw" were at the home of transplanted Virginia planter John Fowler. Another popular genre of border stories (or, perhaps, tall tales) revolved around the blunders of those new to the preparation and service of tea. Samuel Gibson's father recounted the tale of a Presbyterian clergyman who traveled through the West with his own supply of tea. "As he had understood that in the western settlements tea was not always to be had, and as this was to himself an indispensable delicacy, the gentleman took the precaution of depositing a pound in his saddlebags." One day, when he stopped at a house that could not supply his favorite beverage, the clergyman drew out his package of tea and handed it to his hostess, unopened. The woman withdrew, and in due time served up the tea "in the manner of a dish of greens, and set [it] on a plate before him." The visitor asked the woman what she had done with the broth, and she replied that she had thrown that out. "The preacher observed that if she had given him that, that was all he cared for." To further illustrate the domestic deficiencies of Marylanders, Daniel Drake recounted a similar story of a family that had "purchased half a pound of Bohea tea, and boiled it in winter with a ham of bacon in place of greens." As late as 1816, a French emigrant to Kentucky warned her nephew about the quality of western beverages: "you will never see a drop of soup, nor beer. There is tea and dark water that is called coffee, although it does not contain one grain of it."[51]

Divergent culinary traditions also distinguished cohees from tuckahoes. When Hugh Garret's militia company stopped at a house one day to ask a woman for something to drink, "she sat us out a churn full of cream with cups. Dupuy said it was mighty rich buttermilk. Craig said he must be a d—d tuckahoe that he didn't know the difference between cream and buttermilk." In a story illustrating the intersection of regional, ethnic, and social distinctions in the realm of food customs— as well as in electoral politics—Joseph Ficklin claimed that Andrew Steel lost a bid to serve in the Virginia legislature because "they ran him off at the election with Cohee." His opponents "told on him, that his wife came to the door, and said 'Andrew come to your mush. The pegs [pigs] have been in it, and will be in it again.' " Mush, a thick porridge made with cornmeal and water or milk, was a western dish, explained Ficklin. "Knew nothing about mush in eastern Virginia. Called it hominy in eastern Virginia. It (mush) was a Cohee dish." John Fowler, the planter with the tea cups and saucers, won the election.[52]

In reflecting upon social divisions in early Kentucky, another of Shane's informants linked habits of food consumption with religious affiliation and social standing. After describing Fowler's tea equipment and the coach-and-four driven by James Wilkinson, James Stevenson added that the first loaf of bread he had ever seen was at Lewis Craig's Mill. "In those times this was the outside of Presbyterianism," he explained to Shane, "and I looked upon those men as the quality of the land. The Baptists were the great ones." Shane added his own observation in an initialed aside: "They came from an older part of the country. Presbyterianism, therefore, here, was allied with unimposing prospects. Neither great wealth, ostentation, nor influence." In a similar fashion, religious and social tensions may have been at work in the scuffle over breakfast recorded by Daniel Trabue. Breakfast at a tavern with rum toddy, tea, and coffee would have been the fare favored by a genteel Anglican; a simple pan of fried hominy was Baptist or Methodist fare.[53]

Anglo-Americans who ventured outside their own settlements discovered the culinary peculiarities of Indians and Frenchmen. The use of salt, like buttermilk, marked a cultural divide in the western country. Soon after a Shawnee hunting party captured Benjamin Allen and dressed him as an Indian, the group came across a herd of buffalo. Taking this opportunity to kill several animals and pack the meat for transport, the hunters then prepared a portion for cooking. "They gave me a leather purse of salt to salt mine," Allen explained, adding that "[I] never saw any of them use of it." On a militia raid against the Shawnee towns north of the Ohio River, William Clinkenbeard stopped to sample some boiled dumplings that he found still warm and steaming in a tray. Clinkenbeard recalled thinking that "now I would have my belly full," but he could not stomach the Indian food. "They were made of corn and beans with enough of meal in them to make them stick together," he said, but "without any salt."[54]

Sharp disagreements surfaced over preparation techniques and the range of foods considered edible. The culture shock of Euroamericans suddenly confronted with Indian foodways was a staple of backcountry captivity narratives. Daniel Ketcham's Ottawa captors prepared a feast that he later recalled with little relish. After finding two "nice" bear cubs nested in a hollow tree, "they put fire under their kettle, filled [it] with water, threw the two cubs in it, feathers and all, without even ablution, and made their choicest dish of soup." To Ketcham's stunned disbelief, the Indians ate the broth, but not the flesh of the bears; that, "which to the uninitiated white man was so much more desirable, was left to be consumed by the wild beasts." Abel Janney had lived on blackberries for four days but still could not eat the roast wolf his Ottawa captors prepared. "They took the entrails out and stripping the stuff from them between their fingers and threw them on the coals when roasted a little they offered me some, but as hungry as I was my stomach revolted at it; they devoured them like dogs." Janney remembered his welcome to the Ottawa village more fondly: an old woman motioned him to her side and told him that it was her son who had taken him prisoner. "And now I was to be her son also, and so gave me some victuals, water melons and apples, and pitied me very much seeing that I was so exceedingly poor."[55]

On his trading voyage to Natchez with a party of Frenchmen, Joshua McQueen similarly traversed alien culinary terrain. For daily fare, "we lived on Bears oil and rice, stewed up," he told Shane. One day, while out hunting for something to add to the pot, McQueen killed a doe which he cut in half to carry back to the traders' bateaux. As he rounded a bend in the river, he stumbled upon a hunting camp of almost fifty Indians including women and children. "I dare not be afraid," McQueen recalled. "They were cooking there, and I just went on and put my half doe across the pole. . . . An Indian took me by the coat into his wigwam, swung his kettle of lie [lye] corn on, and warmed it, and gave me a horn spoon—buffaloe, black as [an] ace of spades." After he had satisfied his immediate appetite, McQueen began to shove aside the rich fat which seasoned the porridge. The Indian noticed his gesture "and asked me in French what kind of fat. I answered Mukquaw (bear)." No, it was "sha sha, he said, dog meat. After that I slackened off a good deal," McQueen noted.

Later, when the Indians went down to trade with the French boat and to join in a drinking party, the French purchased a "painter" (a colloquial term for a cougar or mountain lion) from them for their mess. McQueen reported that the painter "ate a good deal like mutton" if you did not see its ribs. As McQueen's account suggests, the

French in the Mississippi Valley had adapted their customs to Indian practice. A visitor to the settlement at Vincennes returned to report about unusual foods and strange agricultural practices. "McLean brought back some apples, striped red. People, they said, fenced up their woods, and put in their cattle and let their crop lands lay open." Such a custom, of course, accommodated Native American farming practices; fencing in cattle rather than letting them roam free prevented grazing animals from ravaging Indian planting fields.[56]

In times of relative peace, sharing food was a common ritual of friendly exchange on the Anglo-Indian border. When Elizabeth Poague's family traveled through the wilderness in 1775, they encountered "ten Cherokees and a squaw . . . [who] were friendly and talked—near Cumberland river; after they left they killed a small buffalo, and divided with the whites." On their way from Fort Pitt to the Illinois country in 1766, John Jennings's river party passed four canoes paddled by twenty Shawnees who joined them and "gave us some fresh Meat." Jennings's group "returned the Compliment with Biscuit, & Tobacco." Such hospitality served as an important social lubricant in the border country; Euroamericans may well have adopted this custom from Indian villagers, who were well known for their open-handed entertainment of strangers traveling through their territory. Certainly, as historian Francis Jennings has pointed out, the gift of food and shelter (and sometimes sexual favors) bears little resemblance to European traditions of commercial innkeeping. Christian missionaries, in particular, learned to utilize the softening influence of generosity to their own advantage. One Presbyterian noted that a shared meal of spring fawn transformed a "very Reserved & Distant" Delaware headman into a congenial host. "We Divided the Deer among them & us to every fire a quartr [sic] which came seasonable to them as well as us they having no meat."[57]

Such cross-cultural contacts gradually led to the appreciation and assimilation of unfamiliar foods. Benjamin Allen termed another dish cooked by his Shawnee captors as "elegant," describing it as fat buffalo meat seasoned with buffalo jerky and thickened with meal. Baptist missionary David Jones enjoyed his first hickory nuts—"which [are] part of their food, being much superior to any of that kind in our eastern world"—at the house of a Shawnee headman. When entertaining the chief and his friends, Jones served them a breakfast of "fat buffalo, beavers tails and chocolate." Chocolate drinking, possibly unfamiliar to his Native American guests, was originally an Aztec custom which had become the rage in Europe in the late seventeenth century; the beverage (now sweetened with cane sugar) returned to the North American continent as a fashionable Anglo-American drink. The missionary had recently experimented with drinking his own breakfast chocolate with rum rather than milk, and pronounced it "very useful here in the wilderness, where flesh [is] our chief provision."[58]

Thus food, like clothing, formed a permeable cultural boundary in the border region. Euroamericans rapidly adopted maize, local game, and maple sugar as dietary staples; at the same time, native inhabitants learned to appreciate a variety of European dishes. When the trader James Kenny visited the Beaver Creek settlement of Gray Eyes, a Delaware headman, in 1761, he discovered that his host lived in a shingled house and made "Good Butter." Visiting the Moravian mission towns along the Tuskawaras River a little over a decade later, David Jones also found evidence of livestock herding and dairying. During his captivity among the Shawnee in the summer of 1788, Thomas Ridout was astonished to be served tea by Metsigemewa, his captor's wife. In preparing for breakfast, the Shawnee woman "boiled some water in a small copper kettle, with which she made some tea in a tea-pot, using cups and saucers of yellow ware. . . . When she had done she poured some tea in a saucer, which, with some fried meat on a pewter plate, she gave [to] me." The tea proved to be green tea, and was sweetened with maple sugar. Ridout confessed that "this was a luxury I little expected to meet with," not only because of the distance the tea must have traveled, but also because he was a prisoner and "could hardly expect such fare."[59]

That the culinary diplomacy of the western country also had its limits is suggested by the tragic fate of one of the Moravian mission towns, Gnadenhütten, which was put to the torch by a backcountry militia company in 1782. Falsely accusing the Christian Indians of stealing the European tablewares that they had adopted, the militiamen slaughtered more than ninety of the town's residents, the majority of these women and children.[60] So it was that creative adaptations by Indians and Europeans in matters of dress, housing, and cuisine turned out not to lead very far down the path of cultural syncretism in the western country, nor, indeed, in Anglo-America as a whole. In later years, with the crafting of heroic narratives of Indian conquest and American nationhood, even the tentative first steps in this direction would be forgotten by all but a few.

Kinship

In making decisions about strangers, preconceptions about cultural norms helped group other persons and give them a name. Border residents used clues of appearance, language, and behavior to sort others into simple perceptual categories which emphasized certain differences while underplaying broad similarities in behavior. Local and particular distinctions based on regional or cultural identities continued to have force in the new geographic setting, as did consciousness of ethnic, racial, and wealth-holding differences. Yet because migrants sorted themselves out several ways simultaneously—as cohees and tuckahoes, Irishmen and Dutchmen, gentlemen and common folk, Presbyterians and Baptists—a collective sense of "us" versus "them" failed to coalesce along socioeconomic, ethnic, regional, or even racial lines. Over time, as the Euroamerican population grew and frontier outposts evolved into settled agricultural communities, some of these social boundaries hardened; others virtually disappeared. All such "distinctions and particions" eventually became subsumed under the largest division which traced the fault line of border war: encroaching immigrant and dispossessed native. Endemic warfare proved a powerful solvent for received cultural categories in the late-eighteenth-century Ohio Valley, even as it strengthened the perceived differences between native and newcomer.

To this point, I have been more concerned with those boundaries that set apart rather than welded groups together. Yet identities of inclusion were equally crucial in defining the social landscape of the western country; certainly we must account for sources of cohesion if we are to explain the deceptively homogeneous appearance of the western population perceived by later generations. Here again, the social sciences may be of assistance in thinking about this problem. While historians traditionally pay only passing attention to kinship relations beyond the immediate bounds of the nuclear family, anthropologists, recognizing that kinship is the basic idiom of all social relationships, usually begin their fieldwork by constructing detailed genealogical tables of family relationships in the community under study. "Conceptions of consanguinity and descent," writes one ethnographer, "are analogically applied beyond the bounds of biological relatedness to create systems of fictive kinship." The metaphor of family, in other words, can be extended to all social relationships which express distinctions of inclusion or exclusion.[61]

In the complex cultural geography of the Ohio Valley, conceptions of kinship—both biological and fictive—provided new bases for social cohesion. Even the most casual perusal of Shane's notes offers glimpses of a dense web of kinship connections stretching from east to west and, in time, spinning outward from new frontier settlements. Families and neighbors shared geographic information about western lands and assisted each other in moving to frontier areas. Caleb Williams's father, for example, arrived in Cincinnati from New York State in October 1790: "moved out through the influence of my uncle Joel, one of the proprietors." Often entire families moved west, journeying together for protection or migrating serially as opportunity allowed. Upon arrival, family members sought each other out and frequently settled together in the same station. As the threat of Indian attack subsided and migrants moved out to their own farms, neighborhoods preserved the spatial expression of these family relationships.[62]

Kinship connections structured many of the narratives recorded by John Shane. James Stevenson was born on the Calfpasture River in western Virginia; as a small child, he traveled to Kentucky with his father and mother in the autumn of 1779. "Didn't get ready to come out with Uncle Sam, as he had intended. When my father got to Boonesborough, there was not a sign of a blaze, or trace, to there from Lexington: and Uncle Sam set out to meet us; was so glad to hear we had come." Stevenson calculated the date of his arrival by making reference to other members of his kin network: "That, I think, was two weeks after Aunt Jane came. Uncle Tommy came with my father." As recorded in Shane's notebook, Stevenson's repertoire of early stories included a seemingly random jumble of family accounts and firsthand experiences; his stories moved back and forth in time and space from his rescue by an older brother during an Indian attack, to Aunt Jane's memories as a girl of swimming on her back in the Greenbriar River, to Uncle Billy's actions at the siege of Bryan's Station. Genealogical rather than chronological connections lent coherence to Stevenson's account, revealing the importance of family relationships in the imaginative universe of this informant.[63]

So universal was the expectation that families would migrate together that William McClelland noted as a curiosity one man's refusal to "come to Kentook" with his children. McAfee had settled on the Catawba, McClelland explained, where he had provided his three sons with plantations of their own. When the sons later decided to migrate to Kentucky, the father stubbornly remained behind. "Said they were all gone to Kantook but one Diel [devil] of a Buck (Mrs. Buchanan) & she was gone to Holston." At their parting, McAfee greased his son's saddle; in return, his sons "filled his bag with beans for ginseng."[64]

Fictive kin—neighbors, friends, and co-religionists—also coordinated their removal to the West. As a member of Upper Spotsylvania Baptist Church, Mrs. John Arnold came to Kentucky in August 1781. "There were 180 of us, when we came out. Lewis Craig came then; it was his church that moved out." Perhaps hinting at the impetus for this extraordinary mass migration, Arnold added: "Lewis Craig had not a very great talent for preaching, but was not to be beat at exhortation." In a similar manner, a Catholic colony from Saint Mary's, Charles, and Prince George Counties, Maryland, migrated to Kentucky and settled on Pottinger's Creek near Bardstown in 1785.[65]

Even in the absence of charismatic religious leadership, neighbors frequently migrated together. When Samuel Williams moved to Cincinnati from New York State in 1790, "there were nine or ten families that came at the same time. Had gotten ready the year before, but heard of the Indian difficulties, and put it off a year." Jacob Vanmetre, a "low Dutchman" who had owned a fort on Muddy Creek in the Monongahela country, led a flotilla of twenty-seven family boats down the river together in the spring of 1780. Much like the serial migration of families, neighbors who migrated separately often sought each other out upon their arrival. Nicholas Moseby's family moved into General Scott's Station on the banks of the Kentucky River; their families had formerly lived within a mile of each other in Cumberland County, Virginia, not far from the James River. Of Strode's station, William Clinkenbeard simply observed: "all came out from one neighborhood in Virginia, and as we knew each other there, we worked together here. Some had to stand guard while others wrought."[66]

The experiences of migration and settlement strengthened existing communal ties among immigrants. In the early 1840s, having recently lived through difficult economic times brought on by the Panic of 1837, old settlers recounted with evident nostalgia instances of communalism and aid among neighbors. James Morris recalled that "eight

families of us left New Jersey in May 1788." Five of the families went
to Mayslick together, and settled in a circle around the salt spring.
"Laid off their farms so as to corner in the lick springs, and then settled
in their corners, with port-holes in their cabins, so as that they could
fire from any four, on those attacking the fifth." Their first year
brought many hardships. "The whole of us had to subsist upon wild
meat, except [for] one hundred pounds of bacon, which was left to my
father because it was so old, they didn't claim a share." The "law" of
the settlement was, "that while there was any bread in the settlement,
it should be divided among the company." When one family purchased
a half loaf of bread for the exorbitant price of four shillings and six
pence, the neighbors divided it equally among the children. One day "a
wagon came along from towards Paris, loaded with meal, at 3 and 6 [3
shillings, 6 pence], which we bought with nearly all the money we
had." Warfare with the Ohio Indians further cemented the bonds of
mutual dependence. Morris listed his neighbors killed or captured by
the Indians: "Wood was the first, Flora second, Stites third, Kelsey
fourth, Lawson next year." Lawson's escape, he recalled, "interrupted
the first wedding that ever was celebrated at Mayslick."[67]

Living together in the close quarters of fortified settlements also
forged new relationships. Although group migration encouraged instances of residential segregation in Kentucky, resulting in the "Low
Dutch Station," the "Irish Station," and the preponderance of Jersey
natives at Mayslick, many migrant families traveled and settled with
strangers. That so many of Shane's informants could name these fictive kin fifty years later dramatizes the salience of these new communal bonds. Joseph Ficklin listed thirty-eight residents of Bryan's Station, including several family groups named individually: "I will begin
at my father's cabin, and go round, as well as I can recollect." As
identified by Ficklin's brief comments, the station housed Virginians, a
Jersey native, a Carolina Tory, a hatter, two Dutch widows and their
sons, a Dutch cooper, an elderly preacher, and two of Ficklin's uncles by
marriage. Ficklin recalled childhood scrapes with his elders and described their actions during the siege of Bryan's Station in 1782. Indeed, it may have been the trauma of this event that seared the residents of Bryan's Station into Ficklin's memory.[68]

Captain Nathaniel Hart Jr. recalled a similarly mixed multitude at
Boonesborough in the 1770s. Assisted by the manuscript ledger from
Richard Henderson's company store in his possession, Hart sketched

brief portraits of a Dutchman who came from Carolina with Boone, Simon ("a yellow man, who staid at the Fort"), an Irish indentured servant, a "bound boy" [apprentice], Virginians, Carolinians, Pennsylvanians, "a rough-backwoods-hunter," and "Hynes . . . a free-Negro." Hynes, in Hart's estimation, was "as good a soldier as any we had. Secured a fine tract of land, called Hynes' bent, 5 miles below Boonesboro. He was a respectable Negro, and owned horses, stock, and etc." In addition to his militia service and desire for land, the African American shared at least one other characteristic with the ambitious and acquisitive young white men who poured into the western country: "he was killed by the Indians."[69]

In the minds of Shane's informants, new local attachments never completely overcame an awareness of living with strangers in one's midst. Joseph Ficklin still recalled making fun of the Dutch, "tuckeyho boys" mimicked the accents of Irishmen, and fellow travelers came to blows over the menu of an imaginary breakfast. "Distinctions and particions" continued to mark western settlers off from one another, but so too did conceptions of kinship and fictive kinship offer new bases for social cohesion. Ultimately, westerners would forge new social identities from these mixed materials, based on the evocation of place and a shared history of border warfare.

They see none about them to whom or to whose families they [have] been accustomed to think themselves inferior.

GEORGE NICHOLAS

The Politics of Power

In the political landscape of late-eighteenth-century America, back settlers occupied a barbarous terrain. Popular images of western anarchy and lawlessness prompted metropolitan observers to view frontier inhabitants virtually as "wild men" living "in a perfect state of war" until the arrival of gentry leaders and the formal institutions of church and state. Benjamin Rush, for example, thought first settlers nearly related to Indians in their manners, while Crèvecoeur termed them simply "carnivorous animals of a superior rank." Political theorists influenced by the Scottish Enlightenment commonly agreed that primitivism befell those western migrants who pushed beyond the restraints of civil society. Although prominent figures such as Thomas Jefferson espoused more optimistic views of westward migration, Crèvecoeur spoke for many far more skeptical observers in describing the earliest backwoods settlers as "a kind of forlorn hope, preceding by ten or twelve years" the respectable migrants who followed in their wake.[1]

An evolutionary perspective has continued to characterize modern historical accounts of prestatehood Kentucky. While early chroniclers celebrated the heroic exploits of notable men, recent scholarship has emphasized the absence of developed political institutions and the limitations of a leadership ill prepared for self-government upon separation from Virginia in 1792. Authorship of the first state constitution, for example, is attributed to the fortuitous arrival of a former member of the Virginia House of Delegates. Early politics have been portrayed as an in-group argument among elites over the question of statehood, where, as one historian has observed, "the populace at large heard their own problems formulated," but remained largely silent on the great issue of the day. Another scholar similarly declared that "the voice of the people was silent. All the available evidence indicates that most Kentuckians . . . regarded the question of separation with a general lack of interest."[2] Scholars disagree over the extent of social discord in early Kentucky—there being a heterogeneous population and significant economic inequality—yet it is apparent that the district witnessed little of the organized agrarian unrest seen elsewhere in the American backcountry. Indeed, the only noteworthy episode of civil disobedience was an almost universal (and unchallenged) defiance of the excise tax on whiskey. "The people think of nothing else than cultivating their lands and increasing their plantations," one disgusted partisan observed.[3]

Contemporary theorists remind us, however, that relationships of power and politics transcend the formal trappings of court and constitution and need not wait upon the electoral process. "Power is everywhere," observes Michel Foucault, "not because it embraces everything, but because it comes from everywhere." It "is exercised from innumerable points, in the interplay of nonegalitarian and mobile relations."[4] Power, in other words, pervades all social relationships—not only those expressed by repression or domination, but also those which produce social consensus and cohesion. If ordinary settlers remained mute on the subject of constitutional politics (or if we cannot hear their voices today), then we must turn to the "small politics" of everyday life—expressed through gossip, status contests, and communally defined rules of behavior—for evidence of their thinking about power and authority. And here, of course, John Shane's settler interviews are particularly rich in just such prosaic details.[5]

In recalling their experiences during the early years of settlement, migrants expressed themselves freely on questions of leadership and influence, often recounting stories in which the mobilization of public opinion or the distribution of economic resources played a prominent role. Recurring patterns of opinion within this testimony suggest that in addition to a formal system of constitutional politics, an informal backwoods political culture—shaped in important ways by warfare with the Ohio Indians—defined societal rules and conventions. Questions of power and authority engage all political systems, no matter how small or informal; insights about the political organization of small-scale societies offer an analytical framework for investigating the "micro-politics" of an emergent frontier society. These resources permit an examination of three central questions about backwoods political culture: What were the arenas of informal political activity? Who had a voice, or became a leader in the proceedings? And finally, what, if any, were the intersections between the formal and informal political systems, between politics "large" and "small"?[6]

Context

An initial point requires emphasis: early Kentuckians did not live in a state of nature. Although advocates of separation from Virginia emphasized the capital's distance and the difficulties of judicial and military administration across a mountain barrier, in reality Virginia did a credible job in spreading its loose institutional web to Kentucky and its other frontier regions. An examination of the petitions of Kentuckians to the General Assembly of Virginia suggests that by eighteenth-century standards of communication, legislators responded promptly to requests for local enabling legislation. In perhaps the most noteworthy case, the Assembly moved swiftly in 1776 to secure Virginia's claim to the "western waters" (and to forestall land sales of dubious legality by Richard Henderson's Transylvania Company) by acting on a request from the citizens of Harrodsburg to extend county government to Kentucky. Within four months, the Assembly had created Kentucky County, Virginia, effective on January 1, 1777, and vested the county's franchise in "every white man possessing twenty-five acres of land with house and plantation thereon." Later petitions prompted the Virginia body to authorize salt works, grant town sites, establish tobacco inspection stations, and even mediate disputes over the location of mill dams. In an era before the general incorporation act, this political process was undoubtedly cumbersome, as each proposed enterprise required separate deliberation. Yet seen within the framework of the weak authority structures characteristic of eighteenth-century America, the extension of Virginia's provincial administration achieved notable success.[7]

County courts, justices of the peace, and an organized militia—as imperfect in operation as they may have been—supplied prestatehood Kentucky with the rudiments of an institutional framework and a measure of self-government. Initially, the Kentucky County court was authorized to meet "for the administration of justice" on the first Tuesday of every month. Four years later, due to "the great extent of the county, and the dispersed situation of the settlements," the Virginia Assembly divided Kentucky into three counties—Jefferson, Fayette, and Lincoln—each with its own court, justices, clerks, and militia officers. Further subdivisions soon followed, giving Kentucky nine counties (for an estimated population of 73,677) by the time of the first national census in 1790. The district received its own supreme court in 1782, with jurisdiction over "all treasons, murders, felonies, crimes and misdemeanors committed in the said district." Thereafter, Kentucky litigants need journey to Richmond only for an appeals process, or in the case of a high crime "made triable by the constitution before the general court."[8]

Virginia was much less successful in ensuring an orderly distribution of western lands, however, and land disputes clogged Kentucky courts until well into the nineteenth century. Virginia law eventually recognized five different types of western land claims: settlement, preemption, treasury warrant, poor-right, and military claim surveys. The regulations governing these claims were complex and, in some cases, mutable. In brief, once a claimant obtained a land warrant—no easy task in itself—he had to go through a series of complicated steps to locate, enter, survey, and register his land. Almost every step included a time limitation which had to be met, or the land would once again become "waste and unappropriated." The process, ultimately dependent on "metes and bounds" surveys of dubious precision, was ripe for error—or, in some cases, deliberate abuse.[9]

Virginia compounded these problems by opening the floodgates on the sale of treasury warrants. Not only did the wartime government seek to pay soldiers of the Virginia line with land bounties, it also sought to "increase the annual revenue, and create a fund for discharging the publick debt" by granting unappropriated lands to purchasers

THE POLITICS OF POWER

of state warrants. By the time the land office opened at Wilson Station near Harrodsburg on May 1, 1780, it appeared that Virginia had sold warrants for more Kentucky lands than actually existed for settlement. County surveyor John Floyd forwarded the troubling news to Virginia a few days later: "The state warrants of a late date I fear will be of little value as there were to all appearance military warrants sufficient to cover all the vacant Land in the county of a tolerable quality." Floyd expressed surprise that 1,600,000 acres in state treasury warrants had been lodged by the first of May—more than twice the number of those secured by military claim. The surveyor promised to do all that he could for his "Friends who have sent out warr[an]ts, but I hope their expectations will not be too sanguine as the country is torn all to shatters already by military warrants."[10]

Political Arenas

Despite these larger political assertions, the exercise of authority in early Kentucky was most often a local or personal affair. Indeed, such was the case for much of British North America during the seventeenth and eighteenth centuries, as local interests and personal loyalties mediated expressions of monarchical authority. The imperial crisis of the 1770s and 1780s only invigorated these localistic tendencies. In the wake of the war with Great Britain, a variety of revolutionary committees and quasi-political organizations seized the initiative in public life. The discrediting of royal government and the explosion of popular political rhetoric during wartime threw open the question of who should take part in political affairs. As gentry leaders in state capitals or in the Federal Congress in Philadelphia struggled to set a public agenda, a clamor of local, often less genteel, voices demanded that they, too, be heard.[11]

At the same time that revolution challenged the premises of hierarchical society, settlers moving across the Appalachians further strained habits of social and political deference. Traditional social hierarchy rested on the presumption of gentry rule and patriarchal authority, but migration to the West sundered many bonds of obedience just as surely as it separated families and friends. George Nicholas, the transplanted member of the Virginia gentry who drafted Kentucky's first constitution, lamented in a letter to James Madison that Kentucky's "peculiar character" would "contribute for a time at least to our unhappiness." Kentuckians were all former citizens of "other countries," he explained, using the colloquial term for county or state. "Citizens generally consisting of such men must make a very different mass from one which is composed of men born and raised on the same spot. . . . They see none about them to whom or to whose families they [have] been accustomed to think themselves inferior." While Nicholas acknowledged the changed rules of social intercourse in a new geographic setting, he also signaled his eventual expectation with the phrase "contribute for a time . . . to our unhappiness." In the middle years of the eighteenth century, the tidewater's hierarchical and deferential values had spread westward with Virginia's population into the piedmont and valley—albeit with a certain loss of potency and prestige. Eventually, Nicholas implied, the respectable migrants would prevail in Kentucky as well.[12]

The result was an initial jostle for prerogative and advantage which, perhaps from a distance, looked very much like Crèvecoeur's "perfect state of war." Power, experienced as the relations between landlord and tenant, militia captain and soldier, first-comer and newly arrived settler, swirled and eddied about in a fluid social setting. In numerous small dramas immigrants struggled for political resources of authority and status much as they competed for economic resources of land and labor. At stake was the social order of a new community, where all were newcomers but were by no means equals. Two basic institutions of border life—the fortified station and the militia company—were the arenas in which many of these status contests occurred.

In possessing Kentucky's rich acres, a few migrants enjoyed apparent advantage. Virginia's complicated land laws favored early-arriving claimants with legal knowledge and contacts in Virginia; generous military bounties for officers and a lively trade in land warrants placed many of the choicest Kentucky tracts in the hands of gentlemen. John Breckinridge's brothers, for example, moved from Virginia to Kentucky in 1781 and wrote home requesting that Breckinridge procure military and treasury warrants for hundreds of thousands of acres in the West. By going into partnership with family members and acquiring warrants from nonresidents who may not have known their value, Breckinridge laid claim to nearly 30,000 Kentucky acres of his own by the time he first visited the district in 1789.[13]

Yet those without legal land claims made up the bulk of Kentucky's early population. Many poorer migrants simply squatted on vacant tracts or swelled the population of frontier stations owned by other men. "Most of the people when I came were on leased lands, till times became more safe," one settler told Shane. "Would take a lease for five years, clear as much as they pleased, and enjoy the range till it was gone, and then move." The lease, he explained, "was to secure their privileges, and the lesor thus got his lands cleared." Beyond offering a modicum of physical security in time of war, stations thus became a means of transforming uncultivated woodlands or canebrakes into productive agricultural property. "Wherever a man could get a number of families to go with him, he went out and leased the ground for so many years to get them to help clear," another resident explained. "Todd's, Craig's, and Bowman's were settled in this way."[14]

Like medieval barons, station owners waxed large in the countryside. Even John Strode, who fled to the interior settlements during the "troublesome times" of the early 1780s, continued to lend his name to the small community gathered within his walls. William Moseby's family lived in General Charles Scott's oak-palisaded station on the banks of the Kentucky River; Moseby later recalled that Scott "was looked upon as all and every thing" in the area. Scott's station housed three families and five or six single men as guards; during its early years of occupation, the general, a veteran of both Braddock's Campaign (1755) and the Revolutionary War, maintained a military style of discipline. "The gate was not allowed to be opened till an appointed time in the morning," Moseby recalled, "and it was the rule for these men [the guards] to be in their place." The dogs were let out first and then the men "followed after, to look for moccasin tracks, and etc." Scott, who became Kentucky's fourth governor in 1808, loomed larger than life in the memories of Shane's informants, celebrated equally for his prodigious oaths and his great daring in battle. Moseby claimed that Scott's personal fame had spread even as far as his Indian adversaries, observing to Shane that "his name was all that kept him from being massacred."[15]

So long as danger from Indian attack governed the rhythms of daily life, the conduct of border war served as another important arena for the contest of power. In a pattern of invasion and counter invasion (not finally ending until the Treaty of Greenville in 1795), companies of Kentuckians and Indians raided back and forth across the Ohio River stealing horses, attacking settlements, and taking captives. Virginia law enrolled all free males between the ages of 16 and 50 in the militia, but prior to the arrival of the first militia commissions from Virginia in 1777, men from each frontier station formed an informal defense force. Even after Virginia provided for a full set of officers under the ultimate command of the governor, Kentucky militia companies continued to operate autonomously.[16]

Although English and colonial in precedent, the Kentucky militia company was in many ways a product of two centuries of Anglo-American contact with Indian-style guerrilla warfare. Tragically, it was in the materiel and tactics of forest warfare that the two cultures came to resemble each other most closely. In the border country, Indian warriors utilized firearms, rode horses, and carried metal-edged weapons; their militia counterparts dressed in deerskin, wielded tomahawks, and took scalps. Both sides employed traditional Indian tactics of scouting, surprise, concealment, mobility, and marksmanship, as well as the novel Anglo-Irish strategy of total warfare waged against women, children, and crops. Young men of both cultures gained status by daring raids which were deplored by civic leaders: "the Law of retalliation [sic] was sweet And agreeable," observed William Whitley. To avenge the theft of his horse in 1777, Whitley led several volunteer horse-stealing parties across the Ohio River—an illegal act without the express authorization of the governor.[17]

For the propertyless young men who poured into the western country, such raids may have had an economic as well as a military objective. When nineteen-year-old John Hanks landed at Maysville in 1786, he joined an informal scouting party going out to investigate a report of Indians in the neighborhood. After surprising one Indian who "cleared out," Hanks and his party "got five horses, which were sold when we got to Maysville, and Abraham Dale, my brother and myself, took each a barrel of flour for our pay." Colonel Levi Todd's 170 volunteers crossed the Ohio River in 1787, killed two Indian males and took three women prisoner, and captured horses and "plunder," which were sold at vendue upon their return; the expedition reportedly earned forty-three shillings for each man, a net haul of over 365 pounds. Military expeditions, like stations, were named for their leaders. Successful forays entered oral tradition as Logan's Campaign, or Todd's Campaign; failures became Estill's or Holder's Defeat, or, more fancifully, Harmer's Humiliation and St. Clair's Shame.[18]

The Political Economy of Land

Border politics revolved around many of the same issues currently being debated in Philadelphia: questions of defense, distribution of economic resources, and election of leaders. In the back settlements, however, this discourse often occurred on a personal rather than a theoretical level: Who is a competent captain? How shall our plunder be divided? What are the terms of our lease? In the early years of occupation, this decision-making process was a relatively open one. Whether this political empowerment of ordinary citizens resulted from ideological forces unleashed by the Revolution, new opportunities for prosperity, folkways drawn from the borders of North Britain, or simple distance from civil authority remains unclear. Nevertheless, in the public sphere of fort and station life, a great many voices made themselves heard.[19]

From the outset, the dislocations of migration encouraged shared civic responsibility. Strangers thrown together on the road or in stations made informal compacts and elected temporary leaders. One traveler reported that before his company entered the wilderness they spent a full day making regulations and choosing officers for the trip. Another man recalled that "by common consent every fort, or at least every camp, had its chief." The "law" of the settlement at Mayslick was to divide food stores. In a striking example of participatory democracy, the passengers of a flatboat (who had paid two dollars apiece for passage to Kentucky) voted on whether the boat's owner should continue the practice of drinking coffee with the genteel occupants of another craft lashed alongside; some members of the company were disgruntled that they had not been invited to partake as well.[20]

Landlords and tenants negotiated the distribution of resources in an uncertain economic environment. Although landowners presumably had the upper hand in an area with a high degree of landlessness, ongoing warfare with the Indians and widespread confusion over Virginia's land policies made investment in Kentucky lands a risky proposition. James Beath's experience in attempting to settle a claim was perhaps unusual, but nevertheless illustrative of the risks involved. He arrived at Strode's Station in 1779, was captured by the Indians, taken to Detroit, sold to the British, and eventually released at the close of the Revolutionary War. "After all his scuffles," an informant told Shane, Beath returned to Kentucky and made considerable improvements on his tract, only to discover that "he was likely to lose his land through conflicting claims, and got chagrined, and sold out, and moved over to Ohio, and died in less than 12 months." Much like Beath, William Niblick's brother, a millwright, also "lost his lands by law claims, 500 acres, and concluded to go out on to Red River, where mill sites and business might be expected." Large speculators also found their expectations frustrated in the scramble for western lands. Upon his arrival in 1782, Nicholas Moseby discovered that his numerous Kentucky land warrants were all worthless paper. His partner in land location, James Estill, had been defeated by a party of Wyandots six months before. Although Estill had surveyed "some 40 or 50,000 acres" before his death, he had apparently failed to record his surveys in the land office. "The land in some way was all lost," Moseby's son remembered. "Father moved out with expectation of abundance of land to go on, and it turned out that he had nothing."[21]

Even where land titles were clear, squatters might defy landowners seeking to take possession. When John Floyd, then the deputy surveyor of Fincastle County, visited his valuable Royal Spring tract in 1776, he discovered "a man who has his wife and family there, and has made large improvements and is determined, as I am told, to hold the land at the risk of his life." Floyd finally agreed to sell the tract to the squatter, but Indians killed the man before they could complete the sale. In the same letter, Floyd warned another Virginian that his lands were similarly occupied: "I now inform you that the 1000 [acres] I surveyed for you in 1774 on Elkhorn has 66 acres of corn growing on it and all under a good fence. It is settled by the Bryans and other Tories to the number of 28 men; they talk good and say they don't design to keep forcible possession but would willingly purchase the land." Floyd predicted "civil war" if the Virginia Assembly did not act soon to regularize the procedure for claiming land. Years later, the son of another early surveyor put his finger squarely on the problem: "the dispute . . . often was, *which* of the first comers, come the first."[22]

Where legal possession of the land was so insecure, tenancy appeared a prudent economic strategy. Scotch-Irish emigrants in Pennsylvania, who had been familiar with the practice in Ulster, initially attached no social stigma to tenancy as a means of accumulating capital. Evidence from the Shane interviews indicates that many Kentucky tenants believed they, too, held a strong bargaining position so long as they were needed for defense, clearing land, or to secure a claim.

Settlers recounted numerous stories of station owners bidding for the services of tenants and of landless settlers conspiring—often success-fully—to acquire their own lands. At Stocton's Station, for example, residents reportedly received the land they cleared rent-free for seven years. John Strode, who ignominiously fled to safety in the East, promised settlers the use of his land for nine years; his tenant Isaac Clinkenbeard was able to clear three acres in three days, and even managed to sublet his holding to another man for a year when he no longer wanted the use of it.[23]

John Craig settled two different stations by offering attractive terms to his tenants. Joice Falconer and her husband settled with Craig on Daviess Fork upon their arrival in the fall of 1779. "John Craig owned the land, and had put us there, together, on it. We just went, and cleared, and lived there as long as we pleased," she said. After Indian raiders burned this station in 1781, Craig initiated a second settlement on Clear Creek in 1783; another tenant recalled that Craig promised the married men who moved to this site "a hundred acres apiece, and the single men 50." The Craigs may have overextended themselves in these financial dealings, however. The tenant observed that "John Craig was mostly broken up, speculating in lands . . . and moved to down on the Ohio. Lewis Craig got broke up too, before he died—came to the plough."[24]

Other settlers spoke of landowners who had sold tracts at advan-tageous terms to encourage settlement. "In those days, it was believed that the land never would be settled for [due to the danger from] the Indians," Martin Wymore explained. "Those who had entered land, were glad to get their money back, by selling the land at low prices." Wymore claimed that John Todd had given away town sites in Lex-ington and had sold the outlots at a very low price. "Maxwell, a tailor, bought five hundred acres, at nine pence per acre," he recalled. The physical labor needed to clear frontier lands of their dense native vegetation also proved to be a valuable bargaining chip in the market for land. William Risk, who rolled logs at Billy Keeton's farm for two days, remembered Keeton telling him that "John Baker, I think it was, gave him the hundred acres for clearing twenty acres."[25]

Property owners with outlying tracts bargained for the services of tenants at a distinct disadvantage. Ralph Morgan wished to stay in safety in Bourbon County, and proposed to sell land at a dollar an acre to those who would settle on his claim on Slate Creek. Despite this generous offer, Morgan found few takers. James Wade, hired for ten dollars a month as "spy and hunter to strengthen the place," arrived at Morgan's tract on the second day of June 1789 and found that only "three cabins had been erected in the shape of a three-footed stool . . . and about forty acres of land planted in corn." By that fall, only Wade and his brother remained at the exposed settlement. Wade confessed that he, too, would have left, "but I made it a rule always to fulfil my contract, and I didn't know but that he [Morgan] would hold me to it. Yet he hadn't [held to] his, for he was to have had more men there all the time." In desperation, Morgan finally turned over the running of the place to the Wade brothers, "giving them liberty to bring as many, and what other persons they might choose, and on terms at their own discretion."[26]

Gentlemen landowners at times found themselves hard-pressed to maintain a dignified social distance from the tenants upon whose services they depended. Charles Vancouver hired ten men to help him build a station at the forks of the Big Sandy River; John Hanks remembered that "our wages were to have been a barrel of corn 'a piece,' two bushels of salt for the ten, and a deed or title, to each, for fifty acres of land." The proposed station site, which the native of Holland had purchased sight unseen, was in the mountainous and sparsely inhabited area of eastern Kentucky, which was settled in the main only after 1800. When Vancouver's party arrived there in February 1789, pine trees covered the bottom land and wild turkeys roosted in their branches. The men built a log stockade and a few rough cabins while Vancouver, despite the rugged conditions, attempted to keep up his routine as a gentleman. Hanks marveled that "he would have himself dressed, and his hair powdered, at the fort, every Sunday morning regularly, as prim as in a court, and there was no body there but us men."[27]

Vancouver's training as a gentleman had left him largely unprepared for the harsh realities of settling a frontier station. Indeed, his attempt faltered almost from the start. Within two months the company's horses disappeared; Vancouver seemed to doubt Hanks's explanation that Indians were to blame until the young man showed him the bark rope that the raiding party had left behind. Vancouver next determined to open a store to serve the river traffic he soon expected would come flowing down the Big Sandy River. He traveled to Philadelphia to purchase his wares and returned with a keelboat full of supplies, including whiskey, rum, meat packed in barrels, and even women's clothing.[28]

Few customers reached the remote outpost, however. As Hanks remembered the forlorn scene, "there were setting about there a great many store articles, perfectly useless, such as a barrel of coffee-mills." The young men grew restless and one day began taking target practice at the coffee-mills, which Vancouver allowed for a time, "and then directed them to be put away, and taken care of." In the absence of paying customers, Vancouver began giving away his store goods: when Jenny Wiley returned from a three-year Indian captivity without "a speck of women stuff on her," he sent her over "a suit of new clothes."[29]

A year after his arrival, Vancouver finally abandoned his settlement to the turkeys and the pine trees, retreating to the more safely genteel precincts of Lexington to sell his store goods and prepare for a new undertaking in agriculture. The ownership of slaves was also a part of his new economic strategy. In March 1790, the following advertisement appeared in the *Kentucky Gazette*:

> I have a considerable quantity of valuable Iron mongery, buckles, and buttons, round glass and Queens ware, Men's and Womens shoes, Hats, Norwich camblets and callimancoes, India Chintzes, Muslins, Silks and Callicoes, together with a compleat assortment of British mounted Carpenters and Joiners tools, which, with a variety of other articles, I will exchange at the lowest cash price for young healthy Negroes, two or three yoke of oxen, and a quantity of whiskey. CHARLES VANCOUVER.

In what may have been a final blow to Vancouver's pride, Hanks recalled that "we regarded his land so poor, none of us ever thought of asking him for it."[30]

Traditions of social deference surrounding property ownership also eroded in wartime. In outlying areas, frequent raids left property owners dependent on often-propertyless young men drafted to guard their homes. One senses from the records that these young men enjoyed pressing home their temporary advantage. John Rupard, who was seventy-eight years old when Shane interviewed him in 1843, reminisced at length about the time a station owner had called for his militia company's help after Indians had killed his son and captured two of his slaves. Rupard, then in his early twenties, drew the lot to guard the defeated station while other men pursued the Indian raiders. When the station owner suggested that Rupard take his gun and stand sentry in the field, the young man laughed off his instructions. "He had, what appeared to be very nice sweet-potatoes, in the hill yet; they hadn't been dug yet. I told him that I didn't come there for that purpose [sentry duty]; I just come there to eat sweet potatoes, and court his gals, if they would let me." Rupard recalled that the young women, who were within hearing, seemed much amused by his remark: "I suppose they would have preferred living with a white man, off the frontier, to living there, exposed to the Indians." Undoubtedly sensing where such flirtation might lead, the station owner assigned Rupard to sleep in a cabin about twenty yards from the main house. Rupard responded that "if the Indians came, and attacked his house, I wouldn't fire on them, I would take care of myself." Although this tour of duty did not win him a wife, Rupard noted that it did earn him a certificate for fifteen days' pay that covered his county taxes.[31]

Citizen Soldiers

In the turbulent days of early settlement, a subtle diffusion of power was evident in even the most hierarchical of institutions: the military. Departing from English custom, colonial militia companies had regularly elected their junior officers; now frontier militiamen challenged even the most basic assumptions of military discipline. In impromptu councils of war, officers and men negotiated the terms of their service and the conduct of campaigns: "I was captain," but "we were all heads," recalled William Clinkenbeard. Despite the proud boast that "one Indian to four regulars, and two Indians to one Kentuckian, was the common rating of equal forces," witnesses reported that Kentucky militia companies were plagued by disorder and insurrection. Forced to call for volunteers in his campaign against the Indians of the Northwest Territory, General Anthony Wayne fumed to Henry Knox, Washington's secretary of war, that Kentucky troops would "[steal] a March very wide from the Army—in order to burn a few Wig-wams & capture a few women and Children . . . [so that] they cou'd not meet with any Opposition, until they returned *triumphantly & safe* to their respective homes—leaving the Legion to contend with the difficulty & danger." The reality of Wayne's abortive 1793 fall campaign was even less glorious: after reaching winter quarters at Fort Greenville, one-third of the Kentucky volunteers decamped for home without permission. Returning militiamen may have explained their rapid reappearance by reference to Wayne's mental stability: in Kentucky to this day, the general is known by the sobriquet "Mad" Anthony Wayne.[32]

Former militiamen spoke freely about the confusion which surrounded their campaigns. Their candid and often rueful stories bear little resemblance to the heroic mythmaking which later would surround the "winning of the west." Josiah Collins recalled that part of his company, when ordered to march to the Falls of the Ohio, mutinied and went home. After another (this time successful) foray across the Ohio River—netting "163 head of horses, besides some other plunder gotten from a trader's store . . . [and] one squaw's gown in which were 1,100 silver brooches"—it took Collins's company two days to divide the booty "equally among officers and soldiers according to the agreement under which we had volunteered." Collins confided that he and his brother "got a small mare, a yearling colt and a three-year-old mare, [and] this amounted to 15 pounds more than our share, which we never paid in the world." Joshua McQueen was equally frank about his ethical lapses during wartime. When "they wanted me to go up on O'Post campaign that September [Clark's Vincennes expedition of 1779], and I was tired of the war, and kept out hunting. Told them I wanted to go and see my mamma that season on Mingo bottom." Such manifest deficiency of martial spirit was apparently not uncommon. Captain William Sudduth had to "beat up for volunteers to go a few miles farther" when his troops balked on Edward's Campaign in 1791; of the debate which occurred at the halt, a man recalled, "such a buzz I never heard." On Bowman's expedition against Chillicothe in 1779, troops reportedly "too keen" for plunder allowed their Shawnee adversaries to regroup; an eyewitness attributed the misadventure to Bowman's failure of leadership, for "not foreseeing the consequences" and lacking the "discipline to restrain the men and govern them."[33]

Nor can all the blame be laid at the feet of Kentucky's citizen soldiers. John Rupard retained firm—and often unflattering—opinions about the qualities of the militia commanders under whom he had served. In Edward's Campaign across the Ohio in 1791, he served in Simon Kenton's company of spies, ranging ahead with a few other men to look for signs of the enemy. Rupard dismissed Edwards as a coward, telling Shane with evident sarcasm that he "sent on word to Kenton and Hall, if they saw any danger, to be sure and let him know." Edwards, he observed, "wasn't worth as much as many an old woman." Rupard spoke more approvingly of Colonel McDowell's actions in a similar situation in 1789. When McDowell's advance scouts reported signs of Indians, the commander moved to the head of his troops and proceeded forward cautiously. Finally, when he began to fear that they were being drawn into an ambush, McDowell called a halt and spoke frankly to his men. He "said he considered himself as good a soldier as any of us, that he felt towards us as his children," Rupard remembered. "If we were defeated . . . he would bear the blame of it, after he was dead and gone—and proposed in view of the danger, that we should turn back." Having been consulted in such a fine fashion, the men readily agreed. McDowell, unlike Edwards, understood the consensual nature of the informal political system.[34]

"Big-Men"

The "small politics" of border life thus blurred traditional hierarchies. New sources of social authority challenged received structures of rank and status by which gentlemen in the East had fixed the dependence of others upon them. In frontier stations and on military campaigns a redefinition of power took place as personal qualities of bravery and leadership vied with property and gentle birth in securing a reputation for "influence" or "interest."[35] Anthropologists distinguish between two different types of status rankings: the "ascribed" status of inherited position and the "achieved" status of personal accomplishment. Westerners, while acknowledging the ascribed status of gentleman landowners, nevertheless used qualities of achieved status such as bravery, acquisition, command, even brute survival to distinguish their popular leaders. Deference to social superiors was not automatic; it was earned, by gentleman and commoner alike in the rough and tumble of border life. This, then, is the meaning—the real significance—of the hundreds of tales of border life recorded by John Shane and other western collectors: for ordinary settlers the telling and re-telling of border stories was a culturally distinctive means of ranking the social order of the backwoods community.

A variety of resources and skills brought social acclaim to the aspiring frontier leader. Woodsmen like Daniel Trabue, Spencer Records, and James Wade treasured youthful reputations for hunting prowess—an important social contribution which often meant the difference between survival and starvation in a frontier station. Another episode from Daniel Trabue's salt-making expedition during the "hard winter" of 1779–80 captures the tone of these hunting stories. Trabue, who was only twenty years old at the time, had set out with a small party of Virginians to make salt at Bullit's Lick. Shortly after his party left Harrodsburg, Trabue recalled that "these young men said they was afraid to go on with me. They was afraid of Indians, was also afraid as their was no road or path[,] that I would not find the way, and another thing was we had nothing to eat[,] we might starve to Death." Trabue reminded his companions that they should have provided for their own sustenance, and "as to the Indians we had to run that risk."[36]

After setting up camp for the night, the men went out to hunt for their dinner. Although the others came back empty-handed, Trabue killed a large, fat raccoon, and "negro Jo" prepared it for roasting over the fire. But, as Trabue recalled, "the men began again with their woefull tail. Said they[:] 'We are in a wilderness without any path, nothing to eat but a koon for 6 or 7 Men without Bread or Salt, liable every moment to be Masscreed by the Indians. If we can only be spared until morning we will return to Logan's Fort.'" One man added that "he would return to Old Virginia as quick as he could and them that liked Kentucky might enjoy it but he would not stay in such a country."[37]

Since it was a bright moonlit night, Trabue decided to go out hunting once again. When the other men refused to accompany him, he "told negro Jo to take his axx" and come along. Walking only a short distance to a spot where some of the other men had hunted earlier, Trabue found five wild turkeys roosting in the branches of a sycamore tree. In short time he had "killed all 5 of the largest fatest [sic] Turkeys that I had ever seen." Trabue remembered thinking that surely the men would come running when they heard his rifle fire; to his great disgust, "they stayd where they was at the camp looking at their koon a rosting." Trabue's tale ended happily, however; with the addition of the turkeys to their feast, all ate heartily that night. "The neaxt Day we went on our Jurney and no one turned back." As the now-acknowledged leader of the company, Trabue added, "I went on before."[38]

Cunning in land acquisition also led to achieved status within the backwoods community. Kentucky's land troubles inspired a series of trickster tales (resembling those of African American slaves) in which ingenious but poor settlers outwitted land speculators from the East.

Green Clay, the hero of one such tale, dressed in buckskin, rode a mule, and pretended to be half-witted in order to be hired as cook by a surveying party. The tale included the requisite play on words: "Asked if he understood mathematics. Replied he knew one George Mattox." After secretly copying the surveyors' notes, Clay set out for the land office three days before the others: "Said as he rode a mule, they would overtake him." The wily pioneer made sure to arrive first, however, and entered the surveys in his own name. The tale concluded with a voucher of authenticity: "He never denied the story." While this particular story of Green Clay's land dealings may be apocryphal, Lewis Collins's 1847 *History of Kentucky* notes that Clay, with "slender resources" and "an exceedingly limited" education, acquired large quantities of Kentucky land due to his "retentive memory" and his position as a deputy surveyor for Kentucky county.[39]

An "ingenious Dutchman" was the protagonist of another trickster tale. Jacob Myers came from Pennsylvania and worked at the hazardous task of "chain carrier to one Fox, surveying down on the Ohio River, at a dollar per day." After the surveyors had finished their work, Myers asked the men to survey an unclaimed tract of about five hundred acres for him; when they ungraciously refused, Myers "said they shouldn't have a foot of the land they had already surveyed; swearing to what he said." The surveyors laughed him off because they knew that Myers could neither read nor write. Along with Green Clay, the "ingenious Dutchman" had the last laugh, however. "That night he started on foot for Harrodsburgh, and entered every foot of land, an hour and a half before they came into the office, they having rode." His memory was perfect without the aid of written notes, the narrator claimed. To add insult to injury, Myers "then sued for his wages, and recovered before Colonel Bowman."[40]

On the other hand, ineptitude in land matters could ruin a man's reputation. Perhaps the most famous example comes from the career of Daniel Boone, who surveyed thousands of Kentucky acres yet managed to hold on to very few of them for himself. "All Boone's entries were mighty vague," William Risk observed. Boone also surveyed thousands of acres for other prospective landowners who eventually found themselves in court; according to another settler, "mighty little land ever held under Boon." William Risk related one episode in which officials called upon Boone to establish an entry that he had made for someone near Lulbegrud Creek. When Boone went out to the site to find the tree that he had marked as the corner of the property, " 'twas said he couldn't find the entry, and leaving his company, made one and dirtied (rubbed) over the fresh marks so as to conceal the fraud." Boone's trick was discovered, however, which disallowed the entry; Risk speculated that it was embarrassment over this matter that prompted Boone to leave for Missouri.[41]

Cuthbert Combs witnessed a similar dramatic challenge to another man's ability at locating land. John Howard claimed settlement and preemption rights to an entry at the mouth of Howard's Upper Creek in Clark County; John Holder later laid claim to this same tract in a special land entry designed to cover and, thus, supersede all vague claims in the area. Combs recalled the tense scene when Howard established the validity of his prior claim. "He made a square [on the ground], and said, if they would dig in that square, they would find the broken glass of a green bottle. That if they didn't find it, it wasn't his land, and he didn't want it."[42]

Physical bravery was another highly valued personal characteristic in the backwoods social order. As one man explained, "I was raised on the frontiers of Kentucky, in the midst of the Indian war, where men were only respected in proportion to their valor and skill in fighting Indians, and killing wild beasts; and I verily thought to be a brave skilful [sic] warrior and a good hunter was the greatest honor to which any man could attain." In rough pranks, gruesome animal contests, and crude boasting matches, young men tested each other's mettle: "the fort yard was a great place for wolf baiting," recalled William Clinkenbeard. Such status contests often played upon traditional European fears of the forest and its creatures; indeed, wolves seemed to be singled out for particular animus. Clinkenbeard recounted that Dick Piles once had "run a ring round the neck of a wolf with his knife— drew its skin over its eyes, and let it go." On another occasion, Piles came into the yard with a wolf lashed to his back. He was "holding it by its fore feet around his neck . . . its mouth only tied, and its head sticking out from behind his shoulders beside his own. Piles had dark skin and a big mouth, and he come grinning into the fort gate; tell you, it did look a sight. Threw the wolf down for the dogs to fight with." As a young child, William Niblick watched the bloody animal fights that took place in the fort yard at Lexington. "Would tie a wolf dog with the middle of the rope and then one would take hold at each of the ends and keep it in the middle and make the dogs fight it."[43]

Why wolves in particular should attract such sadistic gamesmanship is difficult to determine from the remove of two centuries. Certainly wolves might prey on valuable domestic stock and were known to raid hunters' stores of meat; but deeper anxieties seem to be at work in these accounts. Psychologists note that one way to cope with the fear of death is to act out fantasies of killing and destruction. Benjamin Allen's description of his father's death provides a clue that wolves may have served as totemic substitutes in some of these fear-displacement performances. While out hunting near Mud Lick Spring in 1790, Allen and his father were surprised by a party of Shawnees. After raising a yell "like wolves howling," the Shawnees seized Allen and shot and scalped his father. The men who later went out to bury Allen's father found his body mutilated almost beyond recognition. "Said the wolves had eaten him nearly up. All they knew him by was the teeth. He had a very pretty full set of wholesome teeth." The linkage is subtle but striking: scavenging wolves, wolf-like Indians, and sudden horrific death were all manifestations of the forces of chaos which threatened border life. Of these, only wolves could be safely challenged and conquered in the bounded universe of the station yard.[44]

Mutilation of enemy dead may have served a similar function. Although wartime atrocities are transcultural phenomena that have spanned the centuries, incidents from the border warfare of the revolutionary era suggest an unusual level of personal violence. David Crouch, for example, related the story of old David Morgan who got "in a scuffle" with an Indian along the Monongahela. After killing the man in a vicious knife fight, and only narrowly escaping death himself, Morgan turned on the corpse. "He then flayed the Indian," Crouch recalled, "and tanned his hide. Was ever after called savage Morgan. My brother Jonathan Crouch saw a razor strap that had been made out of that hide." Two of Shane's informants reported that Harrodsburg residents had fed fallen Indian attackers "to the dogs, to make them fierce." Sarah Graham, who arrived three years after one such incident supposedly took place, was told that the dogs "quarreled and bristled up, ready for Indians as they ate." In recounting a second such episode, Jacob Stevens said that Hugh McGary had "killed an Indian that he found had his [dead] stepson's shirt on, and cut him up and fed him to the dogs." Even among regular troops, postmortem scalping and trophy taking were apparently routine in battle. After Josiah Harmer's disastrous defeat by northwestern Indians in 1790, one of his men cut off an Indian war captain's head and displayed it by the general's marquee. "The soldiers stuck a quid [of tobacco] in each side of the Indian's mouth," a witness recalled.[45] It is tempting to view these brutal incidents as early evidence of Indian dehumanization and racially based Indian hating among white borderers. Yet their context here seems too personal, too immediate, too *intimate* to represent the categorical racialism that would gain respectability by the 1840s. The displacement of fear, the horrific momentum of wartime, and, above all, a desire for personal revenge and reputation are surely other important elements in this volatile psychological mix.[46]

In an environment which celebrated violent masculinity, cowardice met with crude but effective reprisals. Station residents taunted "Virginians and land-jobbers" for their timidity in coming out to Kentucky in the winter (when Indians were less likely to attack) and returning home before "dangerous times" commenced. "Crowd the fort, and eat the provisions, and in the spring go back," one man recalled with obvious disgust, as he told of driving a buffalo into a cabin occupied by fifteen Virginians. When a large British and Indian army surrounded Bryan's Station in August 1782, residents threatened to throw two men advocating surrender over the stockade wall. Humiliation could also take more subtle forms. In southern Ohio, John Smith watched his own bed clothes go up for sale by a militia company returning with his family's linen and other recovered plunder. Smith "was not one of the party" pursuing the Indians and, thus, had to bid for his own property, the informant told Shane. Even children took part in the "rough music" meted out to those lacking courage. Thomas Metcalf recalled that when there was an "alarm of Indians" near Masterson's Station, "some volunteered to go in pursuit, and some packed and went to Lexington." The next day there was fighting among the boys, "who taunted each other with the imputation that their fathers had refused to go in pursuit, or had fled to Lexington." Such impugning of a man's bravery could lead to serious consequences if the target was unwilling to accept the judgment of the community. On a crowded court day in Winchester, John Whitesides accused Stephen Boyle of being "a Tory and coward" for letting the Shawnee captive Blue Jacket escape from their militia company. A witness reported that Boyle "whipped Whitesides three times, and made him cry 'enough' for it."[47]

With a single act of courage, however, an outsider could quickly establish his reputation. One such story was told of an Irishman who accompanied two more experienced woodsmen on a hunt. After they had settled in for the night in the loft of a vacant cabin, seven Indians came in below and kindled a fire in the hearth; the newcomer kept stretching his head forward to see the Indians and the hunters repeatedly pulled him back. At length, however, the boards shifted and the men fell below. "Come on! by J—s, said the Irishman, as he tumbled thro', Come on, boys! by G-d we've got them." As the story concluded, the panic-stricken Indians fled, and the men gathered up their booty and returned in triumph to Harrod's station.[48]

Command ability was perhaps the most valued characteristic among western males. Militia officers led their unruly troops with an unconventional combination of techniques: personal valor, economic incentives, democratized decision making, and public verbal suasion. Rank was no guarantee of success. After being appointed commander of the Jefferson County militia, surveyor John Floyd wrote to a correspondent in Virginia: "I sincerely thank you for your very friendly admonition concerning my personal safety; and I mean always to take your advice when it is in my power; but I have sometimes found it absolutely necessary to descend below my station in a Command, in order to preserve the County in which I have my little Family." Floyd added that "I am now determined to be more cautious than I have been heretofore[,] yet every man in this country must be more or less exposed to danger." Only twelve days later, Floyd was fatally wounded in an ambush.[49]

Militia appointments were confirmed in Virginia but nominated in Kentucky, thus military rank was open not only to gentlemen like John Floyd (as was customary in Virginia) but to virtually any man showing outstanding leadership characteristics. Jacob Stucker, "a poore Dutchman," became militia captain in Fayette through a memorable instance of personal bravery. Daniel Trabue related Stucker's story, opening his tale with the observation that parties of Indians "got very Troublesome" in their neighborhood in 1786. All attempts to pursue them failed, until one day an unexpected snow fell. Lacking an officer to lead them on the chase, Trabue and Stucker joined a hastily organized ad hoc company which tracked the rapidly retreating Indians for hours. Eventually the men tired as night overtook them. "The indians went with all their might. Our men als [all] Did their best," Trabue loyally exclaimed; "Jacob stucker insisted to go on but the men refused." After the men had built a fire and eaten their dinner, Stucker "went himself alone the cource the Indians went, and about 2 Miles he Discovered the Indians' Fire." Making what discoveries he could, Stucker returned to his company and told them the news. "They then fixed up and went to the Indians' camp and fired on them and killed and wounded several of them and got consederable plunder." Trabue described the dramatic scene at the plundered campsite: "Stucker picked up one of the best of the Indians' blankits and roped it around himself and said, 'This will keep me worm [warm] this winter.' " Trabue noted: "This J. Stucker was a poore Dutchman. He soon made a captain and he made a good officer." A fellow officer later termed Stucker "the genteelest illiterate man I ever saw. Very silent man. Distinct bravery, and eternal vigilance."[50]

Daniel Boone, Simon Kenton, Benjamin Logan, and Charles Scott: tales of such border captains abound, men who through a combination of personal bravery, oratorical skill, economic calculation, and commanding physical presence achieved public distinction in the leadership of other men. The career of William Whitley (1749–1813) is perhaps typical. Born west of the Blue Ridge to Irish emigrants, Whitley was, in the words of a biographer, "unknown to early fame" and "grew to manhood in the laborious occupation of tilling his native soil, in which his corporal powers were fully developed, with but little mental cultivation." He made his first trip to Kentucky in 1775, and after living in Harrod's and Logan's forts for a time, settled his own station on the Wilderness Road in 1779. Whitley quickly became known for daring exploits (usually involving the theft of horses) and was appointed militia captain in 1785; his daughter Levisa later claimed that he always restored recovered plunder to the original owners or their friends. Whitley later achieved fame for his personal style and public generosity. Building one of the first brick houses in Kentucky, he emblazoned the front and rear facades with the three-foot-high initials "WW" and "EW" (for himself and his wife Esther) in glazed brick headers (Fig. 11). The border chieftain nevertheless retained his common touch. A public barbecue held for his men and neighbors after a successful campaign against the Chickamauga Cherokees in 1793 was memorable not only for its expansive spread but in particular for the "two well roasted shoats, with an Irish potatoe in each of their mouths, and a sweet potatoe under their tails." Some guests reportedly "were so full of laughter that they rolled off their seats upon the grass, and tumbled over and over." In 1813, at the age of

FIGURE 11. William Whitley's house, "Sportsman's Hill,"
completed before 1794. (Photograph by author)

sixty-five, Whitley volunteered with the Kentucky militia and fell "at
the first fire" in the Battle of the Thames. A witness saw Whitley
"come along shaking his Indian scalp, and heard him say, the bullit had
never been run that was to kill him. He had scarcely more than said it,
when he was killed."[51]

Social authority in early Kentucky thus became concentrated in the
hands of male leaders known for their physical courage and military
prowess, as well as for their ability to mobilize and manipulate wealth.
In hunting and gathering societies such leader-figures are called "big-
men," and this concept may be a useful way to think about the informal political role that such popular leaders played on an American
border. As anthropologist Marshall Sahlins has observed, "the indica-
tive quality of big-man authority is everywhere the same: it is *personal* power." Big-men do not achieve their position through inheritance or election; "the attainment of big-man status is rather the
outcome of a series of acts which elevate a person above the common
herd and attract about him a coterie of loyal, lesser men."[52]

We need not look so far afield to discover a comparable population of
powerful men sustained by personal influence: wartime leaders among
the Ohio Valley Indians achieved their positions in a nearly identical
fashion. In Shawnee society, hereditary chiefs normally headed each
of five tribal divisions; the position of war chief was a temporary one,

awarded during wartime for "great talents, exertion, and bravery." Yet in the last quarter of the eighteenth century, hereditary chiefs—like gentry landowners—found their power eroding as new wartime leaders came to the forefront commanding unprecedented sources of personal prestige. In the words of one scholar, "the abnormal was now normal," as war captains spoke out in councils with ever increasing authority. For the Shawnees, as for the Kentuckians, the political elevation of military leaders was a fateful improvisation resulting from the chronic warfare of the revolutionary era.[53]

Inversion

This hypothesis of big-man hegemony raises questions about the status of women and slaves in the border country. Did the privileging of violent white masculinity affect relationships within the family or household? Did women or enslaved African Americans have any access to sources of social authority or achieved status? To uncover evidence of these domestic power relationships—rarely recorded in any part of Anglo-America in the eighteenth century—we must listen for muted voices in very scattered accounts.

The sparse evidence available suggests that enslaved African Americans had few opportunities to achieve status within the informal political system. Stories of slaves giving the alarm, or fighting off Indians during an attack, indicate that some blacks achieved recognition for their bravery or quick thinking. William McBride, for example, mentioned in passing that "a good woodsman" named Chick helped Joe Gray settle an outside station on Rolling Fork. Gray's settlement, McBride recalled, was "made with his negroes alone, whom he armed. They made good soldiers. He was attacked once." The arming of frontier slaves suggests that some aspects of masculine culture may have transcended race, yet we must be cautious not to read too much into these accounts. Most African Americans, like Chick or Negro Jo, who took up his ax to go hunting with Daniel Trabue, have only fleeting mention in border stories—and then only as supporting characters to whites.[54]

Enslaved African Americans did serve as protagonists in one type of story, however. These were tales of "inversion," which use humor to trivialize or degrade ideas or people normally held in esteem, while at the same time advancing the position of those considered to be inferior. Related in tone to the ridicule that women displayed for the braggadocio of males, slave humor most often directed its barbs toward efforts at maintaining eastern customs and institutions under the primitive and leveling conditions of western life. In one such story, when Captain Watkins told his slaves that they must eat wild turkey in order to save the supplies of bread and bacon for the white people, his bondsman slyly suggested that Watkins reconsider his long-term economic interest. "That will Do very well, master. If we have a plenty of Turkeys we will never Die; but if we have bread and bacon too, we would live a heap longer."[55]

Another slave protagonist managed to poke fun at backwoods architecture, court proceedings, and the pretensions of maintaining a rigid caste system in a raw frontier setting. The story, as told by Benjamin Allen, concerned Tom and Carey, two brothers who belonged to William Angell. When the county court arraigned Tom on the charge of burning John Baker's fodder house, Angell hired Brown, "the great lawyer," to clear his slave's name. During Tom's trial, his brother Carey stood outside the new Clark County courthouse to observe the proceedings. Another eyewitness described the seat of justice at this time as "like a tobacco house, of open round logs in the midst of the cane"; Allen understood that it had cost just sixteen dollars to build. Peeping through the cracks between the logs, Carey kept up a constant banter. " 'Hurra! Massy Brown,' " he would say, " 'Carey got one more ninepence. You clear Brother Tom and Carey treat you, as soon as ever you come out.' " The justices attempted to silence Carey in order to maintain the dignity of the court, but Allen reported they "couldn't stop the fellow from talking." He "would say, 'Massa Bill, Ball sorrel and I could build a better courthouse than this in three days.' " In the end, the charges against Tom were dismissed. Allen concluded with the wry observation: "a treat was a great thing, them times." Slave humor may have targeted white institutions and officials, but one comes away with the distinct impression that in retelling these stories, many ordinary white settlers joined in the laughter as well.[56]

Women also seized a voice in the public sphere of border life. Fearing that "the children's hands would be torn," the women at Strode's Station spoke up against animal baiting. After an alarm at Stocton's Station, "the women would not let the gates be opened, nor any of the men go out, until after dark." At the siege of Boonesborough, when a German immigrant named Tice Brock crept into hiding in Squire

Boone's smith shop, Mrs. Callaway took a brush and brought him out: "Py sure, said he, I was not made for a fighter—I was not made for a fighter." During an attack on McAfee's Station, another woman flushed her own husband from under their bed so that he could fulfill his duty in the settlement's defense.[57]

Perhaps the most telling episode involved another Boone—Rebecca —when she lived with her daughters at Moore's Station on the Clinch River. As a woman later remembered, "the men had gotten very careless, and while the guards were out, they would all go out and play at ball, and those that were not playing, would go out and lie down, without their guns." Boone, her two daughters, and several of the other women determined to play a trick on the loiterers. Loading rifles with the light powder charge customarily used by Indians, the women fired them off on the other side of the fort and ran back in and slammed the gates before the men could get inside. As the women laughed, some of the men "were in so great haste, they run right through the pond. They were all exceeding mad, and wanted, some of them, to have the women whipped, and the men had like to have got to fighting among themselves." The witness added that "*this* quarrel did not grow out of whiskey, for they had none."[58]

What can we make of such stories? More important, what meaning did they hold for John Shane's informants? For years, historians have debated the significance of all the assertive women to be found in western sources. While visions of a "golden age" for westering women have largely faded before undeniable evidence of loneliness, hardship, and personal loss, abstractions about victimization seem equally suspect. Hemmed in as they were by the bonds of patriarchy, Rebecca Boone, Mrs. Callaway, and the other women who shot rifles and wielded brooms nevertheless retained access to sources of social authority and achieved status within the informal political system. Their cause was community security. While bravado and risk-taking secured a man's public reputation, this behavior could also bring about a retaliatory Indian attack against his family or neighbors, and, in the case of a man's death, deprive his dependents of critical food supplies furnished by his hunting. Using the sanctions of moral coercion and public shaming, women staked their claim in the common defense by attempting to curb the rashness of men and, alternately, by ridiculing their overt cowardice.[59]

Words were strong weapons in a face-to-face society preoccupied with the "small politics" of personal reputation. Even a young woman could puncture overweening male confidence with a suitably ironic observation. Eleven-year-old Jane Sprowl grew tired of listening to her brothers sit by the fire and boast of what great things they could do among the Indians. "It is easy to fight Indians," she said, "sitting in the chimney corner, with your bellies' full of mush and milk." Women might also retaliate within their own sphere of dominance. As one man observed: "The women could read the character of a man with invariable certainty. If he lacked courage, they seemed to be able to discover it, at a glance." And, he continued, "if a man was found to be a coward, he stood a poor chance to get his washing, or mending, or anything done."[60]

A few women achieved public renown, and thus were memorialized in their own border stories, for displaying unusual courage. After a party was ambushed on the Wilderness Road, the survivors dressed the women in "big coats . . . and made them ride with sticks on their shoulders," in order to make their appearance more formidable. Sarah Graham remembered that "Sally Thompson, an old maid, raised in my father's neighborhood, came riding up, making her will." In another account, two women at McConnell's Station scalded an Indian to death as he was trying to lift the floorboards of their cabin. "The Indian was trying to lift the slabs, and one of these, a very heavy woman, would always jump upon it, and he hadn't purchase enough to throw her off." To end the standoff, the women poured boiling water through the floorboards. "'Twas said he made a dreadful howling," the informant confided. William Whitley recorded a similarly gruesome account of young Hannah Woods, who took up a broad ax and nearly severed an attacker's arm from his shoulder as his raiding party rushed the door of her family's cabin. While a disabled slave attempted to bar the door, Woods dispatched the Indian, presumably with her ax.[61]

Other women gained notoriety for their ability to handle firearms. William McBride recalled that "Hugh Luper's, Samuel Daviess', General Logan's, [and] Whitley's wives, kept rifles, and were mighty hard to beat, 100 yards." William Whitley, like a number of other border captains, maintained a relatively cordial relationship with his Indian counterparts during times of peace. As his daughter Levisa McKinney later remembered, some time in the 1790s, a large company of Cherokees visited him "looking upon him as a sort of governor of the country—a big captain." Whitley determined to entertain his guests with a shooting match and, as his wife Esther was "a better shot at a mark" than he was, he asked her to participate. Esther Whitley took all the honors. "When beaten, the Indians, astonished, inquired, how she, a squaw, had learned to shoot so well." Esther replied that she "had learned on purpose in order to kill them should occasion ever make it necessary." Whitley's Cherokee guests were no doubt deeply (and doubly) shocked at Esther Whitley's handling of firearms; in Eastern Woodlands culture, strict ritual prohibitions separated women from the masculine realms of hunting and warfare. Backcountry males, on the other hand, seemed less shocked than admiring: in the social order of the frontier community, the physical daring of "soldierly women" blurred even at times the hierarchy of gender.[62]

Public shaming tapped more dangerous emotions, however. Distinctions made between women applauded for their marksmanship and those who earned male censure for playing pointed jokes about courage reflected the ambivalence which surrounded female roles at the end of the eighteenth century. By the mid-nineteenth century, the ideology of domesticity would sanction a woman's efforts to protect her home from the dangerous moral influences of the outside world. At the time of Kentucky's settlement, however, this sort of female activism was still a novelty. Rebecca Boone, her daughters, and the other women who banded together to punish cowards and curb hotheads took public action—political behavior in its most basic form—on what they perceived as a threat to the community's security. They championed the needs of families who, often at great risk, accompanied what amounted to a military occupation force to seize the Ohio Valley. Some women paid a price for this political activity. Rumors abounded about the paternity of one of Rebecca Boone's children, and a Shane informant called Boone's daughter Suzy "a notorious prostitute. Said every Kentuckian ought to try her gait, since she was the first white woman in Kentucky." Assertive frontier women, in general, became caricatured—and thus diminished—in the early nineteenth century as the "reprorious she-males" of the famous Davy Crockett almanacs.[63]

This political discourse had another, more profound, implication. Debates between men and women over issues of community security laid bare deep cultural anxieties about the blurring of the traditionally separate realms of military and civilian life. Did a family gambling on financial betterment by moving west really make the right decision when a father, mother, son, or daughter might be killed or captured at any time? Was death or torture an acceptable risk in the pursuit of a modest competency? In the "small politics" of fort and station life, women and men seemingly articulated divergent positions on this question; yet their joint concerns transcended the gendered terms in which this discourse occurred. In time, of course, all such doubts would be swept away in the crafting of a celebratory and heroic frontier past which transformed assertive backwoods women like Rebecca Boone and Esther Whitley into faithful helpmates and plucky accomplices.

Political Style

By focusing on the struggle over formal constitutional issues, historians of early Kentucky have largely missed the subtle changes taking place in informal political arenas. In frontier outposts and on military campaigns, more egalitarian styles of public participation challenged habits of social deference and the premise of gentry leadership. Yet it would be equally mistaken to overemphasize the autonomy of backwoods life and thus ignore electoral politics and the importance of legal land titles. Returning, then, to the formal political arena and to a question raised at the beginning of this chapter, what, if any, were the connections between the informal and formal political systems, between politics "large" and "small"? Here lies the classic problem of ethnographic history: linking the intimate perceptive universe of ordinary people with the flow of historical events.

For a few men, achieved status within the backwoods social order led to public office. "In consequence of his bravery, in Harmer's Campaign, no one was ever elected to the Legislature . . . with more honor than was McMullin," observed one settler. "Old Michael Cassidy had no earthly claims to office: was a man of no talents. But was elected to the Legislature several times alone because he was not killed that night when Bennet & Spohr were killed," claimed another. Three of Kentucky's first five governors and nearly a third of the early magistrates were militia officers. A Shane informant summed up General Charles Scott's qualifications for office: "not fit for Governor. His military character made him Governor." Many years later, an implacable critic of Turner's frontier thesis would go so far as to claim that "the vulgarization of the judiciary and of officeholding in general was one of the chief accomplishments of that frontier leveling spirit of which so much has been said."[64]

Yet it would be naive to suggest that the election of a few border heroes signaled a wholesale transformation in electoral politics or social structure. As the threat of Indian attack subsided and the countryside grew more thickly populated, Kentucky's once-fluid economic conditions hardened, coming to reflect the disparity of wealth found in areas to the east. Joshua McQueen reflected that it was "easy to have plenty of hogs, and [a] great gang of cattle, and plenty of horses, very soon. But capital and labour were soon as necessary. . . . Cost us nothing, could get nothing." John Hedges explained that for many settlers, tenancy changed from a temporary economic strategy to a permanent social condition. "Some who had leased, enchanted with the abundance of the cane, and the ease of raising cattle, fell too readily from their original purpose of settling themselves, and by attempting to follow up the range, which thus soon ran out, reduced themselves to poverty, and some of them thus lost some of the finest lands in the country." Improvidence, he observed, "once scarcely to be practiced, when the face of things changed, was the ruin of thousands."[65]

An influx of wealthy landowners and their slaves stabilized central Kentucky land values and pushed squatters off their holdings. Benjamin Hardesty described the situation at Bryan's station in the spring of 1785, when John Rodgers (called "negro whipper John") came out to take possession. It was "the time according to the custom of the country" for settling out, he said; "all that didn't—he put them under a rent directly." Revisiting his old neighborhood of Mayslick many years later, Daniel Drake was surprised at the diminishment of the white population. "In a single solitary walk of two miles, which included the spot of our old home, I passed over the foundation—the decayed logs and dust—of no less than twelve cabins." In place of cane, the cabin sites were now overgrown by hemp, the slave-produced cash crop which brought central Kentucky planters great prosperity in the antebellum era. "Their inmates might almost be said to have perished by the hemp," Drake observed of the abandoned homesteads. "The loss of white population . . . has occurred in various parts of Kentucky, and must be referred to the influence of Slavery." Drake recalled his own family's discussions about moving north to the Little Miami Valley to avoid the existence of slavery and the uncertainty of land titles in

Kentucky; he himself had settled in Cincinnati. Drake's perception is supported by other evidence: the 1850 census counted 132,068 Kentucky natives as now residents of Ohio, Indiana, or Illinois—a figure equivalent to almost one-sixth of the total free population remaining in the state.[66]

So, too, did the "respectable migrants" largely succeed in establishing control over constitutional and electoral politics. Despite an upsurge of popular interest in the election of delegates to the constitutional convention of 1791, it was with few exceptions a body of wealthy planters and "solid citizens" who approved George Nicholas's plan of government in April 1792. Kentucky's new constitution, otherwise drawn from the most conservative models of republican government, did contain one political novelty, however: free manhood suffrage regardless of property. As historian Humphrey Marshall observed in 1824, this innovation was a legacy of the settlement era. "For history will perpetuate, what recollection attests, that such had been the condition of the country, such the state of society, and such the habits of the people, that the constitution of the state [of Virginia], had been completely superseded in elections to the legislature, as to the qualification of voters; by all voting, whether they had property, or not."[67] Broad suffrage did not immediately translate into the election of popular leaders to office, however. In Kentucky's first popular gubernatorial election, early pioneer and famed Indian fighter Benjamin Logan polled third behind two wealthier and more educated men.[68]

Yet the ultimate impact of border politics may have been on the *style* of political life. As gentlemen with political ambitions moved to Kentucky, they found that they had to compete with the achieved status of local border heroes; increasingly, they did so by adopting a popular style of public verbal suasion first seen on the battlefield or in the militia company. In 1791, when Kentucky militia companies formed local committees to elect delegates to the constitutional convention, gentlemen like George Nicholas were compelled—possibly for the first time in their lives—to campaign for their seats at mass public meetings. Newcomers to office, like future governor Thomas Metcalfe, now began their political careers with a fiery speech before their militia regiments, rather than a patronage-seeking visit to a local grandee.[69]

Kentucky voters tested the mettle of aspiring politicians by the rules of the informal political system. A famous anecdote from the life of Henry Clay suggests that success in this realm could even turn the tide of an election. Clay's first race for the Kentucky legislature in 1803 looked hopeless, according to an early biographer. He was opposed by "several candidates who were veterans in the business, had occupied the field sometime in advance of him, and besides electioneering warmly for themselves, employed the influence of powerful friends." One day while stump-speaking for his uphill cause, Clay attracted the attention of a company of riflemen going home after a militia muster. The men listened politely until Clay closed his remarks,

> when one of their number, a man about fifty years of age, who had evidently seen much backwoods service, stood leaning on his rifle, regarding the young speaker with a fixed and most sagacious look. . . . "Young man," said he, "you want to go to the legislature, I see?" "Why, yes," replied Mr. Clay. . . . "Are you a good shot?" "The best in the country." "Then you shall go; but you must give us a specimen of your skill; we must see you shoot."

Clay later claimed that he had never shot a rifle before in his life. But he gamely shouldered the man's weapon and luckily hit near the center of a target set at eighty yards. According to his biographer, "this unimportant incident gained him the vote of every hunter and marksman in the assembly, which was composed principally of that class of persons, as well as the support of the same throughout the county." In this latter-day border story, Clay easily won election with the single act of bravado that established his reputation.[70]

In his congressional career, Henry Clay continued to draw upon lessons he had learned in the informal political system. As spokesman for the West and leader of the young "War Hawks" advocating war with Great Britain, Clay adopted a combative style of verbal sparring reminiscent of the physical contests of fort or station yard. In calling for an invasion of Canada in 1813, Clay scoffed at more cautious House members who questioned the justice of the action.

> Canada, said Mr. Clay, innocent! Canada unoffending! Is it not in Canada, that the tomahawk of the savage has been moulded into its death-like form? Has it not been from Canadian magazines . . . that those supplies have been issued, which nourish and continue the Indian hostilities—supplies which have enabled the savage hordes to butcher the garrison of Chicago, and to commit other horrible excesses and murders?

Dreams of conquering Canada soon faded, but the spread-eagle political rhetoric of Clay and other young westerners would become the political idiom of a rising generation of American leaders. Far removed from the cool and reasoned discourse of the revolutionary gentry, this new political style was instead a cultural legacy of border war, a throwback to a time when personal qualities of bravado and canny survival secured public reputation. The new party spirit bubbling up in the 1820s and 1830s preserved a remnant of a western political culture in which a "big-man" had entertained his followers with a grand picnic and a vulgar joke, much like a generation later another border captain would welcome a few thousand of his closest friends to his inaugural reception.[71]

THE POLITICS OF POWER

The stories of their little pioneer log forts are
as epic as the Nibelungen Lied.

LUCIEN BECKNER

5 Indian Times

In the early 1840s, a vigorous controversy broke out in Kentucky newspapers as to the date and location of the state's first settlement. Captain Nathaniel Hart Jr., writing in the *Louisville News-Letter*, claimed this honor for Boonesborough, citing letters and papers he had inherited from his father, "an active member" of Richard Henderson's Transylvania Company. After laying out his evidence for Boonesborough's precedence, Hart concluded that "from the most thorough investigation of all the sources of information to which I have had access, as well as from the tradition of the country with which I have been familiar for the last sixty years, the conviction upon my mind is irresistible, that Boonesborough was the first place in Kentucky occupied by the white man, in 1775, with the view of permanent settlement." If Harrodsburg or any other place claimed priority, Hart would "be pleased to see the evidence to support such claims."[1]

General Robert B. McAfee rose to the defense of Harrodsburg. After "a laborious investigation" of published histories, family journals, and interview notes "taken in personal conversation" with early residents, McAfee revealed in the *Louisville Journal* that "it has been my settled opinion for more than thirty years, that *Harrodstown* (now Harrodsburg) was *permanently occupied in March, 1775,* and *Boonesborough* in the month following (April)." Boonesborough's residents had stolen a march on those of Harrodsburg, however. Boonesborough celebrated the "first settlement of Kentucky" on the 25th of May, 1840, with a grand military encampment drawing "many thousands" of visitors. Former governor James T. Morehead delivered the principal address, diplomatically paying tribute to James Harrod as the "builder of the 'first log cabin' that was ever raised in the wilderness of Kentucky," while drawing his listeners' attention to the first *permanent* settlement commenced at Boonesborough in the following year. Not to be outdone in civic boosterism, a committee of Harrodsburg residents led by Robert McAfee vowed to make the commemoration an annual event—with the following year's celebration to take place in their own town of Harrodsburg.[2]

The controversy over the date of Kentucky's founding prompted a flurry of historical research. The newly organized Kentucky Historical Society appointed a committee of members to report on the date and place of the earliest settlement, "so nearly as could now be ascertained." Daniel Boone's grandson Septimus Schull entered the fray, searching out old settlers who could offer eyewitness accounts of Boonesborough's early years. When John Shane interviewed Schull in 1841, Schull repeated his conversation with James Hays, who "states that he came to Boonesborough with grandfather's family." Unfortunately, Hays was not of much help in settling the contest. Asked about the settlement date of Boonesborough, "the venerable old man drew his hand across his forehead, as if to concentrate all his recollection, and after some delay, said it had been a long time—but the precise year I do not recollect. Says it was in the fall season that the family arrived: though not late, 'for,' says he, 'a snake bit me the day after we got there, and came near to killing me.'" Content to approximate his measure of time, the old settler unwittingly frustrated posterity's attempt to plot Boonesborough's founding on an absolute time line immune to interpretive distortion.[3]

The imprecision of early residents who "never attended much to history" troubled Kentucky's first historians. Too busy founding settlements and fighting Indians to keep careful notes, informants later used a variety of temporal references—"at corn-planting time," "about Christmas," "after Wayne's treaty"—to anchor their experiences in the past. Aspiring frontier historians, imbued with the "scientific" principles of the great antiquarian historians of the early nineteenth century, searched for reliable firsthand accounts of "what actually happened"—which usually implied the naming of a precise date and location. In 1843, Lyman Draper consulted the grandson of Colonel Richard Callaway about a vexing problem. "I have before me several versions of the interesting occurrence of the capture of your mother [aunt], her sister, & a daughter of Col. Boone, in July of 1776." Yet historians could not agree on the particulars.

> Marshall says it occurred on the 14th July '76. Flint follows Marshall in this particular. Col. Floyd states in his letter to Col. Preston, written soon after, that it took place on the 7th. Butler, in his Ky. History, adopts Col. Floyd's version of the affair, both as regards date and facts. Flint's very improbable story, in his life of Boone, I suppose is little to be relied on. McClung says but little about it, and agreeing in date, with Marshall & Flint; but differing from all other narrators of that occurrence, by stating that only *one* Miss Calloway & Miss Boone were taken prisoners. Judge Hall's Monthly Magazine for Sept. 1833, gives an account of that affair, differing in some respects from all the rest, sadly mistaken as to (the) time, placing it in June, 1778.

French, having "never attended much to history," could offer little assistance. His wife recalled, however, that old Mrs. French "said she well remembered, she, at the time, was one of the little girls, and cried to go along."[4]

All such efforts to organize the passage of time are interpretive acts. Like the cognitive mapping of spatial, social, and political boundaries, humans structure their temporal experiences in a variety of ways—by reference to natural or celestial phenomena, by their own age or position in the life course, and by episodic chronologies based on a chosen sequence of events. Each system of time-reckoning depends on a comparison between two parallel processes that bear some relationship to each other. Thus, James Hays related his arrival at Boonesborough to the seasonal appearance of reptiles; Mrs. French dated her sister's captivity by her own age rank as "one of the little girls." Episodic chronologies, employed most often for historical periodization, utilize social rather than natural phenomena. Familiar timeframes include the reigns of monarchs, the birth of a messiah (B.C./A.D.), or the invention of historical epochs like the "Middle Ages."[5]

Clock and calendar time also originated in natural bases of measurement: the movements of the sun and moon. Since the publication of Isaac Newton's *Principia* in 1687, however, these measurements have increasingly taken on the character of "absolute time"—uniform, mathematical, and continuous, flowing without reference to any external events. Newton revolutionized perceptions of time by basing his laws of motion and gravitation on an analogy between time and geometry. In his conceptual system, the moments of absolute time formed a continuous sequence, much like the imaginary points of a straight geometric line. Newton's time was general and ideal, depending on the "objective" authority of science rather than the subjectivities of the social and natural world. In subsequent centuries, Newton's concept of an absolute time line provided a compelling model for historians seeking to locate the events of history in a simple—but precise—temporal continuum.[6]

Early efforts to record western history drew upon both absolute and relative dating systems. Notable events which depended on "reliable sources" (and thus could be located in absolute time) constituted the primary "facts" that scholars with positivistic aspirations used in their historical reconstructions. Occurrences identified only by vague temporal references entered the realm of mythic time; handed down as border stories, some of these accounts eventually found publication in popular frontier collections like McClung's *Sketches of Western Adventure*. Many other stories were simply forgotten, or were captured in the trackless clutter of John Shane's or Lyman Draper's notebooks.

Even the narrative of Kentucky's founding fit uncomfortably into the chronology of absolute time. Because the danger of Indian attack diminished rapidly in more densely populated areas, the same year— 1793, for example—saw the capture of Morgan's Station, the operation of twenty-eight retail stores in Lexington, and the erection of a new state house in Frankfort. Scholars seeking to identify the "closing" of Kentucky's frontier era have variously cited its occurrence at the end of the American Revolution, statehood in 1792, and the production of agricultural surpluses in the mid-1790s.[7]

Absolute and relative time intertwined in the memories of Shane's informants. Less concerned with chronological precision than Draper (who later annotated Shane's notebooks with precise dates where he knew them), John Shane recorded a mixture of specific dates, seasonal references, and attempts at historical periodization. The variety of these dating systems richly documents the efforts of ordinary women and men to give narrative shape and historical meaning to their life stories. Adopting Shane's broad view of what constitutes temporal experience, this final chapter seeks to comprehend the various "times" of Kentucky's early settlers as a means of exploring the topography of indigenous historical perception. It concludes by examining how historians and popular authors reshaped the complex historical understanding of old pioneers into a starkly simplified national drama about the winning of the western country.[8]

Cyclical Time

Anthropologists suggest that consciousness of time may be a fundamental human characteristic. Speculation about the astronomical orientation of prehistoric stone circles in Britain and apparent references to a future life found in cave paintings and burials in Europe argue that an awareness of time touched the lives of our earliest human ancestors. Such elemental methods of time-reckoning depend on the observation of naturally recurring phenomena. The sun's rising and setting, the phases of the moon, the rhythm of the seasons, and the life cycle of birth, death, and rebirth provide a structural framework for the cyclical ordering of human experience. Cycles of nature continue to influence our most intuitive notions of time.[9]

In the western country, subsistence activities and border warfare governed the rhythms of daily life. Often these two cycles intersected. During "dangerous times," security measures accompanied even the most mundane domestic tasks such as crop tending or milking. Other daily activities like the careful barring of cabin doors at dusk and a quick search outside for moccasin tracks in the morning offered even more dramatic evidence of the blurring of military and domestic routines. Milking, for example, was women's work, but men commonly stood guard while they labored. Mrs. Arnold remembered that her husband "was holding the cow by a short rope, while I was milking, when the Indians came. . . . We jumped up and ran into the fort. We got this and some other cows in." An attack at Strode's Station came just as "Mrs. Spaugh had been out to milk, and told her husband, Jacob

Spaugh, to drive the cattle away, as customary, out of the fields into the cane." With experience, a quick dash for cover became almost perfunctory, a subject for rueful humor. Mrs. Shanklin recalled that one day when the apprentice at Clear Station cried out "Indians! Indians!," she "cleared a high fence, into the yard, with both buckets of milk, and without spilling a drop." As she remembered, "they all raised the laugh to see me."[10]

Evidence of a weekly cycle was less clear-cut. Indeed, only one day of the week—Sunday—achieved any measure of distinction in Shane's notes. Frances Lays, for example, planned to return to Virginia on "sabbath morning," but Indians shot him as he turned his horse out to graze. Jane Stevenson's family "never travelled a Sunday" in coming out to Kentucky, except for one Sunday in Powell's Valley when they journeyed about five miles to reach a beautiful clear spring of water. John Rankins noted "it was Sunday morning, when they were not stirring much about the station," when a buffalo bull came into the salt lick with the tame cattle at Boonesborough. "Mat, I think it was, or Kit Hahn took down their gun and went out and shot it. . . . It furnished us beef for some time." Whether employed as a temporal marker or viewed as a day of rest, Sunday exhibited a qualitative difference from the other days of the week.[11]

So, too, did traditional holidays stand out in the landscape of remembered time. Benjamin Allen's family "saw Easter eggshells on the road" when they started from Berkeley County, Virginia, in 1789. On Christmas Eve, 1788, Samuel Potts Pointer sought refuge in Masterson's Station when "the snow fell nearly half [a] leg deep." Robert Shanklin built two cabins outside Clear Station when his family arrived in December 1784; his widow later recollected that "it was New-Year's day, the day when he got into them." Although Shane's interview notes contain scant evidence of holiday observances among backcountry settlers, the use of traditional holy days as temporal markers suggests that these days were nevertheless bounded by a special sense of time.[12]

Far more important in shaping time's contours were seasonal periodicities governing planting, hunting, warfare, and even migration. Spring and fall, for example, were the most popular travel seasons; migrants generally avoided relocation during the growing season or in the wet winter months. A Virginia newspaper published a monthly tally of emigrants passing through the wilderness in the year 1795; the seasonal fluctuations revealed in this list suggest the popularity of an autumn removal after completion of the harvest:

January	72
February	88
March	365
April	1,218
May	717
June	489
July	141
August	74
September	739
October	3,103
November	1,442
December	562
Total	9,010

A number of Shane's informants mentioned the season of their migration; of these, the vast majority journeyed west in the autumn. Isaac Clinkenbeard traveled through the wilderness in 1779; he recalled that "thousands of people came out that fall. More than did for seven or eight years after that." David Crouch's family also came out in "the fall season—we had narry [a] river to ferry at all." Timing of departure was critical, however; emigrants making a late start occasionally found themselves "frozen up in the Monongahela Country."[13]

Annual routines associated with corn cultivation formed a rudimentary calendar—one shared by both native and immigrant inhabitants of the Ohio Valley. Although specific practices varied from place to place, Indian villagers generally celebrated a corn-planting festival in early May or June, a green-corn ceremony in late August or September, and a harvest festival in October. For Euroamericans, the corn crop's progress supplied a similar succession of temporal references. "At corn-planting time," for example, four families moved into Morgan's Station. About the first of May, two hunters "had our corn planted and it was a sort of leisure time." In June, the "corn was made" at the time of an attack on Baker's Station. "When the corn was about as high as your shoulder," the buffalo came into the salt lick at Boonesborough. In the fall, two men "went down to kill the bears—roasting ear time—eating up all our corn. Had to gather it green, to keep them from eating it up." One year, however, "a very forward frost" on the last day of September killed all the corn in roasting ear. The corn calendar influenced the timing of other natural cycles: Josiah Collins later claimed that "about ten or eleven months after the corn of 1780 came in . . . the women began to breed pretty fast." Before that, he explained, they had only had buffalo meat to eat.[14]

Other temporal references documented the intersection of seasonal and military rhythms. John Gass dated his sister's death at Estill's Station by a turn in the spring weather: "it was March . . . that night the snow had fallen." Indians captured William McCutchen's wife "in June or July," while George Fearis stood sentry "while they were reaping at this season." McCutchen later escaped, but "she got in deranged," Fearis said. "She left the Indians just as the buds were putting out, and wandered about from that time till harvest with a camp-kettle, butcher-knife, and fire," living on boiled roots. At Covalt's Station in the Miami country, Indians killed Abraham Covalt "about [the] first of May. Woods were right green." The residents of Lee's Station were out "frosting their tobacco," when Indians "came on them and killed and took several." Recalling one of their own raids against the Indian settlements in southern Ohio, a veteran of Edward's expedition referred to it as the "Blackberry Campaign. So many blackberries. Blackberry time."[15]

Monthly and annual cycles similarly reflected times of security or danger. Settlers observed that Indian military activity waxed and waned with the passage of the seasons and the phases of the moon. The siege of Boonesborough, for example, "came in September; the river was low." Indians carried off eleven horses from Wickersham's Station in southern Ohio "about the full of the moon, first [of] April." A similar raid struck near Georgetown in "warm weather—the first night the men had camped out." William Clinkenbeard later claimed that "Indians were always worse in the spring and fall." Jane Stevenson, whose mother was killed and her aunt and three cousins captured on the Calfpasture River in Virginia, distinguished between the relative dangers of the two seasons. "In the spring they would rather have a prisoner than a scalp," she said, suggesting that an additional mouth to feed in the summer was less problematic for an Indian community.[16]

Experienced settlers anticipated the seasonality of border warfare. Mrs. Arnold recalled that at Bryan's Station on "the first moonlight night in March, you would hear the men hollowing out, boys! put up your horses, if you don't the Indians will get them." As reports from the western country filtered back to the interior settlements, land-lookers from the East timed their visits accordingly. McConnell's fort was crowded in the winter, Jane Stevenson observed scornfully. "It was the continental war going on. Safe for to be among Indians. But as soon as warm weather came on, they put back." William Tyler cited the regularities of his own military service. "In the spring of 1787 . . . I was drafted to guard one month down on McConnell's run while they planted corn. And I then came home and ploughed and planted my own corn. In the fall I was out in the same way, down by Lee's Town. For anything of this kind, we never got a cent."[17]

Early fall was, in turn, the most popular season to attack Indian settlements. Of approximately thirty major armed expeditions cross-ing north of the Ohio River between 1774 and 1794, over half took place during August, September, and October—the crucial months of corn ripening and harvest. In a scorched-earth policy striking at the heart of Indian subsistence regimes, Kentucky militiamen and army regulars routinely targeted native cornfields for destruction. William Whitley served as pilot on one such expedition (Clark's) in July 1780. He recorded in his memoir that they found "Old Chilicotha Town" va-cated, but nevertheless "We Burnt the Town & Cut down their Corn." Proceeding to "Pickaway Town," where they engaged an Indian force, Clark's troops suffered 15 or 16 casualties but gained "about 16 or 17 scalps" in return. Whitley termed their expedition a victory, although it came at a price: Kentucky troops killed an Indian captive—"an Own Cozen [sic] of General Clark's"—by mistake; the Shawnees captured and later burned Captain Hickman. After driving the remaining Shaw-nee villagers from their homes, the Kentuckians "Destroyed about 500 Acres of corn." In a tragic spiral of hate and destruction, the shared cycles of subsistence became the shared cycles of war.[18]

Linear Time

Linear time is social and political rather than ecological; it depends on an analogy to human ageing and death rather than the recurring phases of nature. The concept of chronology—the arrangement of events into linear time—probably dates from the rise of city-states and empires in the ancient world. Sumerians, Babylonians, Egyptians, and early Greeks all recorded episodic chronologies based on linear politi-cal sequences; at the same time, however, they retained fundamentally cyclical views of history. The unification of the Mediterranean world by Roman conquest and, in particular, the adoption of the history of the Jews as recorded in the Bible provided historians with their first chronological sequences that transcended purely parochial events. Jewish tradition contributed one other important temporal concept to historians: the notion of providence and linear progression—the sense that time had a direction.[19]

In the western country, categories of human interaction—the course of settlement and relations with Indian neighbors—shaped perceptions of linear time. Personal and local chronologies based on "coming out," "settling out," and "improving" ran parallel to a military sequence of "friendly" and "unfriendly times." At critical points these time lines intersected: settling outside a station, for example, depended on friendly times, or at least the security of numbers. Timing of occupation also varied from place to place. Interior areas, particularly the rich cane lands along the Kentucky River bottoms, filled up rapidly with homesteaders, while surrounding frontiers remained sparsely inhabited and vulnerable to attack for at least another decade.

What year migrants "came out" depended on a variety of factors. Personal considerations such as age, opportunity, or family situation all played a role; so, too, did larger historical events influence the timing of many arrivals. Population estimates, although not very reliable for this period, suggest that the close of the Revolutionary War unleashed a surge of migration to the West. In 1782, Brissot de Warville estimated Kentucky's population at 8,000 inhabitants; two years later John Filson cited a figure of 30,000. Settler John Hanks offered perhaps the best explanation for this explosion in numbers: "The Indians made peace when Cornwallis was taken, and continued it five or six years."[20]

Migrants were acutely conscious of the risks and opportunities offered by "friendly" and "unfriendly times." Shane's informants frequently used military events to date their arrival in the West, suggesting that the state of Indian-white relations at that time had influenced (or at least shadowed) decisions about migration. David Gass's father first came out to Kentucky in "the year of the Battle of the Point"; Jane Stevenson "moved to Greenbriar in 1775. The year after the battle of the Point." Other migrants came "the year after the sham treaty at Boonesborough [1779]," "the year before Con Jackson's defeat [1780]," "the same year Cornwallis was taken [1781]," "very soon after the

Battle of Blue Licks [1782]," "the year of Harmer's campaign [1790]," the "time of St. Clair's defeat [1791]," and "perhaps in 1795. It was the same fall with Wayne's victory [1794]."[21]

In much the same way, decisions about when to "settle out" weighed perceptions of physical risk against the calculus of economic advantage. Migrants anxious to break the soil of their own farms chafed at planting other men's fields; tenants who lingered too long after danger from Indian attack passed found their services devalued in the "small politics" of economic life. Sarah Graham recalled that the residents of Stephen Fisher's station first attempted to settle out in 1781, but "the Indians beat them back"; her family remained at the station until the fall of 1783. At Craig's and nearby Downing's Stations, "people had scattered out and got scared, and all went in to Downing's Station" during the summer of 1782. By the fall of 1784, however, "a few scattering families had settled out" near Jessamine Creek and in other central areas. A resident of Bryan's Station noted that when Rogers "came out and took possession" in the spring of 1785, "I reckon the half were gone" before the landowner could put them under a rent. When John Rankins reached Boonesborough in May 1784, "the picketing of the fort was gone, but the cabins were occupied and the bast ends stood. . . . That fall they began to move out." He explained that "the fear of Indians about Boonesborough was done away before we got there. Bush's Station, and McGee's, and Strode's Station were outside when we came." William Clinkenbeard remarked that "we were seven years in the fort [Strode's] before we got out. I then bought twenty-five acres of land on Wolf Creek of old man Parvin." His brother Isaac settled on a "corn right" farm in Bourbon County in 1790. Strode's, he recalled, was "called inside, then."[22]

Settlers abandoned the safety of "outside" stations—settling their own farms even farther out—with even more caution. Masterson's Station lay only five miles outside of Lexington; in 1788, "it was peace then about Lexington and Cross-Plains, but not to the right of Lexington, about Masterson's. Every few weeks troubles broke out about there." When John Wilson's family arrived in soon-to-be-organized Scott County, "there were but few settlers in this county, as early as 1790, the year we came to Kentucky." His family lived in Lexington for two years before settling out on their own farm. "My father had bought land before he came out to live; but was afraid to settle on it for fear of the Indians. I was the oldest son. Every time I went out after the horses, I expected I might be killed." Wilson's fears were justified. "The first night we came to Scott County . . . the Indians took a man and his wife prisoners, on Lane's run, the other side of Georgetown." His mother, Wilson recalled, "was very much alarmed at that occurrence, and importuned my father (though she was a woman of courage, and would have fought) to move down to Campbell's Station" until "corn-gathering time—say in October."[23]

Those who settled outside during "unfriendly times" often risked death or capture. After Congress enacted the Northwest Ordinance in 1787, the federal government used first negotiation and then force to secure cession of Indian lands northwest of the Ohio River. The result was a general renewal of border war in the early 1790s. Samuel Spence settled on a farm at Eagle-ridge near Georgetown in 1791. Times seemed safe enough, recalled his brother; we "had no more idea of Indians then, than I have now, not a bit." One February night in 1794, Spence returned home after a log rolling and found that his wife had collected sugar water from their tapped maple trees. When Spence told his wife that "he would go out and kindle a fire under the furnace, and boil it down that night," she advised him that it was "best to leave it till next day"; he was tired and the hour was late. "But it was a beautiful, clear moonlight night, and the people were just settling out, and had everything to do," explained his brother. Spence lit his fire and returned inside to eat his supper; on his second trip outside to check his kettles, someone shot him in the chest. "When he was shot, he was not more than ten steps from the Indians," his brother told Shane; "I've measured it many a time."[24]

Settling out was also a time of painful separation. Daniel Drake's family left the "stirring" settlement at Mayslick for the "seclusion" of a new farm in 1794. His mother, he remembered, was particularly affected. "None but those who have lived where they saw many persons every hour in the day, can fully estimate the feeling of loneliness which comes into the heart when only trees and a few domestic animals can be seen." For the first two years in their new cabin, often entire days would pass without seeing an outsider. The family drew closer emotionally, he recalled; any visitor became a notable occurrence. "I well recollect that when anybody came, I was all the time afraid he was about to start away. The coming of a negro on an errand was a welcome event, and the visit of a boy, even on business, was a matter of delight." Reflecting back on this solitary time, Drake dated his social aptitude and love of company to his youthful longing for companionship.[25]

What settlers termed "improving" usually began in densely settled areas safe from Indian incursions. Strictly speaking, "improvements" in Anglo-American tradition were any alterations to the landscape rendering it more profitable by cultivation, enclosure, or occupation. Virginia law, for example, recognized "any house or hut, or . . . other improvements" as the basis for claiming settlement and preemption rights to western lands. For Shane's informants, however, improving usually meant the erection of commercial or public facilities and the amelioration of existing housing stocks. Migrants arriving in the early 1790s often commented on the improvements they encountered. When Major Bean came down the river in the fall of 1790, he recalled that "Hornbachs mill was built, and the people were scattered, or began to be, out of Stroud's and Constant's stations. Winchester not settled yet." James Hedge spent the winter of 1791–92 in Paris. "Old man Kelly, first merchant in Paris," kept a small store there and "did a good deal of trafficking." Harris, a potter, "who had some money, turned in to improving: built a frame house, 1792."[26]

The chronology of economic expansion moved swiftly in interior areas. In 1784, the town of Lexington consisted of thirty cabins scattered around a log stockade; eight years later it was Kentucky's metropolis, boasting twenty retail stores, eleven ordinaries, two wheeled carriages, and "one brick house in six." Craftsmen from the East flocked to the booming western town. Benjamin Wood and his brother Joseph migrated from Allenstown, New Jersey, to set up their tailoring business in Lexington. In the summer of 1792, Benjamin Wood wrote home that "our little town that we see every day is improving so fast that it is alterd since we came to it so much that it is almost beyond exception and Expression. I bleve [believe] thare is about twenty Buildings now on hand and most of them elligant one's[,] sum brick and sum stone. . . . Thar is sixty more buildings to go up this summer." The merchant Ephraim January, he reported, was building a new brick store fronting seventy feet along the street. And their own tailoring business was prospering as well. "Thare is about thirty taylors in town and the most of them gits Work plenty[.] for our parts we never was in such a way of busaness in our lives[.] we get from fore Dollars to five for making a sute of close and git as much as whe can turn our hands tow[.] it makes well for us this summer thare has been a grate many commers and goers[.] it has maid cash plenty." Wood could not predict how much larger Lexington would grow, but to his mind, "the more the better for us."[27]

In recalling the commercialization of the western landscape, settlers' perceptions of linear time often took on a Whiggish momentum. The choice of the word "improvement" was in itself significant. While longtime residents seemed ambivalent about some aspects of temporal change—lamenting, for example, the destruction of Kentucky's once-rich game supplies and its lush native vegetation—they displayed few reservations about the arrival of other aspects of metropolitan culture. Perhaps influenced by the recent controversy over Kentucky's "first settlement," Shane's informants volunteered information about a variety of other pioneering enterprises. Cockey Owings from Baltimore "built the first Iron-works," according to Major Bean; "his improvement was the first out that way, outside of Stroud's Station." Another man recalled the "first water mill I saw, was on Dick's river, tother [sic] side of Lewis Craig's Station." Elijah Foley claimed that "Colonel Bowman built the first mill on Cane-run, the first in the state, I think." James Stevenson remembered the rapid transformation of even the most mundane aspects of material life. "After the Revolutionary War, goods from England and France came in so that all the East was flooded"; in Kentucky, "tin-cups were about the first goods imported."[28]

Chronologies of civic improvements proved equally memorable. While few settlers commented on the legal business conducted at county courts, a number described the construction and improvement of local courthouses. Several informants noted, for example, that the Bourbon court met at Strode's Station before moving to Winchester after the town's establishment in 1793. James Hedge recalled that in Paris, "old man Jackson kept the first Court-house." After building a new brick courthouse in Paris in 1792, they "moved the frame Courthouse off, and kept the Post-office in it." Jesse Graddy recounted a similar elaboration of public facilities in Woodford County. When the county was first laid off in 1788, the court met a few times at Shannon's meeting house, a log church. Then, Graddy recalled, "in 1789, when the first court was established, I had the job of building the Court-house. The whole [job] cost just $22.50, and I made a dollar a day at that. Hired two or three days, Ben Guthrie to saw some plank too." Graddy described the courthouse's simple construction: "Buckeye logs—just hewed straight inside, a platform for the judge, a place for the bar, and some benches. Occupied two years, till the other house was built." Woodford County's second courthouse was stone, he recalled; the third was brick "and now last year renewed and repaired at a cost of some $6000."[29]

While expressing pride in these accomplishments, informants nevertheless remained candid about the limitations of early civic and commercial efforts. William Sudduth, who served as a justice of the peace in Clark County, described the first courthouse at Winchester as "put up of round logs, unstopped. . . . There was an open crack behind the judge's bench. I set my hat there one day, and while I was on the bench, it was stolen." As late as 1792, a new arrival in Lexington could still describe Kentucky's metropolis as "principally a log village," while another resident recalled that "part of the stockading of the fort was standing here in the middle of the street" long after he arrived in 1798. Jeptha Kemper considered Lexington's first store a meager affair. "You could have put it all in one waggon. If there had been much buying, two or three families would have bought it out." Other commercial "firsts" bore even fewer traces of the local boosterism at play in the controversy over Kentucky's first settlement. Near Danville, Sarah Graham's father built a wooden still for two brothers from England who, she claimed, produced the "first whiskey made in Kentucky." Graham suspected, however, that the immigrant distillers had little benefited the community. "Fourteen persons, that I knew their faces, committed suicide, and I never thought before, it might have been this still."[30]

In recounting their personal narratives, migrants periodized linear time by references to shared experiences of arrival, orientation, and social and spatial elaboration. Stories about "coming out," "settling out," and "improving" created simple temporal boundaries in an episodic chronology which did not depend on the precision of absolute dating for its inherent meaning. Equally influential in structuring the remembered past was a concurrent sequence of "friendly" and "unfriendly times." Here, variation in circumstance among localities influenced the timing and duration of the settlement sequence. The intertwining of these chronologies of settlement and warfare helps to explain a seeming paradox of Kentucky pioneer life: the simultaneous presence of Latin schools and log stockades, of Indian raids and coaches-and-four. Socioeconomic divisions among migrants undoubtedly contributed to differing material conditions, but so, too, did temporal and spatial complexities play a role in the bifurcation of cultural styles still evident in the state today.

History

Beyond the universal experiences of migration and settlement, notable events supplied Kentuckians with shared temporal landmarks in the topography of western time. In reflecting on the times in which they had lived, Shane's informants repeatedly returned to particular "occurrences" which they placed in the chronicle of "early times." Migrants wove their own remembrances into the larger narrative of western history by singling out these extraordinary events and recounting their own roles in them. Notable events also marked points of intersection between indigenous and scholarly historical perceptions. Early historians simplified the rich contingency of personal experience by letting landmark events stand for whole classes of pioneering experiences. And, as individual settlers rarely viewed themselves as historical agents for the nation or for "civilization," aspiring authors also supplied their activities with an interpretive direction—one that would, over time, trumpet America's "manifest destiny" to fill up the continent. A modern social historian might argue for a more generous definition of what constitutes history, but western settlers and their earliest historians clearly placed great emphasis on discrete events as the marrow of historical experience.[31]

The "hard winter" of 1779–80 was one such remarkable time. Writing from the Bear Grass settlements near the falls of the Ohio, surveyor John Floyd left a contemporary description of that January's weather: "When I attempted to write in December the ink froze in the pen and it is no better yet, as the Snow has never melted off the south side of the cabbin [sic] since the first of last month. . . . it is certainly an uncommon winter as the cane seems to be all dead by the hard frosts." Adding to their miseries, Floyd reported that the demand for food from arriving settlers had outstripped the supplies on hand. Flour, he wrote, was as "dear as gold dust"; "corn has sold at the Falls for 165 Dollars per Bushel and people seem desirous to have every other article in proportion to that. Money is of no account here."[32]

Those who experienced "the Violence of this Winter" later spoke of it with awe. Joice Falconer and her family spent the winter in a rough V-shaped log pen called a half-face camp. Coming out in the fall of

1779, the family arrived at the future site of Craig's Station on Christmas Eve. "From that time, to March 10, 1780 (the day Calloway and Hart were killed at the Borough) there was not any thaw, and the ground was covered with snow," she recalled. "Through all this winter, these five families, with the rest of the company that was at Craig's Station continued there in half face camps—the cracks covered over as well as could be with cane—and the cane in a great body all around them." William Clinkenbeard and his brother Isaac also arrived in the fall of 1779. William recalled that they "drove two cows out, that died of that hard winter. Go through the cane and see cattle laying with their heads to their side, as if they were asleep; just literally froze to death." Many settlers lost their cattle that winter, Clinkenbeard remembered; wild animals suffered as well. "A great country for turkeys, and they had like to have starved to death—a heap! a heap! of them died." A visitor to Harrodsburg dated the decline of the buffalo to this same period. "Should an Indian ware [war] take place in the spring I am confident numbers must perish for want of provision as that Grate magazeen of providential blessings peculiar to this Countrey now has faild (The Buffalo) which is accasioned by the extream hard Winter."[33]

In the narratives of early historians, the "hard winter" of 1779–80 came to symbolize the hazards of migration and settlement—and the rewards of perseverance. In his 1847 *Historical Sketches of Kentucky*, Lewis Collins (quoting Davidson) described it as "a winter of unexampled severity," when "famished wild animals would come up in the yard of the stations along with the tame cattle," and when the human sufferers would divide "a single jonny-cake" into a dozen parts, and make it serve for two meals. Departing subtly from participant accounts, the historian also lent his story narrative direction by stressing the providential blessing that awaited the survivors. "A delightful spring, and the rapid growth of vegetation, promised to repay them for the hardships they had undergone. The peach-trees they had planted five years before, were loaded with fruit, and the apple-trees were also in a thriving condition. Plenty and happiness smiled upon the settlement." God, in short, smiled upon the conquerors.[34]

Border warfare also supplied a dense chronology of historical references. Attacks, campaigns, and defeats punctuated the passage of remembered time. Many of these incidents were primarily localistic in their importance; as John Shane traveled throughout the countryside, the significant events he documented varied from place to place. In Bourbon and Clark Counties, for example, informants spoke about the attack on Strode's Station in March 1781. In Jessamine and Woodford, they recounted the death of Scott's son in the spring of 1789. In Bath and Montgomery, informants described the taking of Morgan's Station in April 1793. The instinctive attractions of a local history perspective, which serves to connect individuals with their own immediate surroundings, assured the form's survival from oral to written accounts. Lewis Collins, for example, divided his *Historical Sketches* into two unequal parts: a general historical narrative followed by a much longer county history compendium, in which incidents of border warfare figured prominently.[35]

A few military events achieved universal significance. One of the most widely discussed was the battle at Blue Licks on 19 August 1782, which drew more than 160 men from central Kentucky stations. Many families lost sons or fathers that day; at least sixty officers and men were killed in the defeat, including Daniel Boone's son Israel. Mrs. January recalled that "sixteen went to the Blue Licks Battle from Harrodsburg under Colonel McGary. Eight returned. My father was one killed." Hugh McGary's actions in precipitating the battle—in particular, his reported challenge to "let all those who are not cowards follow me"—became the source of immediate (and continuing) historical controversy. In time, as memories faded of the long litany of defeats and victories that made up the two-decades' long contest for the western country, historians would style Blue Licks as "the last battle of the American Revolution," thus simplifying and rationalizing the complex concurrent struggles for American empire and American independence.[36]

Another significant battle cleaved historical time into two parts: "Indian times" and those that came after. General Anthony Wayne's defeat of a confederacy of western Indians at Fallen Timbers in 1794, along with the signing of the Treaty of Greenville in the following year, closed the epoch of border warfare for most Kentuckians. For Shane's informants, Wayne's victory over the Indians served as the pivotal moment in the settlement of the western country; it created a common historical reference point much like World War II serves as a watershed for those born in the twentieth century. Chilton Allen mused in hindsight that "the Revolutionary war in the western country did not close before the year of Wayne's Treaty." Sarah Graham recalled that "it was after Wayne's Battle . . . that we had peace." Other memories of peacetime were more pragmatic. Jesse Daniel found that it was safe to move out to Shelby "after Wayne's war." Jeptha Kemper recalled that "they hung men for stealing horses after the treaty by Wayne, in numbers. It was all attributed to the Indians before." John Hedge remembered Wayne's victory because "after peace was made, they got to make salt upon Sandy [River]." Caleb Williams later lamented that "when peace was made, Cincinnati was a very dull place. Nothing there but soldiers wives, and soldiers drinking."[37]

After peace, as is customary, historians took to the field. John Filson, Harry Toulmin, and Gilbert Imlay had previously published promotional tracts aimed at metropolitan audiences, but which now served as fledgling historical efforts as well. In 1812 Humphrey Marshall published his *History of Kentucky*, which he revised and expanded to two volumes in 1824. *Kentucky Gazette* editor John Bradford reprinted a series of sixty-six "Notes on Kentucky" history from 1826 to 1829. Other historians and tale collectors followed in their wake, often paraphrasing each other as they went along. John McClung, for example, specialized in Indian stories in his 1836 *Sketches of Western Adventure*. For his authorities he cited Filson, Marshall, and Bradford. McClung noted that he had gathered "but a small portion of the minor details" from the individuals involved, and added the disclaimer: "had I chosen to have given admission to *mere rumors*, related by persons who had received them from others, I might have given a host of anecdotes, partaking strongly of the marvellous, and some of them really worthy of being inserted, could I have been satisfied of their *truth*!" McClung, like many of his contemporaries, evinced greater faith in published accounts than in the gathering of his own data.[38]

Aspiring historians were not the only ones in the field. Border residents themselves attempted to make sense of their experiences and pass on their knowledge to future generations. A few determined pioneers set down their own records on paper. With erratic spelling and fractured syntax, William Whitley, Daniel Trabue, Spencer Records, and others like them laboriously wrote out their memoirs in their later years. A few memorialists sought editorial help from more educated men. When Lyman Draper acquired Spencer Records's memoir in the 1860s, it had been rewritten and copied by a neighbor who polished its grammar and form. Other memoirs remained in manuscript, scrawled across pages of foolscap in rusty iron-gall ink, displaying little punctuation and less literary form. These were the accounts of men who set down the truth "plain" as they saw it; high-flown rhetoric and thematic coherence had little place in their interpretive schemes.[39]

Most often this historical discourse took place in the form of oral reminiscence. The editor of the Frankfort *Commonwealth* warned in 1835 that "the perils, toils, sufferings, and achievements of the Pioneers of Kentucky, live now principally in the traditionary knowledge of their descendants. Few written memorials exist." Years before John Shane and Lyman Draper began interviewing old settlers, they told and retold their stories to families, friends, and neighbors. Often it was this post-heroic second generation of listeners who committed participants' oral traditions to writing. Daniel Drake, who recorded his own memoirs for his grown children in 1847, recalled that when he was a child, "Indian wars, midnight butcheries, captivities, and horse-stealings, were the daily topics of conversation." Drake loved to listen to neighborhood storytellers who spoke about the past. Old Billy Johnson "was a great talker, had a historical memory, had lived in Jersey and Virginia before he came to Kentucky, and I learned (imperfectly) many things from him." Old Rector was another garrulous neighbor, "a large coarse Leather Stocking," who "had a never-ending vein of disjointed narrative of the past. . . . How much my own historical and autobiographical reminiscences are modeled after him!"[40]

John Shane tapped into—and recorded for posterity—this same rich vein of oral tradition. Ephraim Sowdusky was a typical informant in that he recounted a multigenerational series of border stories handed down from his father, grandfather, and uncles: "father said he could see an Indian, most any day at all, during the 60 days of the siege of Harrodsburgh, by watching two or three hours." The family's collective memory reached back to the time of his great-grandfather, an educated man (said to be able to speak seven languages) who had migrated to America from Poland. A product of a predominantly oral backwoods culture, Sowdusky was unsure of how his ancestor had spelled his name: "I never got any writing from my grandfather," he said. While his uncles made use of the Anglicized form Sandusky, "my father retained the Polish form."[41]

Although print materials now carry a more authoritative voice, oral accounts must have had their own satisfactions. The performance of storytelling communicated not only the content but the emotional texture of past events. James McIlvaine, whom Shane interviewed, had often conversed with Joe Young about early times. Shane recorded "that the old man [Young] told him about the attack on Morgan's Station, and how he hunted three years for his wife before he found her. Found her at last on the Ohio River. The Indians had traded her to the French." Young, he recalled, "always cried freely talking about it." A Woodford County informant similarly reported that he had "seen Mrs. Hutton set and cry, when she related the incident of Miss Woods." Richard French, whose grandmother ran bullets during the siege of Boonesborough, said, "I have heard her speak of Blackfish a great deal. I heard her talk of the manner in which the Indian chief gave the command. It was a shrill voice as she ever heard. Then followed the firing."[42]

Not all participants were willing to speak of their experiences, however. When Marcus Richardson met a former Indian captive in Frankfort and asked him "to tell me of the whole affair," the man referred him to his published captivity narrative. "Oh says [he,] you have read it all—all I can tell you." Richard French's uncle, Jack Callaway, was similarly reticent about his time spent as an Indian captive. French commented that "there was one quality in Jack that I never admired. He wouldn't talk of his captivity; and if you appeared anxious to know, by asking civil questions, he would observe a sullen silence." His mother, French added, "never could bear an Indian's presence. Her father was killed and her brother Jack, two sisters, and a cousin were taken by them."[43]

But Indian hating was by no means universal in the western settlements. Alexander Hamilton's father had spoken freely, even fondly, of his time as an Indian captive. After singing a traditional ballad of "about thirty verses" composed on the subject of his father's capture and ransom, the younger Hamilton said that his father always remembered the gentle treatment he had received from the Shawnee women. Archibald Hamilton had been just seven years old when he and his two sisters were taken prisoner on Carr's Creek, Virginia, by a party of twenty-seven Indians. After reaching the Shawnee town of Pickaway, the Council met and "determined they would sell them." Attempting to reassure the children, "the squaws made motion to them . . . not to be afraid, they wouldn't kill them." While negotiations went forward for his ransom, Archibald lived with an Indian family and was incorporated into his foster mother's work routines. "While with her, he had to carry about the papoose in a blanket tied about his neck. The boys would sometimes throw corn-cobs at him, as he went about. If he didn't want to carry it, he would pinch its legs, and make it cry more, and she would call and take it." On another occasion his foster mother intervened on his behalf: "His Indian father told him one morning to get up and make a fire. He was sleepy. The Indian drew out his tomahawk from under his head, flung it and cut him a gash. She scolded and raved about it so, that the Indian went off."

Hamilton's captivity lasted for two years. His son still recalled one woman's effort to reach out across the cultural divide. At the time of his departure, "his mother squaw took him and dressed his hair in Indian fashion with bear's oil, and told him to go home and tell his people she had treated him well." As was typical of many redeemed captives, the young boy clung for a while to his Indian identity. When dressed in European clothes from the King's store at Pittsburgh, "he threw them all off but enough to make a breech-clout." Without a trace of embarrassment or dismay, his son explained that "he had been an Indian so long, he had forgotten English."[44]

Other borderers sought connection with the past by traversing the "sacred ground" of past battles. As incident piled upon incident, the recently conquered landscape became thick with Anglo-American historical references. William Risk's father was caught in Estill's Defeat near Mount Sterling in March 1782. Years later he returned with his son to walk over the site of the clash. As the younger man recalled, his father "said they fought three hours. He has shown me the trees they fought behind." In Fleming County, Fielding Belt often rambled over the site of Holder's Defeat and collected artifacts from the battle. He showed Shane the "squaw axe" and tomahawks he had spotted in newly plowed ground. "Another tomahawk I found, was on the north side of Battle Run," Belt said. "Had a British stamp, such as we now see on British metallic goods, like [a] four leaf clover." Other veterans were more interested in establishing the exact topography of battle. Belt recalled that "about thirty, maybe thirty-one years ago, Captain Holder came here to see if he could designate the battle ground. Was commander in the battle fought on Battle Run." Holder first "fixed on an opposite hill, on the north side, as the spot—about where the better tomahawk and that knife were found." But after consulting with Captain Cassidy "who was with them in the same engagement" and walking over the site together, "they then agreed on a hill, the round of a hill, on one of the then traces, just to the south side of Battle Run."[45]

The coming of peace saw the return of other war veterans. Native Americans, too, came to ponder the landscape of memory. Cuthbert Combs recalled that an Indian named Old Blackbeard once camped near Clay's Lick. "Old Blackbeard was called the oldest Indian any where," according to Combs. "Said this was all his country once. Could give no account of the mounds. Had been up Copper Creek, a company of them, but after what we didn't know." Shortly after the turn of the nineteenth century, a party of three Indians, "one very old, and two younger, that were said to be his grandsons," camped near Mount Sterling. Jesse Daniel, who was a boy at the time, spent some time in the Indians' camp. He described the elder man as "an old Indian, very grey. Tallest Indian I ever saw. No spare flesh about this Indian." Daniel said they "came up through Bourbon, up Grassy Lick, and by my place here. 'Twas said, by those who might have been more with them, that as soon as they came in view of the Pilot Knob, they gave great demonstrations of joy." The Indians told Daniel that they were Shawnees. "Visited several licks about there—seemed to know them all. I soon found by his chat, he seemed to be acquainted with the ground he was on."[46]

Forgetting

But the reconciliation of old enemies suggested by these visits was not to occur. As the original combatants of border warfare died off, new generations of historians and writers shaped their accounts along increasingly racist and nationalistic lines. Where settlers' stories had often been tinged with ambivalence or regret, later conquest narratives breathed moral certainty. Indian opponents lost their humanity in proportion to pioneers gaining their heroism. A military victory that had taken twenty years and untold deaths to achieve now became the inevitable triumph of a superior race. As historians and popular authors reshaped and simplified the messy complexities of remembered experience, politically inconvenient details dropped out: the recognition of Indian humanity and individualism, perceptions of ethnic diversity and social conflict among the Euroamericans themselves, and even lingering doubts about the environmental and social transformations that migration had set into motion. By the end of the nineteenth century, the solipsism of the victors was complete: historian Frederick Jackson Turner gazed out across the landscape of the western country and saw only "free land" there for the taking.[47]

John Shane compiled his historical collections on the cusp of these transformations. When he wrote in his notebook of the "open contest" between "truth and fancy, history and fiction," in the recording of western history, he spoke partially of his own dilemma. Shane, the careful empiricist, deplored seizing "any local incident, and rendering it the subject of embellished detail." Yet he also longed to ascribe higher significance to what he had learned, understanding that "there are many aspects to be taken of events, which were not visible to those who were the agents in bringing them about."[48]

Shane carried on a running personal debate about the nature of historical truth. Squeezed into blank spaces in the pages of his interview notebooks can be found a series of memoranda in which he experimented with—and, in turn, challenged—his own historical interpretations. To the modern reader, the shift in tone from western settler to western historian is jarring—but instructive. Following popular nineteenth-century convention, at several points Shane attempted to distinguish between the essential characteristics of European migrants: the Germans ("laborious"), the Scotch ("daring and enduring"), and the English (prideful and profligate). He also repeatedly sought to explain the defeat of the Indians. These efforts usually involved an evolutionary justification, one that was increasingly persuasive for nineteenth-century white Americans.

> Even now the contrast between the whites and indians is not a contrast of numbers, but of condition. And it has ever been, less a contrast of personal bravery, than of domestic refinement and useful culture. . . . Art, with her handy care, gathered the nettle from the thickets, and the wool from the Buffalo till stronger enterprize should invite more fitting materials. Thus the indians were literally killed off; and of necessity their social existence has perished from the lands. . . . It was not, in truth, our superiority in war, or warlike implements. It was the plough that overturned the Indians.

The skeptical researcher is tempted to ask if he had read his own notes.[49]

Yet, only a few pages later, after outlining the chapters of a prospective history, Shane sounded a more cautionary note about the practice of historical interpretation: "In order safely to indulge in such embellishment, or in order to give scope to a lively fancy, we must have been a personal observer at the time of the scenes described—or of the times portrayed: that from all we beheld, our judgement might make a selection of what shall be deemed worthy the graphic pen." He concluded with an avowal of the empiricist's creed: "the patient acquisition of the simple facts is the clue to the true spirit of the times: they are that spirit itself."[50]

The tension between narrative convention (the "graphic pen") and the rich complexity of "simple facts" continued to haunt John Shane. He never organized his materials into the monumental history of the western country that he set out to write. Instead, he searched until his death for the chimera of perfect historical understanding. John Shane was perhaps, in the end, too scrupulous a scholar to craft an account that betrayed the ambivalent and conflicting perceptions of his pioneer informants. It would take a later, more chastened generation, to tell the truth about western history: the triumphal and patriotic narratives that characterized the "winning of the West" did not originate with the participants.

Postscript

Like John Shane, I have learned some larger lessons about history while contemplating his dilemma. First, I have discovered that even the most troublesome sources, when used with care and a critical perspective, can yield important insights. All of our sources are flawed; history writing will never be an exact science. By being candid about how we make our judgments—on what kind of evidence or theory we base our claims—historians can go a long way toward bridging the contemporary chasm between popular and scholarly views of the past.

In studying the late-eighteenth-century Ohio Valley, I have also learned to be wary of simple stories and the imperatives of narrative convention. Tracing the linkages between experience, perception, memory, and historical text in the western country, one discovers disjunctures at every point. It occurs to me that the creation of historical narrative is much like the workings of an individual's memory: over time, details give way to a generalized representation. Like an individual's half-forgotten doubts and discarded ideas, subtlety, paradox, and conflicting testimonies tend to be lost in the streamlining of historical narrative. Our evidence is often ambiguous; we should be more candid about its variant readings.

Certainly I am not alone today in raising questions about history writing and the nature of historical truth.[51] What I hope to contribute to this discussion is a greater appreciation for vernacular history—the means by which Americans have woven their own personal stories into the larger narratives of national and even international history. The phenomenon of historical "forgetting" in the Ohio Valley (and the role historians played in this cultural cleansing) has convinced me that we need to listen more attentively to the voices of ordinary people as they attempt to make sense of their experiences. Vernacular interpretations of the past are pervasive and persistent. We ignore them to our peril in the current "history wars" over the ownership of historical knowledge. We ignored them to our loss in the writing of western history.

Item List of John D. Shane's "Historical Collections"

No complete guide to Shane's collection currently exists. Archival research for this project failed to locate at least five bound volumes of his "Historical Collections" and "Collections in Church History" which were listed in the 1864 catalog of materials auctioned at his death. This is probably not a major problem in assessing Shane's interview collection, however, as Lyman Draper examined Shane's notebooks before the auction and pronounced some of the now-missing volumes as almost empty, or of little interest. Where appropriate, Draper's comments on these materials are noted in the item list below.[1]

Shane's extant "Historical Collections" are divided among three repositories. The Draper Manuscripts of the State Historical Society of Wisconsin include Shane's volumes 1–6, 8, 11, 13, 14, and 16. The Presbyterian Historical Society in Philadelphia owns volumes 12 and 17; volumes 7, 9, 10, and 15 are missing, but one of these is most likely an unidentified volume of Shane's historical collections found in the John Day Caldwell Papers at the Cincinnati Historical Society.[2]

Of Shane's "Collections in Church History," the Presbyterian Historical Society owns volumes 1, 3, 5–7, 9–11, and an unnumbered volume entitled "Baptist Coll."; volume 2 is in the John Day Caldwell Papers at the Cincinnati Historical Society; volumes 4 and 8 remain unlocated.

I have compiled the following item list of Shane's "Historical Collections" from the 1980 microfilm edition of the Draper Manuscripts (State Historical Society of Wisconsin), Shane's manuscript notebooks at the Presbyterian Historical Society, and those at the Cincinnati Historical Society. Information on volume 17, which was not available for examination at the Presbyterian Historical Society at the time of my visit in July 1991, comes from a published guide to the microfilm edition of their collection.[3]

Each entry below lists: Shane's item number, name of informant or source, location (if known), date (if known), Shane's page number (if known), and Draper's reference number in parentheses, where appropriate. (Under the notation system used for the Draper Manuscripts, a citation to "11 CC 1" refers to page 1 of volume 11 of Series CC, the Kentucky Papers.) Shane labeled some of his short entries as "mem." or "memoranda," and these are noted below as [mem.]. Other bracketed notations are my own descriptions or additions, or Draper's quotations; the latter are marked with "Draper" preceding the comment. Unnumbered items at the end of each section appear to have been added at a later date.[4]

VOLUME 1 (11 CC)

Bourbon County, Kentucky

1. Isaac Clinkenbeard, 1–4 (11 CC 1–4)
   Duncan Oliphant Richart [mem.], 4 (11 CC 4)
3. Mrs. Hinds, 33 (11 CC 5)
   Thomas Cunningham [mem.], 33 (11 CC 5)
4. Patrick Scott [1844], 33–37, 45–46 (11 CC 5–9, 17–18)
5. Jesse Kennedy, 37–38 (11 CC 9–10)
6. John Gass [1843], 39–43 (11 CC 11–15)
7. Henry Parvin, 43–44 (11 CC 15–16)
8. Joseph Lucky, 45 (11 CC 17)
   [Mems.], 45 (11 CC 17)
   Daniel Thatcher, 45, 68–69 (11 CC 17, 44–45)
   Cunningham family [mem.], 46 (11 CC 18)
9. John Hedge, 47–51 (11 CC 19–23)
   Old Mr. Gass [mem.], 51 (11 CC 23)
10. Mr. Wigginton, 52 (11 CC 24)
11. John McKinney's family, 53–54 (11 CC 25–26)
    Isaac Cunningham, 54–55 (11 CC 26–27)
    George Reid [mem.], 55 (11 CC 27)
    Jane Fisher [mem.], 56 (11 CC 28)
12. James Brackenridge, 56–61 (11 CC 28, 33–37)
    Plat of North Middletown, n.p. (11 CC 29–32)
13. Dr. George N. Hall, 62 (11 CC 38)
14. North Middletown Record Book of Trustees, [1818–45], 63–65 (11 CC 39–41)
    Capt. J. H. McKinney, 1850, 65 (11 CC 41)
    [1850], 65 (11 CC 41)
    Elias Darnall, 65 (11 CC 41)
    Hickman S. Evans, 66 (11 CC 42)
    Mrs. Charles Hedge, 66 (11 CC 42)
    William Bryan, 66 (11 CC 42)
    James McClintock, 66 (11 CC 42)
    James Matson, 67 (11 CC 43)
    W. C. Lyle, 67 (11 CC 43)
    Joel Lyle, 67 (11 CC 43)
    B. F. Harris, 68 (11 CC 44)
    Mrs. Susannah Harris, 68 (11 CC 44)
    Mrs. Sheets, 68 (11 CC 44)
    Paris Citizen, 1848–49, 69–71 (11 CC 45–47)

James Wright, 71 (11 CC 47)

Mrs. John Spencer, 1856, 71 (11 CC 47)

Western Citizen, 1851, 72–73 (11 CC 48–49)

Clark County, Kentucky

1. Patton Harrison, 1 (11 CC 51)
2. Cornelius Skinner, 1 (11 CC 51)
3. —— Stevenson, 1 (11 CC 51)
4. Septimus Schull, 1–3 (11 CC 51–53)
   Chilton Allen [Shane remarks suggested by], 3 (11 CC 53)
5. William Clinkenbeard, 4–16 (11 CC 54–66)
6. Benjamin Allen, 17–29 (11 CC 67–79)
   [Mem. on roads in Clarke], 29 (11 CC 79)
   Col. Thomas Hart, 29 (11 CC 79)
   James Keys, 29 (11 CC 79)
   Paul Evans, 29 (11 CC 79)
7. Cuthbert Combs, 30–31 (11 CC 80–81)
8. John Rankins, 31–33 (11 CC 81–83)
9. John Alexander, 33–34 (11 CC 83–84)
10. William Niblick, 34–35 (11 CC 84–85)
11. Matthew Anderson, 35–36 (11 CC 85–86)
12. William Risk, 36–40 (11 CC 86–90)
    Plat of land division in Clarke, 41–42 (11 CC 91–92)
13. Maj. Jesse Daniel [ca. 1843], 42–45 (11 CC 92–95)
14. Thomas Easton [1843], 45–47 (11 CC 95–97)
15. Mrs. Gough [1843], 47–48 (11 CC 97–98)
    Boone's Creek [mem.], 48 (11 CC 98)
16. John Rupard [1843], 49–54 (11 CC 99–104)
17. Maj. Bean, 55–56 (11 CC 105–6)
18. Daniel Spohr, 57–60 (11 CC 107–110)
    Mr. Moore, others [mem.], 61 (11 CC 111)
    Mrs. James Simpson, 61 (11 CC 111)
    [Mem. on distances from Winchester], 61–62 (11 CC 111–12)
    Mrs. Rev. Tommy Boone and son, 62 (11 CC 112)
    Isaac C. Skinner, 62–63 (11 CC 112–13)

Fayette County, Kentucky

Contents [2 pages] (11 CC 115–16)

[Mem. 1] Capt. Andrew Scott, 1, 51, 62 (11 CC 117, 149, 160)

[Mem. 2] Tumbleson, 1 (11 CC 117)

[Mem. 3] McDowell papers, 1–3 (11 CC 117–19)

[Mem. 4] Private notes: plans [Shane's?], 3 (11 CC 119)

[Mem. 5] Private notes: A difference, 3–4 (11 CC 119–20)

[Mem. 6] List of works mentioned in Morse's *Gazetteer*, 1823, 4 (11 CC 120)

[Mem. 7] Indian warfare, 4 (11 CC 120)

[Mem. 8] Finley [query], 4 (11 CC 120)

1. Col. John Graves [ca. 1845], 5–9, 60 (11 CC 121–25, 158) [page 9 copied in Draper's hand]

2. [next page, numbered 29, marked out by Shane; listed in contents as D. Bryant]

3. William Tyler [1852], 30, 61 (11 CC 128, 159)

4. —— Wymore, 30–34, 61 (11 CC 128–32, 159)

   [Mem. on publications], 34 (11 CC 132)

5. Elijah Foley, 35–37 (11 CC 133–35)

6. Mrs. Falconer, 37–40 (11 CC 135–38)

   [Mems.], 40 (11 CC 138)

   Judge Marshall's library [mem.], 40–42 (11 CC 138–40)

   Robert Carlisle [mem.], 42 (11 CC 140)

   John Lowry [mem.], 42 (11 CC 140)

   Capt. John Nest [mem.], 42 (11 CC 140)

7. Ephraim Sowdusky [before 1854], 43–48, and in Jessamine County volume, 6 (11 CC 141–45, 220)

8. James McConnell, 48–49 (11 CC 146–47)

9. Col. Roger Quarles, 50 (11 CC 148)

   [Mems.], 50 (11 CC 148)

10. J. M. C. Irwin, 51 (11 CC 149)

    William Trimble [mem.], 51 (11 CC 149)

    Andrew McClure [mem.], 51–52 (11 CC 149–50)

11. Mrs. Morrison, 52–56 (11 CC 150–54)

    James Wardlaw [mem.], 56 (11 CC 154)

12. [James Stevenson?], 56–57 (11 CC 154–55)

    Robert Kenney [mem.], 57 (11 CC 155)

    [Mems.], 58 (11 CC 156)

13. Samuel Matthews, 59–60 (11 CC 157–58)

    [pages 60–62 are continuations from previous pages]

14. Mrs. Dunlap [ref.], 62 (11 CC 160)

    William A. Leavy [mem.], 1849, 62–63, 64 (11 CC 160–62)

    Benjamin Hardesty [mem.] 1848 or 1849, 63 (11 CC 161)

    Hawkins Jones [mem.], 63–64 (11 CC 161–62)

    Thomas Henderson [mem.], 64 (11 CC 162)

    [References for interviews], 65–66 (11 CC 163–64)

15. Mr. and Mrs. Darnaby, 66–69, 81 (11 CC 164–67, 179)

16. —— Ware, 69–70 (11 CC 167–68)

17. John F. Shryock, 70 (11 CC 168)

18. —— Hardesty, 71–73 (11 CC 169–71)

    Henry Parvin, 74–77 (11 CC 172–75)

    [Mem. of references], 77 (11 CC 175)

    T. P. Dudley [mem.], 78 (11 CC 176)

    [Mems.], 78 (11 CC 176)

19. ——, 79 (11 CC 177)
20. [Mem.], 80 (11 CC 178)
    —— Cochran [mem.], 80 (11 CC 178)
    [Mems.], 81 (11 CC 179)
21. Waller Bullock [1852], 82–83 (11 CC 180–81)
22. William McClelland, 83–86 (11 CC 181–84)
    [Mem. on lost vol. of *Kentucky Gazette*], 86 (11 CC 184)
    Gen. [Thomas] Metcalfe, 87 (11 CC 185)
    M. T. Scott, 87–88, 91 (11 CC 185–86, 189)
    R. Pindell, 89 (11 CC 187)
    —— Wheeler, 90 (11 CC 188)
    R. W. Wooley, 90 (11 CC 188)
    Samuel Laird, 90, 92 (11 CC 188, 190)
    Caleb Williams, 1855, 93–99, 109 (11 CC 191–97, 207)
    Notes copied from Davidson's *Kentucky*, 100–101 (11 CC 198–99)
    [Mem. on early roads], 102–3 (11 CC 200–201)
    Mr. Barlow, 103–4 (11 CC 201–2)
    [Mem. on old spring], 104 (11 CC 202)
    Abraham Van Meter [1856], 105–7 (11 CC 203–5)
    [blank], 108 (11 CC 206)
    [continuations], 109 (11 CC 207)
    [blank], 110 (11 CC 208)
    John I. Van Meter [1856], 111–15 (11 CC 209–13)

Jessamine County, Kentucky

1. Thomas Butler, 1 (11 CC 215)
2. Thomas Steel, 1–2 (11 CC 215–16)
3. Robert Gwynn [1842], 2–3 (11 CC 216–17)
4. Mrs. Shanklin, 3–7 (11 CC 217–21)
5. Mrs. Ephraim January, 7–10 (11 CC 221–24)
6. Mrs. Samuel Scott, 10–13 (11 CC 224–27)
7. John Lowens, 13–14 (11 CC 227–28)
8. Capt. Joe F. Taylor, 14–19 (11 CC 228–33)
   [Mem. on Indians, Scots, & Germans], 19–20 (11 CC 233–34)
   Dr. A. Young, 20–22 (11 CC 234–36)
   —— Holloway, 22–23 (11 CC 236–37)
   John Mahan, 23–24 (11 CC 237–38)
   John Garrison, 24–25 (11 CC 238–39)

Woodford County, Kentucky

1. Mrs. John Arnold, 1–5 (11 CC 241–45)
2. Lewis Arnold, 5 (11 CC 245)
3. Maj. P. N. Obannion, 5 (11 CC 245)
4. Hugh Garret [lives in Jessamine], 6 (11 CC 246)
5. Jerry Wilson, 6 (11 CC 246)

6. James Stevenson, 7–11 (11 CC 247–51)
   [page 12 blank]
7. Isaac Howard, 13 (11 CC 253)
8. Ben Guthrie, 13–17 (11 CC 253–57)
9. William McBride, 17–23 (11 CC 257–63)
10. Stephen Shelton, 24–29 (11 CC 264–69)
    [References], 29 (11 CC 269)
11. William Moseby, 30–34 (11 CC 270–74)
12. —— Tillery, 34–35 (11 CC 274–75)
13. Maj. Herman Bowmar, 36 (11 CC 276)
14. Mrs. Wilson, 1841, 36–39 (11 CC 276–79)
15. ——, 39–43 (11 CC 279–83)
16. —— Hockersmith, 43–44 (11 CC 283–84)
17. ——, 44–45 (11 CC 284–85)
    [Mem. on Glenn's Creek], 1852, 45 (11 CC 285)
18. D. C. Humphrey, 45 (11 CC 285)
    Miss Martha Markham, 46–47 (11 CC 286–87)
    [Mem.], 47 (11 CC 287)

Franklin County, Kentucky

1. Mr. Swigert, 1 (11 CC 289)
   [Mem.], 1 (11 CC 289)
2. Judge Ben Monroe, 1–3 (11 CC 289–91)
   Alexander Hamilton, 4–6 (11 CC 293–95)

Shelby and Henry Counties, Kentucky

1. Samuel Graham, 1 (11 CC 297)
2. Samuel Campbell, 1 (11 CC 297)

VOLUME 2 (12 CC)

Bath County, Kentucky

1. James Wade, 1–29 (12 CC 11–41)
2. Walker Kelso, 30 (12 CC 42)
3. Samuel Treble, 31–32 (12 CC 43–44)
4. Mrs. Sarah Graham [d. 1844], 33–41 (12 CC 45–53)
5. Capt. James Walker, 42 (12 CC 54)
6. William Craycraft, 42–43 (12 CC 54–55)
7. Col. James Lane, 43–45 (12 CC 55–57)
8. Col. Putnam Ewing, 45 (12 CC 57)
9. Abel Morgan, 45–46 (12 CC 57–58)
10. James McIlvaine [post-1843], 46 (12 CC 58)
11. William Boyd, 1841, 46–49 (12 CC 58–61)
12. Thomas Cartmill, 49 (12 CC 61)

13. Col. William Sudduth [d. 1845], 49–52 (12 CC 61–64)
14. Josiah Collins [1841], 52–66, 85–98 (12 CC 64–78, 97–110)
15. Jarvis Brummagin, 66–67 (12 CC 78–79)
    "A Sketch of the Life of W. Sudduth" [copy], 1840, 67–84 (12 CC 79–96)
16. Joseph Smothers, 84–85 (12 CC 96–97)
17. Peter Cutwright, 98–99 (12 CC 110–11)
18. Benjamin Snelling, 99–101 (12 CC 111–113)
19. George Trumbo, 101–3 (12 CC 113–15)
    Col. James Workman [mem.], 103 (12 CC 115)
    John Berry [mem.], 103–4 (12 CC 115–16)
20. James Hedge, 105–8 (12 CC 117–20)

Montgomery County, Kentucky

1. Samuel Gibson, 1–5 (12 CC 121–25)
2. Capt. Marcus Richardson, 5–7, 34–36 (12 CC 125–27, 154–56)
3. John Coons, 7, 36 (12 CC 127, 156)
4. Jeptha Kemper, 7–13 (12 CC 127–33)
5. Jacob Stevens, 13–18 (12 CC 133–38)
6. John Hanks, 18–24 (12 CC 138–44)
7. John Craig, 24–26 (12 CC 144–46)
8. John Frame, 26 (12 CC 146)
9. George Yocum, 27–31 (12 CC 147–51)
10. Robert Evans, 31 (12 CC 151)
11. Mrs. Sharp, 31 (12 CC 151)
12. Maj. Black, 31–32 (12 CC 151–52)
13. John McClure, 33–34 (12 CC 153–54)
14. John Crawford, 36–43 (12 CC 156–63)
15. Rev. David Barrow's Journal & some notes [copy], 1795, 1797, 43–66 (12 CC 163–84)
16. Texas, correspondence, extracts [copies], 1842–43, 66–67 (12 CC 186–87)
    James Dunlap [mem.], 68 (12 CC 188)
17. John Sappington, 68–70 (12 CC 188–90)
    [Mem. on Spohr], 70 (12 CC 190)
    William Barrow [mem.], 70–71, 90–92 (12 CC 190–91, 210–12)
    [Mems.], 71 (12 CC 191)
    [Shane mem. on Indians & whites], 71–77 (12 CC 191–97)
18. William Camper, 77–78 (12 CC 197–99)
    Samuel Morris [mem.], 79 (12 CC 199)
19. David Thompson, 79–81 (12 CC 199–201)
20. Richard French, 81–90 (12 CC 201–10)
    Charles Hazelrigg [mem.], 92 (12 CC 212)
    [Mem. on Missouri migration], 1840, 92–93 (12 CC 212–13)
    [Mems.], 93 (12 CC 213)
    Jonas Hedge [mem.], 93 (12 CC 213)

Capt. John Hulse [mem.], 94 (12 CC 214)
[documents from a Montgomery County land suit inserted here]

Nicholas County, Kentucky

1. David Crouch [ca. 1843], 1–5 (12 CC 225–29)
—— Milligan [mem.], 6 (12 CC 230)

Fleming County, Kentucky

1. Capt. George Stocton, 1–2 (12 CC 231–32)
2. —— Bartlett, 2 (12 CC 232)
3. Col. Thomas Jones, 2–4 (12 CC 232–34)
4. George McIlvaine, 4 (12 CC 234)
5. Hugh Drennon, 4–5 (12 CC 234–35)
6. Andrew Thompson, 5–6 (12 CC 235–36)
7. Samuel McCoy, 6 (12 CC 236)
8. Mrs. Stagg, 6–8 (12 CC 236–38)
9. Samuel B. Finley, 8–9 (12 CC 238–39)
10. Daniel Deron, 9–14 (12 CC 239–44)
    [Mem. on Upper Blue Licks], 14 (12 CC 244)
11. Fielding Belt, 15 (12 CC 245)
12. David Strahan, 16 (12 CC 246)
13. Samuel Potts Pointer, 17–20 (12 CC 247–50)
14. Thomas McKinney, 21 (12 CC 251)
15. Jacob Lawson, 21–24 (12 CC 251–54)
    [Mem.], 24 (12 CC 254)
    Mrs. Dr. McDowell [mem. on location of *Kentucky Gazette* file, other papers],
    24 (12 CC 254)

Scraps

[Excerpts copied from the Washington *National Intelligencer*, the Danville (Kentucky) *Wednesday Mercury*, and the Baltimore *American*, on various topics],
1842–43, 1–5 (12 CC 263–67)

Court of Appeals, Virginia

[Excerpts copied from land suits dealing with Fairfax's patent, etc.], 1790s, 1–6 (12 CC 269–74)

Medical and Agricultural Register and *Rural Magazine*

[Excerpts copied from the Boston *Medical and Agricultural Register*, 1806, and the Philadelphia *Rural Magazine and Literary Evening Fireside*, 1820, on various western topics], 6–16 (12 CC 274–84)

Scraps &c &c Continued from "Historical Collections, Vol II"

[Excerpts from the Philadelphia *Rural Magazine* continued from previous volume], 1–2 (12 CC 285–86)

APPENDIX A

General History

[Shane's outline for a western history? Includes subsections on antiquities, the mastodon, mounds, the French, Spaniards, traders, Boone], 1–2, 7–8 (12 CC 287–88, 293–94)

VOLUME 3 (13 CC)

Historical Statements obtained during conversations held with many individuals, as per names prefixed [in Shane's hand]
[contents preceding and index at end]

34. Jesse Graddy [ca. 1842], Woodford County, Kentucky, 130–34 (13 CC 130–34)
35. Jane Stevenson, Woodford County, Kentucky, 135–43 (13 CC 135–43)
36. [blank]
37. William Curry Jr., Ohio, 145–50 (13 CC 145–50)
38. Robert Jones, Kentucky [1842], 151–65, 176–81 (13 CC 151–65, 176–81)
39. Thomas Paslay, Kentucky, 166 (13 CC 166)
40. [John?] Scrimsher, Kentucky, 167–69 (13 CC 167–69)
41. Maj. Herman Bowmar, Woodford County, Kentucky, 170–74 (13 CC 170–74)
42. Lewis Collins, Mason County, Kentucky, 182 (13 CC 182)
43. Thomas McJilton, Owen County, Kentucky, 183–84 (13 CC 183–84)
44. Nathaniel McClure, Grant County, Kentucky, 185–86 (13 CC 185–86)
45. [Benjamin Ethington?], [Franklin County, Kentucky], 187 (13 CC 187)
46. [—— Spence?], [Ohio], 188–90 (13 CC 188–90)
47. ——, Kentucky, 191–92 (13 CC 191–92)
48. ——, Kentucky, 193–95 (13 CC 193–95)
49. ——, Kentucky, 196 (13 CC 196)
50. [John I. Jacobs], Kentucky, 197 (13 CC 197)
51. ——, Ohio, 198–99 (13 CC 198–99)
52. [Copy of an 1834 letter on family history of Gen. Andrew Jackson], 200–201 (13 CC 200–201)
53. James Morris, Mason County, Kentucky, 202–5 (13 CC 202–5)
54. [Mems.], 206 (13 CC 206)
55. ——, Ohio, 207 (13 CC 207)
56. William Richey, Mason County, Kentucky, 208 (13 CC 208)
57. —— Suggett, Scott County, Kentucky, 209 (13 CC 209)
58. Lewis Flannigan, Scott or Owen County, Kentucky, 1842, 210 (13 CC 210)
59. Fielding Bradford, Scott County, Kentucky, 211 (13 CC 211)
60. Hugh Dickey, Kentucky, 212 (13 CC 212)
61. Mrs. Gen. John Poage, Greenup County, Kentucky, [1841], 213–15 (13 CC 213–15)
62. ——, 216 (13 CC 216)
63. John McCoy, Kentucky, 217 (13 CC 217)
64. [Samuel McDowell?], Kentucky, 218–25 (13 CC 218–25)
65. Capt. John Dyal [or Dial], Kentucky, 226–37 (13 CC 226–37)
66. George Fearis, Kentucky, 238–44 (13 CC 238–44)
67. Samuel Boyd, Lewis County, Kentucky, 245–46 (13 CC 245–46)
68. [Lawson], Kentucky, 1842, 247–49 [removed by Draper and placed in 9 BB 58]
69. Capt. James Ward, Mason County, Kentucky, 250–78 [removed by Draper and placed in 9 BB 58]
70. [listed in Shane's index as Capt. James Ward's interview, but this is apparently a mistake]

VOLUME 4 (14 CC)

1. Needham Parry [copy of his diary], Adams County, Ohio, 1794, 1–9 (14 CC 1–9)
2. Daniel Kain, Clermont County, Ohio, 10–13 (14 CC 10–13)
3. James Bousby [or Beasley], near Cincinnati, Ohio, 13–16 (14 CC 13–16)
5. Thomas Bennington, Brown County, Ohio, 17 (14 CC 17)
6. Charles Cist, Cincinnati, Ohio, 18 (14 CC 18)
7. Extracts, Frankfort *Palladium*, 1798 [on early Ohio government], 19 (14 CC 19)

Cincinnati, Ohio

8. Museum [list of antiquities including sketches of Indian artifacts identified as coming from mounds], 20–23 (14 CC 20–23)
9. [Mems., including note on collection of Indian curiosities], 23–25 (14 CC 23–25)
10. Mrs. Sophia Williamson, 26 (14 CC 26)
11. Dr. Elijah Stack, Cincinnati, Ohio, 27 (14 CC 27)
12. Smith Buckingham [son of former interviewee], Ohio, 1859, 29, 31, 33 (14 CC 29–33)
13. Mark Buckingham, 33 (14 CC 33)
    [blanks and continuation], 34–36 (14 CC 34–36)
    Family record of Joel Williams's family, 37 (14 CC 37)
    Dr. Spence, Clermont County, Ohio, 38 (14 CC 38)
    Whitelaw Read, 39 (14 CC 39)
    Extracts from a ms. journal [on Pennsylvania], 40 (14 CC 40)
    Henry Cushing, Loveland, 1862, 41–42 (14 CC 41–42)
    —— Pollock, Ohio, 43 (14 CC 43)
    Dr. Hall, Oxford, Ohio, 44 (14 CC 44)
    Rev. D. Owen Davies [correspondence dealing with Synod debate over support for Union cause], Ohio, 1862, 45–47 (14 CC 45–47)
    [Mems. including biography of William Templeton], [1861–63], 49–54 (14 CC 49–54)

VOLUME 5 (14 CC)

From the Record Book of New Providence Church [1773–1833], transcribed by Robert B. McAfee, 1822, 1–43 (14 CC 102–44)
[blank]

1. Mahan's School [mem.], 45 (14 CC 146)
2. William Mahan [mem.], 45 (14 CC 146)
3. The Church, 45 (14 CC 146)
4. The Baptist Church [mem.], 45 (14 CC 146)
5. Dr. & Mrs. Cleland, 45–46 (14 CC 146–47)

6.–14. [Brief notes on McAfee documents, Magruder, Rev. Samuel Shannon, Tory principles of Scotch people], 46–48 (14 CC 147–49)
[blank], 49–130
[brief notes], 131–36 (14 CC 191–201)
[Notes on Imlay's *Topographical Description*] (14 CC 202–3)
Works on Kentucky history desirable for the library of the Kentucky Historical Society (14 CC 203–5)
Books [list] (14 CC 206)
[blank] (14 CC 207–13)
Stations [Imlay quotation and list, other notes on Imlay] (14 CC 214–23)

VOLUME 6 (15 CC)

[Draper: "Rev. John D. Shane's 'Historical Collections'—1858. This is apparently Vol. VIth of the series—the last figure torn off of the outside numbering."]
1. Col. Francis Flournoy Jackson, Clark County, Kentucky, 5–12 (15 CC 5–12)
2. John Lewis, Franklin County, 1855, 13–16 (15 CC 13–16)
3. John T. Lyle, Fayette County, 17–22 (15 CC 17–22)
4. Frank Bell, Scott or Franklin County, Kentucky, 23–24 (15 CC 23–24)
5. Glass Marshall, Fayette County, Kentucky, 25–29 (15 CC 25–29)
   David A. Sayre, Lexington, Kentucky, 30–33 (15 CC 30–33)
   D. C. Humphrys, Woodford County, Kentucky, 34–38 (15 CC 34–38)
8. Gen. William O. Butler, Carrollton, Kentucky, 41–47, 55–66 (15 CC 41–47, 55–66)
9. Richard Butler, Carrollton, Kentucky, 1858, 49–50, 71–72 (15 CC 49–50, 71–72)
   Mrs. Brown, Springfield, [Kentucky?], 1858, 51–53 (15 CC 51–53)
11. To Synod at Lebanon, Kentucky, 1858, directions, 67–68 (15 CC 67–68)
12. John R. Lyle, Kentucky, 69–70 (15 CC 69–70)
   [continuations and blanks]
   Rev. Samuel V. Marshall, on the Madison packet, 1858, 75–78 (15 CC 75–78)
   Col. Robert Innes, Fayette County, Kentucky, 80 (15 CC 80)
   —— Giltner, Carrollton, Kentucky, 81 (15 CC 81)
   Robert Wickliffe Sr., Lexington, Kentucky, 1859, 83–86 (15 CC 83–86)

VOLUME 7

[Draper: "2pp. no value whatever"]

VOLUME 8 (15 CC)

[Draper: "mostly blank"]
Books in Louisville Library [mem.], 1 (15 CC 105)
[blank] (15 CC 106–14)

Letter from Nathaniel Hart, of Woodford, to Mann Butler, 1833 [on early settlement; copy from archives of the Kentucky Historical Society (KHS)], 1–3 (15 CC 115–17)
[blank] (15 CC 118–20)
Todd Papers [copies of letters from KHS], 1830s, 4–9 (15 CC 121–26)
[blank] (15 CC 127–30)
Henderson & Luttrell's letter [copy from KHS; also other letters], 1775, 10–13 (15 CC 131–34)
Henderson's Journal [copy from KHS], 1775, 14–24 (15 CC 135–45)
[blank] (15 CC 146–156)
[Levi Todd's Narrative, copy from KHS, identified by Draper], 1774–79, 25–30 (15 CC 157–62)
[blank] (15 CC 163–64)
[Correspondence concerning the Henderson Journal, copies from KHS], 31–34 (15 CC 165–68)
[blank] (15 CC 169–192)
[Correspondence concerning Dunmore's Treaty, copies from KHS], 35–39 (15 CC 193–97)
[Insertion]
[Draper: "Memoranda—I transcribed the following from Rev. John D. Shane's Vol. XII, Histl. Colls., which mostly relates to religious matters—& which, together with Vol. XVII, of the same character, & 8 vols. on Transylvania University (transcripts), & a vol. on the Adelphi Society of Transylvania University, Ky., I have sold to Mr. Saml. Agnew, Philada., at cost, for the Presbyterian Histl. Society."] (15 CC 201–32)

VOLUME 9

[Draper: "wanting"]

VOLUME 10

[Draper: "72 pps.—Notes of W. V. Butler—R. Wickliffe—not of much value"]

VOLUME 11 (16 CC)

[Draper: "Small val."]
Memoranda of the Preston family [copy from the papers of John Brown, 1842], 5–37 (16 CC 5–37)
Todd papers ["obtained of Mrs. Robt. S. Todd, Franklin?, Kentucky, copied and returned, 1854] 39–49 (16 CC 39–49)
Capt. Thomas Steele, Franklin County, Kentucky, 52 (16 CC 52)

Capt. Isaac Wilson, Buck Run, 54–55 (16 CC 54–55)
R. J. Breckenridge, Danville, Kentucky, 1854, 58–59 (16 CC 58–59)
Historical account of the congregation at New Londonderry [copy], 60–63 (16 CC
60–63)
Index of Frankfort *Commonwealth*, 1833–43, 64–95 (16 CC 64–95)

VOLUME 12 (OHIO CHURCHES)

[Now at the Presbyterian Historical Society, Philadelphia. See note by Draper
above.]
  1. Gravestone inscriptions, 5–8
  2. [Thomas Harris] Barlow, planetarium, 15–16 (LCD copy: 15 CC 201–4)
  3. Peyton S. Symmes, 55 (LCD copy: 15 CC 205–6)
  4. Capt. Strader, 59 (LCD copy: 15 CC 206)
  5. Rev. J. G. Montfort, Glendale, 60
  6. Clement Burt, 1856, 61 (LCD copy: 15 CC 207)
  7. Judge James Hall, 1859, 63–64 (LCD copy: 15 CC 207–10)
  8. Col. Robert Wallace, Covington, 69–70
  9. Newspapers, 71
  10. Rev. L. G. Gaines, 73
  11. Caroline & Adelaid Hamilton, 75
  12. Mrs. Cobb, 83
  13. Rev. Samuel S. Wilson, 1858, 85 (LCD copy: 15 CC 210)
  14. George C. Miller, 87
  15. John F. Keys, 89
  16. [Charles] G. Shane, 1858, 92 (LCD copy: 15 CC 211)
  17. Old Mr. Dickey, 95
  18. Charles Cist, Cincinnati, 97 (LCD copy: 15 CC 211–12)
  19. Rev. Cabell Harrison, 101
  20. —— of Indiana, 1858, 101
  21. Mrs. Sophia B. Williamson, 105 (LCD copy: 15 CC 213)
  22. Rev. Sayres Gazley, 1858, 107
  23. Col. William Schillinger, 113
  24. 1st Pbyn. Church papers, 121
      [Shane's numbering sequence becomes irregular from this point on]
  31. Elijah Stack, M.D., 179
  28. Mrs. Richardson, 183
  29. Stephen Wheeler, 184 (LCD copy: 15 CC 213)
      Henry Shane, 192 (LCD copy: 15 CC 214)
  27. Rev. J. E. Spillman, 193
  25. Lincoln Harpham, 194
  26. Dr. Orr, 195
  30. Lay & Brother, 194

1. The *Kentucky Gazette* [part of the first number, 1787, copied by JDS], 1–3 (16 CC 181–85)

The *Lady's Mag. & Repository of entertaining Knowledge*, Philadelphia [copied excerpts], 1792, 3–5 (16 CC 189–91)

G. B. Kinkead, Lexington [letter on his family's early history, 1847, copied by Shane in 1853], 1–5 (16 CC 193–97)

Judge J. B. Monroe [mss. on Adair County, Kentucky, and John Adair intended for Collins' *Kentucky*, copied by Shane in 1853], 1–39 (16 CC 199–237)

Dr. Marshall, Woodford County, Kentucky, 41–49 (16 CC 239–47)

H. T. Duncan, Fayette County, Kentucky, 51–53 (16 CC 249–51)

[John] Kinkead, Fayette County, Kentucky, 54 (16 CC 252)

D. A. Sayre, Lexington, Kentucky, 55–57 (16 CC 253–55)

Joseph Ficklin, Fayette County, Kentucky, 59–87 (16 CC 257–85)

Mrs. Phillips [1854], Dayton, Ohio, 91–93 (16 CC 289–91)

D. C. Humphreys [1854], Woodford County, Kentucky, 94–98, 120–23 (16 CC 292–96, 318–21)

John Steele, Fayette County, Kentucky, 99 (16 CC 297)

Mrs. Col. William Rodes, Fayette County, Kentucky, 100 (16 CC 298)

Col. J. R. Dunlap, Fayette County, Kentucky, 102 (16 CC 300)

Capt. D. S. McCullough, Lexington, Kentucky, 103 (16 CC 301)

Col. John Steele and his son Tom, Woodford County, Kentucky, 104 (16 CC 302)

Judge Ben Monroe, Frankfort, Kentucky, 106 (16 CC 304–5)

Judge Adam Beatty, Mason County, Kentucky, 108 (16 CC 306)

James Houston, Cane Ridge, 109 (16 CC 307)

William Bryan, Paris, Kentucky, 110 (16 CC 308)

Rev. J. K. Lyle, Nicholasville, Kentucky, 111 (16 CC 309)

Rev. Robert Stuart, Nicholasville, Kentucky, 112 (16 CC 310)

List of members of Union Pres. Church, Clark County, Kentucky, 1853, 113 (16 CC 311)

Samuel Graham, Shelby County, Kentucky, 114–15 (16 CC 312–13)

John Lewis, Franklin County, Kentucky, 116–19, 124 (16 CC 314–17, 322)

[continuations and mems.] 120–27 (16 CC 318–25)

[blank] (16 CC 326–32)

[tombstone inscription], 136 (16 CC 334)

[blank] (16 CC 335)

Hugenot family [notes on item #540 in Shane sale] 138–52 (16 CC 336–50)

[Mem.] from old medical books at Joseph A. Humphrey's, 163–65 (16 CC 361–63)

Joseph A. Humphrey, Journal of visit to Mammoth Cave, 1842 or '43, other notes, 165–68 (16 CC 363–66)

VOLUME 14 (17 CC)

Charles Eccles, Georgetown, Kentucky, 5 (17 CC 5)
Capt. John Wilson, 1855, Scott County, Kentucky, 6–25 (17 CC 6–25)
Benjamin Jones, Scott County, Kentucky, 26–27 (17 CC 26–27)
[blank] (17 CC 28–41)
A list of marriages performed by Robert Marshall, 1793–1831, in Scott, Wood-
ford, Bourbon and Fayette Counties, Kentucky, 42–49 (17 CC 42–49)
Mrs. Sarah A. E. Roche and her son, John Smith Roche [interview and copies of
family records], 1856, Scott County, Kentucky, 53–66 (17 CC 53–66)
Journal of John Roche, Professor in Transylvania University [copy], [1824–25],
66–96 (17 CC 66–96)

VOLUME 15

[Draper: "wanting"]

VOLUME 16 (17 CC)

1. Mrs. Rev. John Howe Brown, [1855], Lexington, Kentucky, 2 (17 CC 105)
   Rev. John H. Brown correspondence [copies], 1852–53, 5–15 (17 CC 108–118)
2. [John] Floyd Correspondence [copies], 1779–83, 16–48, 54–85 (17 CC 119–51,
   157–88)
3. Rev. R. M. Cunningham, personal account [copy], 49–53, 159–62 (17 CC 152–
   56, 262–65)
4. Capt. Nathaniel Hart [Jr.], Woodford County, Kentucky, Hart's ledger: "Ledger
   A" of the Henderson company [copy], with comments, 86–106 (17 CC 189–209)
   Capt. Nathaniel Hart [Jr.], published letters & notes, 106–10 (17 CC 209–13)

VOLUME 17 (ILLINOIS CHURCHES)

[At the Presbyterian Historical Society, Philadelphia. See notes on Vol. 8 above.]
1. Edward Craig & wife, Morgan County, 1856, 19–24 (LCD copy: 15 CC 214–
   15)
2. Rev. J. G. Berger, Springfield, 25–26
3. Mrs. Sarah Anderson, Morgan County, 27–29 (LCD copy: 15 CC 215–18)
4. [Mem.], 37
5. Rev. Gallaher, Morgan County, 38–44 (LCD copy: 15 CC 218–21)
6. James Craig & wife, 45–48
7. Rev. Thos. A. Spilman, 36
8. Mrs. William C. Posey, near Jacksonville, 49–50
9. Dr. Edwin Reese, 51

10. Daniel McAfee, 52–54 (LCD copy: 15 CC 221–22)
11. Mrs. Elizabeth Reaugh, 30–33
12. David A. Rannels, 105
13. Mrs. Lucy Scott, 107
14. Richard Yates, 110
15. Walter McCormick, Morgan County, 111, 142 (LCD copy: 15 CC 224–26, 229–31)
16. [Mem.] on works in State Library, Springfield, 113 (LCD copy: 15 CC 226–27)
17. Daniel Huey [or Gray?], near Jacksonville, 114 (LCD copy: 15 CC 227–28
18. Mrs. Agnes Prentice, Jacksonville, 115

VOLUME [ILLEG.]

[At the Cincinnati Historical Society—probably one of missing volumes: 9, 10, or 15.]

1. Davidson's *History of the Presbyterian Church in Kentucky* [published 1847], notes and corrections
2. Judge James Hall, Cincinnati, papers
3. Book table. Books have & want. Printed in west, or about west
4. Lane Seminary, history
5. Rev. John Andrews, Pittsburgh
6. J. S. Wheate, Esqr., Wheeling, books
7. Neville B. Craig, Esqr., on "Olden Time"
8. References, directions
9. Isaac Watson, Esqr., Pittsburgh
10. Georgetown College Library, books
11. Prof. E. N. Elliott, Georgetown, Kentucky, lead ore, trilobites
12. W. H. Whitney, Esqr., on newspapers
13. Rev. J. W. Blythe, at the General Assembly, Pittsburgh
14. Rev. Dr. Charles Hodge, at the General Assembly, on printing catalogues of books, pamphlets
15. Louisville *Literary News*, letter
16. Mrs. Ellett's *Women of the American Revolution*, authorities cited
17. Butler's *History of Kentucky*, authorities cited
18. [Miscellany, largely citations to publications]
19. "The Medical Repository," notes on natural history, history
21. Samuel Moseby Grant [July 1851], Independence, Missouri

John D. Shane's Interview with
Jane Stevenson, [ca. 1841–1842]

For readers unfamiliar with John Shane's historical collections, I have transcribed the following interview with Jane Stevenson of Woodford County, Kentucky (DM 13 CC 135–43), taken shortly before her death. The interview is undated, but probably took place in 1841 or 1842, when the informant was in her early nineties. Shane ends his nine-page transcription with the following note about his subject:

Familiarly known as "Aunt Jane." Had been bedridden for many years, previous to her decease. The time I obtained the preceding notes, she was very much enfeebled in body, scarcely could speak audibly, or for a moment at a time. Yet her mind was clear, and her memory held what she wished to communicate, without incoherence of thought, or even broken expression. It was on account of her bodily weakness, that I deferred securing further information to a more favorable time. That time never came.

Shane's interview with Stevenson is typical of his collection in that she structures her narrative around encounters with Native Americans and by her own experiences of coming out, settling a station, moving out, and helping to found local institutions—in this case, a Presbyterian meeting house in Woodford County, Kentucky. It is also somewhat atypical of his earlier interviews in that the account is relatively brief and somewhat sparse in detail, doubtlessly due to the informant's advanced age and frail health. Because Jane Stevenson came of age and moved west during the height of the armed struggle for the Ohio Valley, it also lacks some of the complexity of perspective found in other accounts more influenced by the advent of peaceful times. Nevertheless, Stevenson has a story to tell, and she communicates it with considerable effect.

In transcribing Shane's notes, I have largely retained his spelling, capitalization, and punctuation, while spelling out most abbreviations for the sake of clarity. Because Jane Stevenson died before he could check his notes with her, Shane included none of his customary marginal notations and elaborations with this interview, although he did insert a few bracketed queries on points about which he was unclear. After acquiring Shane's notebook at auction, Lyman Draper underlined the proper names and added topic headings in the right-hand margins of the pages; I have reproduced several of these headings in brackets.

By including this small sample from Shane's settler interviews, I hope to suggest the immediacy as well as the formulaic nature of the accounts he recorded.

No. 35. Jane Stevenson.

Jane Stevenson, wife of Samuel Stevenson, was born Nov. 15—1750, in Augusta County, Virginia.

The first fort I ever was in, a little girl was taken out of it, but from July to November older than me. She was but 7 years old. And was 7 years gone; untill [sic] Brocade's campaign [Draper: Bouquet's Campaign]. We walked out and got some haws. They, some of the company, pulled down the limbs, and handed us some of the haws. I wouldn't go any farther. And when I came, went into another cabin, wouldn't go into Mammy's, she would know I had been out. Presently the alarm came. They had gone about 200 yards farther, and the Indians took them.

Where we lived was about 35 miles from Staunton. No Lexington then. The country was newly settled. Where Crawford was killed, was some 15 miles from Providence Meeting-house, down towards Staunton. Old Mr. John Brown preached there then. The men carried their guns to meeting, as regular as the congregation met. At Providence Meeting-house. The woman was told, bonie Alex.? Crawford was killed. Well said she, and indeed [Shane: Mr. C.? or M? the lady or man who told her?] M [blank] he must take better care next time. This was a year or two after my mother was killed. I was only 9 or 10 then.

I was forted from the time I was 7 years old, 1757, and was never rid of the Indians till I moved to this place.

Carr's Creek was in about 7 miles of us. We were on the Calf-pasture. Mother was killed when I was about 8 years old. Mr. Crawford lived higher up towards Staunton than the Calf-pasture.

The settlement on Carr's Creek was taken twice [Draper: Carr's Creek Massacres]. The first time it was taken, Aunt escaped in the woods. Had but 2 children then, and while she escaped that way, the rout of the Indians was down the river.

The second time it was taken, I had an uncle and a cousin killed. This Aunt and her 3 children, were taken prisoners and carried to the towns. Two of the children died there. The remaining child was brought in at the treaty following Brocade's Campaign [Draper: Bouquet's]. Aunt wasn't brought in, and Uncle went out that same fall and brought her, but didn't get home till next March.

In less than 3 hours, in 2 hours, they killed and took 63 [Draper: Carr's Creek Massacre, 1763]. They no doubt had the ground all spied out. What they would do they knew. And then they came in like race horses. One Jim Milligan, who got away from them at the Ghanty [Draper: Gantey] Mountains, said the Indians there had 450 prisoners; that he had counted as they passed along. These, besides what they had killed, and a parcel, who at that time were before, in a hunting company.

Two little boys, Jimmy Woods & Jimmy McClung were taken——they went to Staunton when they got back, and had their ears recorded.

The year the Indians took Carr's Creek settlement [Draper: 1763] a second time, they were greatly bad. Almost seemed as if they thought they would make their way to Williamsburgh that year. Shot the cows mightily with bows and arrows.

Simon Girty was from Virginia. He and old John Craig were schoolmates together in Virginia.

We moved to Greenbriar in 1775. The year after the battle of the Point. [Two sentences are struck out here.] There were but one or two families that were not dutch and half-dutch, in that whole settlement. [Shane: what settlement?] But never was a settlement of kinder people. They were great for dancing and singing. 1. William Hamilton. 2. Samuel McClung.

The hard winter was such in Virginia, as well as here.

When I started to Kentucky, I was 100 miles back from Daddy's. My father came from Ireland, when he was a boy. But then he lived on the frontier long before he was married.

John McKinney, the schoolmaster, came out with us. He was nearly killed at the Battle of the Point. We brought him out. We waited on the road a week or so, after we had left Greenbriar, for another family. Were about 2 weeks ? getting to Blackamore's station.

We never travelled a sunday, but one in Powell's Valley, about 5 miles till we came to a beautiful clear spring of water. It must have been 70 miles we travelled in Powell's valley, for we kept all the way down till we crossed at Cumberland ford.

The morning before we came to the ford of Clinch, (Blackamore's station was 10 miles beyond that,) these murders were committed. A mother and 4 children; in sight of the fort too. The husband was in the field, but escaped. A girl about half grown, and 3 little boys tomahawked and scalped, who were talking while their brains were boiling out. The grandmother asked them if they saw their little brother? What had become of him? Said they didn't know. These were dutch people. We staid there good part of a day. Their Aunt sat on a stump, in sight of the fort, and cried all day.

Went by Blackamore's Station next day, and didn't see the smoke of a chimney after that till we got to Boonesborough.

The pretty springs of water, and the woods, rendered Powell's Valley so exceedingly beautiful, I could have stopped very freely in it. A rock road all the way down, and mountains to one side of us.

Just before we got to the foot of the Cumberland Mountain, the company three-quarters of a mile ahead of us, had all their horses stolen. They could do nothing better than just turn their feather beds loose. They could do nothing with them. About their cattle? We never saw any Indians, and were not interrupted.

I was most afraid coming down Cumberland Mountain. The place was narrow and rocky. Stood up on either side, not broader than a house. Woods more beautiful in Cumberland Valley than any other place.

We come to Lexington in October. [Draper: 1779?] It had been settled the previous April. There were every sort of people there, and that was what took us away. We had no notion of raising our children among that sort of people. Frances McConnell was the first man I knew when I got to Lexington. I had known the McConnell's in Pennsylvania.

We went down to McConnell's station second April 1780. It was not settled till the day we went there. It took its name from Frances McConnell, and lay between Frances and William McConnell's places, & about between 1 & 1¼ miles from Lexington. Right where Royall's mill now is—on the rail-road. There was a grave yard there. James, Frances, and William McConnell, were cousins to Alexander and John McConnell.

Robert Edmiston, from Pennsylvania. Daniel Campbell, from Pennsylvania. William Hadden. John Brookey. All Presbyterians I think. All at the station were presbyterians, except two Mooneys, and they were raised presbyterians. John Nutt, Matthew Harper, John Stevenson, killed or taken at the Blue Licks from McConnell's station. [Shane: These 3.]

First summer we came out, Daddy stood sentry, while we milked. Things came on sooner that spring than ever I knew them. In the winter we were crowded. It was the continental war going on. (Safe for to be among indians.) But as soon as warm weather came on, they put back.

Mr. Brookey didn't come out till the winter following. 1780–81. The first of March 1781, John Brookey went out to cut the first log to build his house. The Indians thought to take him. In the spring they would rather have a prisoner than a scalp. They shot him through the shoulder, and it came out in the hollow of his back. He was a very round shouldered man, and the bullit holes were 15 inches between the places. There was no doctor at the station. But he was taken care of and fed and nursed, on just what we had, and in 4 weeks was able to pick up an axe and hew. I was out, bringing in a pail of water, when I saw the Indians after Brookey. A parcel of children were out at the time; some here, some there. Some got in, and some hid in hollow logs. One so near the passing Indian, who didn't see him, that the boy could see his gun was empty. (lock down.)

The company from Lexington were out in a few minutes, (they heard the gun) and set their dogs on them. They had stripped, and left their clothes behind, in coming to catch Brookey. Their things were all gotten; and one indian was wounded. The Indians had gotten within 60 yards of the fort. When Brookey's tree had fallen, he heard a stick crack, and looking round, saw that the Indians had almost gotten between him and the fort.

After the first campaign to Ohio had gone out, John Haggin was in it, (this after Brookey's affair I think,)—one David Hunter determined to go the other side of the river, as a place of more secure safety. Before getting off however he had a dream—that either the women & children, or that he himself would be killed. Henderson. He came down to bid us goodbye, and seemed to stay and stay. He started, and was shot, just in the hollow, about half way between McConnell's station & Lexington.

One Mitchell, was the first that I knew killed by the Indians on the Wilderness road. That was in 1776. When they got back to the first stations on Powell's valley, in June? 1776, they found the place all deserted, and every thing standing, even to the milk-pails on the stumps, as if they had been abruptly forsaken. Mitchell was killed just on this side of the Cumberland Mountain.

[Jane Stevenson's husband, Samuel, apparently speaks up now] Benjamin Blackburn, William Elliott, and Samuel Stevenson, (my father) came out in April, and got back I think in June. Took Billy Campbell with them, whom they got at one Jimmy Gilmore's, over the Kentucky river. Campbell was a wheelwright by trade. He took in a parcel of buffalo horns in a bag, to make spoons of. Daddy and Billy Elliott spelled him so as to enable him to get his bag in, by walking, & letting him ride some. Blackburn was so stiff with fear, we could hardly get him along. Had to light his pipe for him two or three times a day.

Moses McElwaine, (so says Samuel Stevenson) was never taken but the once, (He has a son now living over in Ohio, back of Urbana) that was in 1779. Cartwright the surveyor was with him. This was up in Clarke. One McCormick, that had known him when a boy in Ireland, was a trader among the Indians, and sent McIlvaine back. McCormick afterwards came with the company to the attack on Riddle's station, to avoid the imputation that he favored the Americans, and had sent away McElwaine. But said he never unloaded his gun.

Cartwright told McElwaine he had better not speak so loud, the Indians might be about. He thought there was no danger, untill his horse was shot under him. The horse fell on his leg. One of the Indians was going to kill him, but the other prevented, and showed the horse was holding his foot. He paid the Indian. McCormick afterwards came in, and he paid him.

Daniel Barton was taken over on North Elkhorn, a little beyond Georgetown, at the same time that Samuel Hodge was killed. That day, 12 months, to the very day, from the time he was taken, he returned.

White was killed at Todd's station, down on South Elkhorn, the day we left Lexington to go to McConnell's station. The boy, his son, that was with him, went to go home to his friends in Virginia, through the Wilderness, but took sick and died somewhere on the way, perhaps at Augusta, Virginia. Mrs. Blanchard, a daughter of that Mr. White.

Robert or Charles Knox, started to go on foot up to Lexington, and was killed before he got there. He lived at the upper, we at the lower end of the station, so I didn't see him when he started. He was shot in the thigh. The Indians took him off a piece, but found he could not travel, and shot him. We had moved down to McConnell's station but about a week.

Alexander McConnell had been out to kill a deer, and had skinned and swung it up. He then came in and borrowed a chestnut dun horse, having a white main and tail, of William McConnell, and went out to bring it in. Five Indians were on the look out. This horse was shot from under him, but fell on his leg, the one indian wanted to kill him but the other indian showed that only the horse was on his leg.—This was Thursday to Tuesday he was gone.—McConnell couldn't kill the indian that had saved his life twice. He was the other side of the log.—He got the Indians cappo, blue, (in the night, & he wanted to be dark) and set his gun, and pipe, and tomahawk down.—I heard him tell the story many times, and he never varied a word of it.—Tuesday evening, about sundown, he came in. His wife ran out to meet him, but they had to carry her in, she fainted away, overjoyed.

They had killed the horse, and cut off the main and tail to dye for moccasin purposes, &c. They could make it any color, almost, they pleased.—He shot the two guns first. Then shot the others alternately, and both indians fell into the fire, and flared up the ashes and light.—It is said the place where this happened, was never improved, till some 4 or 5 years ago, and that then they discovered the guns. This somewhere a little below Limestone.

We raised 4 crops, and then moved out. That was in 1784. 80–81–82–83.

The first meeting house was built in 1785. Mr. Rankin gave us time about with Lexington. He preached at first out here in private houses. At Capt. William McConnell's. (No kin to the McConnell's at McConnell's station. This William McConnell moved to St. Louis a great while ago.) Here. McElvain's, & Samuel Kelly's. He came in the fall, and the next spring we raised the house. Elders—This Capt. McConnell, Samuel Kelly, Hugh Campbell, (moved afterwards to Missouri) and another.

Was 17 days in the harvest, and every day in the river. When a young woman. Swam the Cowpasture, 300 yards wide, many a time on my back.

[Shane:] Mr. Trabue of Scott Co., Ky., obtained of "Aunt Jane," information, such as was necessary in order to obtain a pension.

Notes

ABBREVIATIONS

CHS   Cincinnati Historical Society
DM   Draper Manuscripts
JDS   John Dabney Shane
LCD   Lyman Copeland Draper
PHS   Presbyterian Historical Society

INTRODUCTION

1. Crèvecoeur, *Letters*, 46–55; Gorn, " 'Gouge and Bite' "; Onuf, "Liberty, Development, and Union."

2. Bailyn, *Peopling of British North America*, 112–13; Onuf, "Liberty, Development, and Union," 181; Mitchell, *Commercialism and Frontier*; Hahn and Prude, *Countryside*; Turner, *Frontier in American History*.

3. Geertz, *Local Knowledge*, 58.

4. Nobles, "Breaking into the Backcountry," 649.

5. Jakle, *Images of the Ohio Valley*, 15. For a useful introduction to the literature of Native American testimony, see Calloway, *World Turned Upside Down*.

6. The apt phrase "neocolonial" comes from Wiebe, *Opening of American Society*, 17–18.

7. For an overview of the literature of what is called the "New Western History," see Limerick, *Legacy of Conquest*; Cronon, Miles, and Gitlin, *Under an Open Sky*; and Edmunds, "Native Americans, New Voices."

CHAPTER ONE

1. JDS interview with Ben Guthrie, ca. 1840s, DM 11 CC 253; JDS interview with Mrs. Joseph Stagg, ca. 1840s, DM 12 CC 237–38.

2. Classic essays on the early Ohio Valley include Marshall, *History of Kentucky*; Doddridge, *Notes*; Mann Butler, *History of the Commonwealth*; and McClung, *Sketches of Western Adventure*. Useful bibliographic guides may be found in Coleman, *Bibliography of Kentucky History*; Watlington, *Partisan Spirit*, 235–64; and Cayton, *Frontier Republic*, 178–86.

3. This long "second generation" of frontier historians (which actually began with Theodore Roosevelt) was largely caught up in debates surrounding Frederick Jackson Turner's frontier thesis. For important works that touch upon the Ohio Valley, see Roosevelt, *Winning of the West*; Turner, *Frontier in American History*; Abernethy, *Three Virginia Frontiers*; Barnhart, *Valley of Democracy*; and Elkins and McKitrick, "Meaning for Turner's Frontier."

4. Nobles, "Breaking into the Backcountry," 643. See also Tillson, "The Southern Backcountry," 397. On Maine's "Revolutionary settlement" and the aspirations of settlers there, see Taylor, *Liberty Men*. For ethnohistorical works that have transformed our understandings of early American frontiers, see Merrell, *Indians' New World*; White, *Middle Ground*; Usner, *Indians, Settlers, and Slaves*; and Dowd, *Spirited Resistance*. On the continuing failure of ethnohistory to transform the master narratives of American history, see Merrell, "Some Thoughts on Colonial Historians."

5. Marcus and Fischer, *Anthropology as Cultural Critique*, 18. The classic definition of the ethnographic method may be found in Malinowski, *Argonauts of the Western Pacific*. Over the past decade a number of historians have utilized ethnographic insights and techniques to recover the meaning of expressive action in past societies. For works that have influenced my approach to the Shane materials, see Le Roy Ladurie, *Montaillou*; Isaac, *Transformation of Virginia*; Breen, *Tobacco Culture*; and Davis, *Fiction in the Archives*.

6. Isaac, *Transformation of Virginia*, 5. Historians who have made use of Shane's materials include Rohrbough, *Trans-Appalachian Frontier*; Eslinger, "Great Revival in Bourbon County"; Aron, *How the West Was Lost*; Faragher, *Daniel Boone*.

7. For an important exception, see Faragher, "They May Say What They Please."

8. Crèvecoeur, "Sketch," Durrett Collection, 4; Jakle, *Images of the Ohio Valley*, 3–5; Whitaker, *Spanish-American Frontier*, 67–70.

9. Richard White stresses the broad range of interactions between Europeans and native peoples in the upper Ohio Valley in *Middle Ground*. See also McConnell, *Country Between*; Hinderaker, *Elusive Empires*.

10. Tanner, *Atlas*, 43–53. See also White, *Middle Ground*, 223–56; Crosby, *Ecological Imperialism*, 209–15; Hunter, "History of the Ohio Valley," 588–93; Jerry Clark, *Shawnee*, 81–84; Francis Jennings, *Ambiguous Iroquois Empire*; and Francis Jennings, *Empire of Fortune*. On the "play-off system," see Wallace, *Death and Rebirth of the Seneca*, 111–14.

11. Tanner, *Atlas*, 60.

12. Downes, "Dunmore's War," 313; JDS copy of a letter from John Floyd to [William Preston], 21 April 1775, DM 17 CC 169; Scribner, *Revolutionary Virginia*, 7:770.

13. For a detailed account of the military conquest of the western country, see Tanner, *Atlas*, 68–91. For an excellent overview of these events from a Native American perspective, see Calloway, *American Revolution in Indian Country*.

14. Bonnie Smith, "Gender and the Practices of Scientific History," 1169. Turner reportedly had access to Draper's and, presumably, Shane's manuscripts while he was an undergraduate at the University of Wisconsin; see Smith, "The Draper Manuscripts," 45. On Shane's extant papers, see Appendix A.

15. Evan L. Reed to H. V. McChesney, 5 October 1945, Shane biographical file, KHS. Wilson, biographical sketch of John Dabney Shane, in *Presbyterian Historical Almanac* (1865), quoted in Rothert, "Shane, the Western Collector," 4; "Supplementary Material Relating to the Journey of Dr. Charles G. Shane" (1831–32), typescript, folder 7, box 21, Shane Collection, RG 196, PHS.

16. Miller, *Revolutionary College*, 123–27, 163–81, 251–53; May, *Enlightenment in America*, 320–21. On the relationship of Presbyterianism to insurgent religious movements in the nineteenth century, see Hatch, *Democratization of American Christianity*, 60–62.

17. Green, *Inaugural Address*; Union Theological Seminary, *Plan*, 7–8; ibid., *Catalogue*, 12–13; Rothert, "Shane, the Western Collector," 6.

18. "Description of a Minister," 1860, sermon manuscript, folder 16, box 21, Shane Collection, PHS; sermon no. 140, in "Notes of Sermons" (bound manuscript volume), 74–75, Shane Collection, PHS; sermon no. 178, "Education. Pbyns.," in "Notes of Sermons," 88, Shane Collection, PHS.

19. Wilson, quoted in Rothert, "Shane, the Western Collector," 5; James Alves to Lyman C. Draper, 10 February 1846, DM 2 CC 32; Wilson, quoted in Rothert, "Shane, the Western Collector," 4.

20. Hubbard, *Catalogue*. This brief review of Shane's library holdings is by no means exhaustive. Richard D. Brown offers many suggestive insights for an analysis of this type in *Knowledge Is Power*, 197–217.

21. Hubbard, *Catalogue*, title page; Gilmore, *Reading Becomes a Necessity*, 20–21; Hesseltine and Gara, "Draper and the Shane Papers," 332–33.

22. "Another Patriot of the Revolution Gone," unattributed newspaper clipping, 1838, JDS scrapbook, DM 26 CC 11; "Another Revolutionary Soldier Gone," printed broadside, 1838, JDS scrapbook, DM 27 CC 84; "Bye-Gone Years," unattributed newspaper clipping, 1839, JDS scrapbook, DM 26 CC 1.

23. Ralph Waldo Emerson to John Boynton Hill, 3 July 1822, quoted in Lowenthal, *Past Is a Foreign Country*, 118; Watson, *Liberty and Power*, 198–227.

24. "Anecdotes of Old Gen. Scott," unattributed newspaper clipping, n.d., JDS scrapbook, DM 26 CC 10; "Gen. John Armstrong," unattributed newspaper clipping originally published in the *New York American*, n.d., JDS scrapbook, DM 26 CC 5; "A Visit to Simon Kenton," *The Ladies Companion* (November 1841), JDS scrapbook, DM 26 CC 4. Although it is impossible to know when Shane compiled these materials, the articles appear in rough chronological order, suggesting that he added them as they came into his hands.

25. JDS to [Charles G. Shane], 11 February 1841, folder 3, box 18, Shane Collection, PHS.

26. On oral tradition, see Vansina, *Oral Tradition as History*. On Cane Ridge, see Conkin, *Cane Ridge*; Boles, *Religion in Antebellum Kentucky*, 20–30; and Eslinger, "Great Revival in Bourbon County, Kentucky," Chapter 5.

27. On nineteenth-century historical narratives, see Ross, "Grand Narrative," 651–77; and Appleby, Hunt, and Jacob, *Telling the Truth*, 91–125.

28. Malinowski, *Argonauts*, xv; Clifford, *Predicament of Culture*, 26. On the use (and misuse) of ethnography's disciplinary authority by historians, see Rosaldo, "From the Door of His Tent," 77–97; and Ginzburg, *Clues, Myths, and Historical Method*, 156–64.

29. Unbound volume dated 13 October 1856 in JDS miscellaneous papers, folder 8, box 18, Shane Collection, PHS. On David Rice, see Weeks, *Kentucky Presbyterians*, 14–15; and Boles, *Religion in Antebellum Kentucky*, 9–10.

30. Frish, *A Shared Authority*. In analyzing Shane's interviews, I have also profited from Grele, "On Using Oral History," 570–78; and Portelli, *The Death of Luigi Trastulli*.

31. JDS interview with Jane Stevenson, ca. 1840s, DM 13 CC 143; JDS interview with Andrew Thompson, ca. 1840s, DM 12 CC 235; JDS interview with John Rankins, ca. 1840s, DM 11 CC 83. For examples of interviews which contain many marginal notations, see, for example, JDS interview with Isaac Clinkenbeard, ca. 1840s, DM 11 CC 1–4; JDS interview with Maj. Jesse Daniel, [ca. 1843], DM 11 CC 92–95; JDS interview with James Wade, ca. 1840s, DM 12 CC 11–41; and JDS interview with Daniel Deron, ca. 1840s, DM 12 CC 239–44.

32. JDS interview with Josiah Collins, [1841], DM 12 CC 97. Two other informants related much the same story about Boone's wife. See JDS interview with Captain Nathaniel Hart [Jr.], [ca. 1843], DM 17 CC 195; JDS interview with Robert Wickliffe Sr., April 1859, 15 CC 83–86. For the gender implications of this humor, see Chapter 4.

33. JDS interview with Josiah Collins, [1841], DM 12 CC 78.

34. JDS interview with Mrs. John Arnold, ca. 1840s, DM 11 CC 241. Michael Frish notes that any written transcription of an oral interview, even one recorded on tape, must "abandon the pretense of literal reproduction, in order to craft the document into a form that will answer to the needs of successful presentation and communication." See Frisch, *Shared Authority*, 84.

35. JDS memorandum, ca. 1840s, DM 12 CC 194; JDS interview with Mrs. Shanklin, ca. 1840s, DM 11 CC 217; JDS interview with Josiah Collins, [1841], DM 12 CC 78; JDS interview with [a Cincinnati woman], ca. 1840s, DM 13 CC 18; JDS interview with Josiah Collins, [1841], DM 12 CC 78.

36. JDS memorandum, ca. 1840s, DM 12 CC 195. For an example of Draper's interviewing technique, see Redd, "Reminiscences of Western Virginia."

37. U.S. Bureau of the Census, *Century of Population Growth*, 207; Tanner, *Atlas*, 66.

38. No complete demographic study is available, but see Weissbach, "Peopling of Lexington, Kentucky"; and Purvis, "Ethnic Descent."

39. JDS interview with William Niblick, ca. 1840s, DM 11 CC 85. For a fascinat-

ing recent account of children's perceptions of war, see Tuttle, *"Daddy's Gone to War."*

40. Escott, *Slavery Remembered*, 6–7. See also Davis and Gates, *Slave's Narrative*.

41. Barsalou, "Content and Organization," 236; Drake, *Pioneer Life*, 23. In a suggestive essay, Clyde A. Milner II observes that western memoir writers seem most concerned with coming-of-age stories which celebrate regional identity. See Milner, "View from Wisdom," 205–6.

42. JDS interview with Mrs. John Arnold, ca. 1840s, DM 11 CC 241; JDS interview with Lewis Arnold, ca. 1840s, DM 11 CC 245; JDS interview with James Wade, ca. 1840s, DM 12 CC 11; JDS interview with Ephraim Sowdusky, ca. 1840s, DM 11 CC 141; JDS interview with James McConnell, ca. 1840s, DM 11 CC 146.

43. A preliminary search of Kentucky tax records for 1800 suggested the scope of these problems. Out of eighty informants' names appearing in a list of Kentucky taxpayers for that year, twenty-nine names were borne by more than one person. There were ten John McClures listed, for example, none of whom were living in the same county that Shane's subsequent interview took place. Only fifty-one informants could be tentatively linked to a single tax record, and the validity of this connection rests on the assumption that there was only one person bearing that name in both periods, or that informants resided in the same county in 1800 in which they lived at the time of their interview. Age distribution is another complicating factor: many of Shane's informants were still relatively young in 1800 and may not yet have acquired any taxable property. Not all informants supplied their birth date, which would allow one to control for differences in position in the life cycle. Because of these questions, further analysis of informants' tax records has thus far not been attempted. The first two federal census schedules for Kentucky are not extant; an enumeration of Kentucky taxpayers for 1800 can be found in Clift, *"Second Census."*

44. JDS interview with John Crawford, ca. 1840s, DM 12 CC 161; Garcia, " 'A Great Deal of Money,' " 197; JDS interview with George Yocum, ca. 1840s, DM 12 CC 149; JDS interview with Patrick Scott, [1844], DM 11 CC 8.

45. JDS interview with William Clinkenbeard, ca. 1840s, DM 11 CC 55. On the consumer and capital property of early settlers, see Perkins, "Consumer Frontier," 490–92.

46. JDS interview with Samuel McDowell, ca. 1840s, DM 13 CC 225; JDS interview with Abel Morgan, ca. 1840s, DM 12 CC 57.

47. JDS interview with Col. John Graves, [ca. 1845], DM 11 CC 121; JDS interview with Capt. George Stocton, ca. 1840s, DM 12 CC 231.

48. JDS interview with Jesse Kennedy, ca. 1840s, DM 11 CC 10; JDS interview with Mrs. John McKinney and son, ca. 1840s, DM 11 CC 25; JDS interview with [Martin] Wymore, ca. 1840s, DM 11 CC 132. In a recent examination of the social circumstances of "middling sorts" in eighteenth-century America, Stuart M. Blumin associates this concept of social intermediacy with "very modest levels of social and economic aspiration, closer to the bottom of society than to the top." See

Blumin, *Emergence of the Middle Class*, 1, 17–65. McKinney's "wildcat" was probably the *Lynx rufus rufus*, a twenty-pound predator native to Kentucky.

49. JDS to Lyman C. Draper, 9 July 1858, DM 32 CC 40. Shane's only known publication is a sermon preached before the West Lexington Presbytery at the opening of its September 1858 session. See Shane, *Bush in the Flame*.

50. Clifford and Marcus, *Writing Culture*, 13.

51. JDS interview with Jacob Stevens, ca. 1840s, DM 12 CC 136; Thelen, "Memory and American History," 1121. William F. Brewer argues for a "partially reconstructive" theory of human memory in "Memory for Randomly Sampled Autobiographical Events," 27–28. On Lyman Draper's search for the precise date of the Boone and Callaway captivity, see JDS interview with Richard French, ca. 1840s, DM 12 CC 201–10.

52. JDS interview with Joseph Luckey, ca. 1840s, DM 11 CC 17; JDS interview with John Hedge, ca. 1840s, DM 12 CC 117.

CHAPTER TWO

1. JDS interview with Capt. John Dyal, ca. 1840s, DM 13 CC 226–27.

2. Crèvecoeur, "Sketch," Durrett Collection, 10–15. On the "four stages theory," see Meek, *Social Science*, 2.

3. For works that have been of particular importance in shaping my approach to landscape perception, see Tuan, *Topophilia*; Tuan, *Space and Place*; Meinig, *Interpretation of Ordinary Landscapes*; Gould and White, *Mental Maps*; Lowenthal and Bowden, *Geographies of the Mind*; Downs, "Cognitive Mapping"; and Jackson, *Maps of Meaning*.

4. The best guide to this literature is Jakle, *Images of the Ohio Valley*.

5. Tuan, *Topophilia*, 63; see also Tuan, "Thought and Landscape."

6. Imlay, *Topographical Description*, 22. The phrase "western continent" comes from Filson, *Discovery*, 39.

7. On the geopolitical challenge of the West, see Meinig, *Shaping of America*, 1:348–70; Wiebe, *Opening*, 131–42; and Onuf, *Origins of the Federal Republic*, 163–71.

8. Wade Hall, "Along the Wilderness Trail," 288; JDS copy of Rev. David Barrow's journal, 12 May 1795, DM 12 CC 163.

9. Wade Hall, "Along the Wilderness Trail," 289–90; Blair, "Mary Dewees's Journal," 202. Historical geographers and folklorists continue to recognize that the Blue Ridge marks a distinct cultural boundary between piedmont and valley. See Zelinsky, "Where the South Begins"; Glassie, *Pattern in Material Folk Culture*, 64–79.

10. Wade Hall, "Along the Wilderness Trail," 292–93; Tuan, *Landscapes of Fear*.

11. Imlay, *Topographical Description*, 9; Lawrence Butler, "Letters," 369; Carter, *Road to Botany Bay*, 149.

12. Crèvecoeur, "Sketch," Durrett Collection, 8.

13. James Hall, *Letters from the West* (1828), quoted in Faragher, *Sugar Creek*, 242.

14. JDS interview with Mrs. Webb, [1842], DM 13 CC 51; Cayton, " 'Separate Interests,' " 65. On the persistence of cultural boundaries, see Barth, *Ethnic Groups and Boundaries*, 9.

15. Harley, "Maps, Knowledge, and Power," 289. See also Monmonier, *How to Lie with Maps*; and Nobles, "Straight Lines and Stability."

16. On the concept of "natural frontiers," see Sahlins, *Boundaries*, 34–49.

17. On Filson's map, see Jillson, *Filson's Kentucke*, 136–44; Jillson, *Pioneer Kentucky*, 26–29; and Durrett, *John Filson*.

18. Enoch Smith Sr., Survey Book, 1780–92, 5, 44. On Kentucky land surveys, see Thomas Clark, *Historic Maps*, 45–49.

19. See Table 1.

20. JDS interview with [a Woodford County informant], ca. 1840s, DM 11 CC 279; JDS interview with James Wade, ca. 1840s, DM 12 CC 11; JDS interview with George Yocum, ca. 1840s, DM 12 CC 147; JDS interview with David Crouch, [ca. 1843], DM 12 CC 225.

21. JDS interview with David Crouch, [ca. 1843], DM 12 CC 225–26.

22. JDS interview with David Crouch, [ca. 1843], DM 12 CC 226–29. Serviceberries, or Juneberries, are the small purple-black fruits of genus *Amelanchier*, a member of the rose family. On cattle grazing and droving as a regional specialization rather than a Turnerian "stage of development," see Macmaster, "Cattle Trade in Western Virginia"; and McDonald and McWhiney, "Antebellum Southern Herdsman," 147–66.

23. JDS interview with John Crawford, ca. 1840s, DM 12 CC 157; JDS interview with Jacob Lawson, ca. 1840s, DM 12 CC 251; JDS interview with James Wade, ca. 1840s, DM 12 CC 11; JDS interview with Jane Stevenson, ca. 1840s, DM 13 CC 135. "Laurel" was the common name used by early settlers for the flowering evergreen shrub *Rhododendron maximum*, indigenous to North America; the mountain laurel, *Kalmia augustifolia*, was commonly called "ivy."

24. JDS interview with Patrick Scott, [1844], DM 11 CC 18; JDS interview with James Wade, ca. 1840s, DM 12 CC 11; JDS interview with Mrs. Samuel Scott, ca. 1840s, DM 11 CC 224. On Scotch-Irish and Anglo-American borderers as "nomads," see Calloway, *American Revolution in Indian Country*, 22.

25. U.S. Bureau of the Census, *Century of Population Growth*, 207; Heckewelder, "Narrative," 34–42. On the expansion of white settlement north of the Ohio River, see Tanner, *Atlas*, 87–91; and Cayton, *Frontier Republic*, Chapters 1–3.

26. James Breckinridge to John Breckinridge, 25 October 1784, quoted in Dicken-Garcia, *To Western Woods*, 95. See also Klotter, *Breckinridges of Kentucky*, 3–13; and Harrison, "A Virginian Moves to Kentucky."

27. Austin, "Journey," 525–26.

28. Ibid., 518, 527.

29. Ibid., 523–24. As a narrative convention, the Edenic myth has gained credence from the undoubted economic inequality that existed in early Kentucky;

yet while purporting to treat the aspirations of poorer migrants sympathetically, it actually portrays them as dupes and victims. For the perpetuation of this image, see Moore, *Frontier Mind,* 11–43; Channing, *Kentucky,* 3–35; and Teute, "Land, Liberty, and Labor," 2–5, 172–75.

30. Unfortunately, information on book ownership and access to print culture in the southern backcountry is, at best, sketchy. In one study, analysis of 2,400 inventories drawn from all geographic regions of Virginia between 1770 and 1861 (with the majority falling between 1790 and 1830) found that almost half "failed to record a single book or periodical." A much smaller group of Kentucky probate inventories from the early 1780s revealed that only a third of the recent immigrants owned a book, most often a Bible, testament, spelling book, or dictionary. See Kett and McClung, "Book Culture," 110; and Perkins, "Consumer Frontier," 491.

31. "Letter from a gentlman [*sic*]," *Virginia Gazette,* 11 May 1782, quoted in Dicken-Garcia, *To Western Woods,* 75; and Hazel Faye Garcia, "Communication in the Migration to Kentucky," viii. Garcia's study included a systematic examination of Virginia newspapers from 1769 to 1792, Pittsburgh and Kentucky newspapers from their beginnings in 1786 and 1787, respectively, to 1792, and a non-systematic random reading of Massachusetts newspapers over the same period.

32. Many western settlers came from what William J. Gilmore has termed a "minimal access zone" to print communication—isolated, sparsely settled, or newly settled areas. See Gilmore, *Reading Becomes a Necessity,* 141–53.

33. JDS copy of the Record Book of New Providence Church, DM 14 CC 102.

34. JDS interview with Capt. John Dyal, ca. 1840s, DM 13 CC 226; JDS interview with John Gass, [1843], DM 11 CC 11; JDS interview with Benjamin Stites, 1842, DM 13 CC 55–56. On John Cleves Symmes's controversial land speculations, see Cayton, *Frontier Republic,* 61–63.

35. JDS interview with William Niblick, ca. 1840s, DM 11 CC 85; JDS copy of Levi Todd's Narrative, DM 15 CC 157–58; Young, *Westward into Kentucky,* 67; JDS interview with Benjamin Allen, ca. 1840s, DM 11 CC 67.

36. JDS interview with Patrick Scott, [1844], DM 11 CC 6; JDS interview with Jesse Graddy, [ca. 1842], DM 13 CC 133.

37. *Virginia Gazette and Weekly Advertiser,* 11 December 1788, quoted in Dicken-Garcia, *To Western Woods,* 128.

38. On direct observation and conversation as principal sources for information and learning, see Brown, *Knowledge Is Power,* 158.

39. JDS interview with William Craycraft, ca. 1840s, DM 12 CC 54; JDS interview with Capt. Marcus Richardson, ca. 1840s, DM 12 CC 154.

40. JDS interview with Col. John Graves, [ca. 1845], DM 11 CC 121.

41. JDS interview with [a woman in Cincinnati], ca. 1840s, DM 13 CC 9–10; JDS interview with Asa Farrar, ca. 1840s, DM 13 CC 1.

42. JDS interview with Mr. and Mrs. Ned Darnaby, ca. 1840s, DM 11 CC 164; JDS interview with David Crouch, [ca. 1843], DM 12 CC 229; JDS interview with Jane Stevenson, ca. 1840s, DM 13 CC 137; JDS interview with [a Woodford County informant], ca. 1840s, DM 11 CC 280; JDS interview with Mrs. John

McKinney and son, ca. 1840s, DM 11 CC 25; JDS interview with Mrs. John Arnold, ca. 1840s, DM 11 CC 241.

43. Young, *Westward into Kentucky*, 44; JDS interview with Mrs. Samuel Scott, ca. 1840s, DM 11 CC 225; JDS interview with Daniel Deron, ca. 1840s, DM 12 CC 239; JDS interview with James Wade, ca. 1840s, DM 12 CC 12; JDS interview with [Martin] Wymore, ca. 1840s, DM 11 CC 128. On livestock mutilation as a "message of terror," see Anderson, "King Philip's Herds," 623.

44. Filson, *Discovery*, 114; JDS interview with Mrs. Sarah Graham, ca. 1840s, DM 12 CC 45. On the wilderness trace, see also Speed, *Wilderness Road*; and Pusey, *Wilderness Road to Kentucky*.

45. JDS interview with William Boyd, 1841, DM 12 CC 59–60; JDS interview with —— Hardesty, ca. 1840s, DM 11 CC 171. A recent archaeological survey documented more than 150 stations in central Kentucky alone. See O'Malley, "*Stockading Up.*"

46. Carmony, "Spencer Records' Memoir," 373–74. On diverging European and American views of warfare, see Ferling, *Wilderness of Miseries*, 155–70.

47. JDS interview with Elijah Foley, ca. 1840s, DM 11 CC 133.

48. JDS interview with Benjamin Stites, 1842, DM 13 CC 56–57; JDS interview with Levi Buckingham, ca. 1840s, DM 13 CC 89.

49. Heckewelder, "Narrative," 34–39 (quotation on p. 38); Tanner, *Atlas*, 88. For a perceptive analysis of the role of Appalachian settlers in early Ohio, see Cayton, "Marietta and the Ohio Company."

50. Tolzman, *First Description of Cincinnati*, 54–55.

51. JDS interview with Capt. John Dyal, ca. 1840s, DM 13 CC 228; JDS interview with Jane Stevenson, ca. 1840s, DM 13 CC 139; JDS interview with Sarah Graham, ca. 1840s, DM 12 CC 46; JDS interview with Mrs. John Arnold, ca. 1840s, DM 11 CC 241; JDS interview with Mrs. [Samuel] Pierce, ca. 1840s, DM 13 CC 7.

52. JDS interview with Ben Guthrie, ca. 1840s, DM 11 CC 256; JDS interview with Mrs. Mary Perkins, vol. 7, box 2, John Day Caldwell Papers, CHS. On the spatial construction of gender relations, see Tivers, "How the Other Half Lives"; and Moore, *Space, Text and Gender*. For a recent creative attempt to understand the experience of captivity, see Demos, *Unredeemed Captive*.

53. JDS interview with Mrs. Sarah Graham, ca. 1840s, DM 12 CC 46; JDS interview with William Moseby, ca. 1840s, DM 11 CC 272; Faragher, *Daniel Boone*, 132.

54. Drake, *Pioneer Life*, 25; Tuttle, "*Daddy's Gone to War*", 173.

55. JDS interview with [a Woodford Co. informant], ca. 1840s, DM 11 CC 282; JDS interview with Mrs. Sarah Graham, ca. 1840s, DM 12 CC 53. On slave life in early Kentucky, see Lucas, *From Slavery*, xi–xv; and Eslinger, "The Shape of Slavery."

56. JDS interview with David Crouch, [ca. 1843], DM 12 CC 228; JDS interview with Mrs. Sarah Graham, ca. 1840s, DM 12 CC 47; Harrison, "A Virginian Moves to Kentucky," 207; JDS interview with Elijah Foley, ca. 1840s, DM 11 CC 135; JDS interview with Col. John Graves, [ca. 1845], DM 11 CC 125.

57. JDS interview with Col. Putnam Ewing, ca. 1840s, DM 12 CC 57; JDS interview with James Wade, ca. 1840s, DM 12 CC 38.

58. JDS interview with Col. John Graves, [ca. 1845], DM 11 CC 122–23. On the Madoc legend, see Filson, *Discovery*, 95–97; Durrett, *Traditions*; Schwartz, *Conceptions of Kentucky Prehistory*, 11–15; and Morgan, "From a Death to a View," 83–85. On popular misconceptions about Indian occupation of Kentucky, see Henderson, "Dispelling the Myth."

59. JDS interview with John Gass, [1843], DM 11 CC 12; JDS interview with Mrs. [Samuel] Pierce, ca. 1840s, DM 13 CC 8; JDS interview with Col. John Graves, [ca. 1845], DM 11 CC 122; JDS interview with Robert Gwynn, [1842], DM 11 CC 217; Drake, *Pioneer Life*, 20; JDS interview with William Clinkenbeard, ca. 1840s, DM 11 CC 59.

60. JDS interview with Jane Stevenson, ca. 1840s, DM 13 CC 135; JDS interview with David Crouch, [ca. 1843], DM 12 CC 225; JDS interview with Capt. Joe F. Taylor, ca. 1840s, DM 11 CC 228; JDS interview with [Martin] Wymore, ca. 1840s, DM 11 CC 129; JDS interview with Mrs. Morrison, ca. 1840s, DM 11 CC 151; JDS interview with —— Stevenson, ca. 1840s, DM 11 CC 51. On horse theft by Ohio Indians, see McConnell, *A Country Between*, 161.

61. JDS interview with William Clinkenbeard, ca. 1840s, DM 11 CC 58; JDS copy of Levi Todd's Narrative, DM 15 CC 159; JDS interview with Mrs. Sarah Graham, ca. 1840s, DM 12 CC 46; JDS interview with [a woman in Cincinnati], ca. 1840s, DM 13 CC 16; JDS interview with Stephen Shelton, ca. 1840s, DM 11 CC 266–67; JDS interview with Mrs. Gough, [1843], DM 11 CC 98; JDS interview with Gen. [Thomas] Metcalfe, ca. 1850s, DM 11 CC 185; Hammon, "Journal of James Nourse," 265.

The South's only native bamboo, *Arundinaria gigantea*, is now nearly extinct in Kentucky, replaced by the European import which Americans have erroneously named "Kentucky bluegrass." On Kentucky's presettlement landscape, see McHargue, "Canebrakes"; Campbell, "Present and Presettlement Forest," 141–81; Crosby, *Ecological Imperialism*, 157–58; and Worster, "Transformations of the Earth," 1087–88.

62. JDS interview with —— Hardesty, ca. 1848–49, DM 11 CC 169; JDS interview with Ben Guthrie, ca. 1840s, DM 11 CC 255.

63. JDS interview with Josiah Collins, [1841], DM 12 CC 109; JDS interview with John Rankins, ca. 1840s, DM 11 CC 82. A recent study identified 622 Kentucky place-names associated with saline deposits; see Boisvert, *Kentucky Salt Licks*, 8. On hunting in early Kentucky, see Aron, *How the West Was Lost*, 5–28.

64. JDS interview with James Wade, ca. 1840s, DM 12 CC 30; JDS interview with Samuel Gibson, ca. 1840s, DM 12 CC 125; JDS interview with Thomas Butler, ca. 1840s, DM 11 CC 215.

65. Quoted in Henderson, Jobe, and Turnbow, *Indian Occupation*, 18; JDS interview with James Wade, ca. 1840s, DM 12 CC 29; JDS interview with Benjamin Allen, ca. 1840s, DM 11 CC 72. The Henderson, Jobe, and Turnbow study documented at least fifty contact-period occupation and/or utilization sites in Kentucky.

66. JDS interview with John Crawford, ca. 1840s, DM 12 CC 163; JDS interview

with Robert Gwynn, [1842], DM 11 CC 216; JDS interview with William Clinkenbeard, ca. 1840s, DM 11 CC 59.

67. JDS interview with Samuel Gibson, ca. 1840s, DM 12 CC 124; JDS interview with George Trumbo, ca. 1840s, DM 12 CC 113; JDS interview with James Wade, ca. 1840s, DM 12 CC 38. On Indian communication routes and the impact of expanding white settlement, see Tanner, "Land and Water Communication Systems"; and Dowd, *Spirited Resistance*, 112–13.

68. JDS interview with James Wade, ca. 1840s, DM 12 CC 38; JDS interview with Joshua McQueen, ca. 1840s, DM 13 CC 121; JDS interview with John Hedge, ca. 1840s, DM 11 CC 20; JDS interview with William Clinkenbeard, ca. 1840s, DM 11 CC 61; JDS interview with Joshua McQueen, DM 13 CC 121; Aron, "Significance of the Kentucky Frontier," 315.

69. Lakoff and Johnson, *Metaphors We Live By*, 3.

CHAPTER THREE

1. Young, *Westward into Kentucky*, 70–73. For a detailed description of salt-making at Bullit's Lick, see Bentley, "Letters of Thomas Perkins," 145.

2. Young, *Westward into Kentucky*, 73.

3. Crèvecoeur, *Letters*, 51–52. For a revisionist view of western pugnacity, see Gorn, " 'Gouge and Bite.' "

4. Bentley, "Letters of Thomas Perkins," 148; Filson, *Discovery*, 29.

5. Turner, *Frontier in American History*, 23; U.S. Bureau of the Census, *Century of Population Growth*, 207; Purvis, "Ethnic Descent," 259; Teute, "Land, Liberty, and Labor," 63. On the debate over surname analysis as a guide to ethnicity, see Purvis, "European Ancestry"; and Akenson, "Accepted Estimates," 102–19.

6. Knobel, *Paddy and the Republic*, 104–28; Polenberg, *One Nation Divisible*, 243–50; Cohen, *Symbolic Construction*, 104–7; Sollors, *Invention of Ethnicity*, ix–xx.

7. Robert Johnson to Gov. [Patrick] Henry, 5 December 1786, in Palmer, *Calendar of Virginia State Papers*, 4:191; JDS interview with John Hedge, ca. 1840s, DM 11 CC 19. See also Bliss, "Tuckahoe."

8. On the larger context of cultural interaction in early America, see Breen, "Creative Adaptations." See also White, *Middle Ground*; and Merrell, " 'Customes of Our Countrey.' "

9. JDS interview with Mrs. Morrison, ca. 1840s, DM 11 CC 152. On Pennsylvania's role as a distribution center for migrants to the south and west, see Lemon, *Best Poor Man's Country*, 71–97.

10. On the "coding" of strangers in antebellum America, see Halttunen, *Confidence Men*; Lofland, *World of Strangers*; and Wiebe, *Segmented Society*, 21–52.

11. Cohen, *Symbolic Construction*, 12.

12. JDS interview with John Hedge, ca. 1840s, DM 11 CC 19; Cresswell, *Journal*, 101; Isaac, *Transformation of Virginia*, 43; Blair, "Mary Dewees's Journal," 202. On gentility, see Bushman, *Refinement of America*.

13. Cresswell, *Journal*, 103; JDS interview with Mrs. Sarah Graham, ca. 1840s, DM 12 CC 45. A 1761 "List of Goods for Presents to the Indians" from the Ohio Company Papers describes numerous silver ornaments including gorgets, arm bands, nose rings, ear bobs, chains, rings, broaches, bells, and medals "to be made by Willm Evens Jeweller near St. Johns Turnpike Who has the Patterns for them." Quoted in Henderson, Jobe, and Turnbow, *Indian Occupation*, 305.

14. JDS interview with Alexander Hamilton, ca. 1840s, DM 11 CC 295; JDS interview with John Gass, [1843], DM 11 CC 12–13.

15. JDS interview with James Wade, ca. 1840s, DM 12 CC 17; JDS interview with George Fearis, ca. 1840s, DM 13 CC 241–42; JDS interview with William Clinkenbeard, ca. 1840s, DM 11 CC 60–66; JDS interview with Mrs. Shanklin, ca. 1840s, DM 11 CC 218.

16. JDS interview with John Hanks, ca. 1840s, DM 12 CC 138; JDS interview with Benjamin Stites, 1842, DM 13 CC 60, 65. On the incorporation of selected elements of European dress by Ohio Indians, see McConnell, *Country Between*, 211.

17. JDS interview with William Clinkenbeard, ca. 1840s, DM 11 CC 66; Carmony, "Records' Memoir," 366; JDS interview with William Clinkenbeard, ca. 1840s, DM 11 CC 63; William Whitley's Narrative, DM 9 CC 43; JDS interview with Robert Jones, [1842], DM 13 CC 176; JDS interview with Caleb Williams, 1855, DM 11 CC 193.

18. Janney, "Narrative," 470–71; JDS interview with Joshua McQueen, ca. 1840s, DM 13 CC 124.

19. Young, *Westward into Kentucky*, 55–56.

20. JDS interview with Benjamin Allen, ca. 1840s, DM 11 CC 71.

21. JDS interview with George Yocum, ca. 1840s, DM 12 CC 150; JDS interview with Benjamin Allen, ca. 1840s, DM 11 CC 72.

22. JDS interview with William Clinkenbeard, ca. 1840s, DM 11 CC 66; JDS interview with John Rupard, [1843], DM 11 CC 99.

23. Young, *Westward into Kentucky*, 140; JDS interview with Asa Farrar, ca. 1840s, DM 13 CC 4.

24. JDS interview with Mrs. Sarah Graham, ca. 1840s, DM 12 CC 49; JDS interview with James Stevenson, ca. 1840s, DM 11 CC 247; Redd, "Reminiscences," 339; Still, "Westward Migration," 331.

25. Still, "Westward Migration," 331; Redd, "Reminiscences," 338; JDS interview with Capt. Nathaniel Hart [Jr.], [ca. 1843], DM 17 CC 192; JDS interview with Jeptha Kemper, ca. 1840s, DM 12 CC 128; JDS interview with Henry Parvin, ca. 1840s, DM 11 CC 173. On the frontier as a "marrying ground," see Gary Nash, "Hidden History of Mestizo America," 947. On race as a cultural construct, see Fields, "Ideology and Race."

26. JDS interview with William Clinkenbeard, ca. 1840s, DM 11 CC 59.

27. Jones, *Journal*, 88.

28. Forty years ago historians searched the colonial era for qualities that unified Americans and distinguished them from their Old World predecessors; today, the recognition of cultural conservatism among migrants posits a very different rela-

tionship between European cultures and their American offshoots. On transatlantic cultural connections, see Breen, "Persistent Localism"; Allen, *In English Ways*; Landsman, *Scotland*; and Roeber, "In German Ways?"

David Hackett Fischer recently made a forceful argument for the primacy of British regional influence in the shaping of American social institutions. His work, however, is flawed by a static concept of cultural diffusion which largely ignores the complex intermingling of cultural inheritance and creative adaptation at work in early America. See Fischer, *Albion's Seed*; and, for a critique, Jack Greene et al., "*Albion's Seed*."

29. Young, *Westward into Kentucky*, 72.

30. Carmony, "Records' Memoir," 334. The incident Records speaks of was the notorious Gnadenhütten Massacre which took place in March 1782.

In response to nativist hostility to Irish Catholics, Protestant descendants of Ulster immigrants, formerly known as "Irishmen," began to adopt the name "Scotch-Irish" in the mid-nineteenth century. On the evolution of this term, see Jones, "Scotch-Irish," 284–85; and Keller, "What Is Distinctive," 69–72.

31. JDS interview with Jacob Stevens, ca. 1840s, DM 12 CC 135–36; JDS interview with William Clinkenbeard, ca. 1840s, DM 11 CC 64.

32. JDS interview with Josiah Collins, [1841], DM 12 CC 70; JDS interview with Capt. Nathaniel Hart [Jr.], [ca. 1843], DM 17 CC 193–94; JDS interview with Jane Stevenson, ca. 1840s, DM 13 CC 135.

33. JDS interview with Capt. Nathaniel Hart [Jr.], [ca. 1843], DM 17 CC 191; JDS interview with John Gass, [1843], DM 11 CC 13; Young, *Westward into Kentucky*, 137. A. G. Roeber discusses the English use of the name "Dutch" for both German and Dutch speakers in " 'Origin of Whatever Is Not English among Us,' " 220n. William Clinkenbeard was one of the few settlers to distinguish between the "High Dutch" (Germans) and the "Low Dutch" (Dutch), explaining to Shane at one point that a "good many Dutch came about Shepherdstown (Va.); [there is a] difference between high and low Dutch." See DM 11 CC 66.

34. JDS interview with Capt. Nathaniel Hart [Jr.], [ca. 1843], DM 17 CC 193; JDS interview with Josiah Collins, [1841], DM 12 CC 102; JDS interview with Capt. Nathaniel Hart [Jr.], [ca. 1843], DM 17 CC 208.

35. JDS interview with George Trumbo, ca. 1840s, DM 12 CC 113; JDS interview with Dr. George N. Hall, ca. 1840s, DM 11 CC 38; Young, *Westward into Kentucky*, 84; JDS interview with Joseph Ficklin, ca. 1850s, DM 16 CC 267; Carmony, "Records' Memoir," 361–62.

36. JDS interview with William McClelland, ca. 1850s, DM 11 CC 182. On the long tradition of Irish jokes, see Secor, "Ethnic Humor."

37. Ferling, *Wilderness of Miseries*, 78. On "interethnic image-making" in the nineteenth century, see Knobel, *Paddy and the Republic*, 21–38.

38. JDS interview with Samuel Potts Pointer, ca. 1840s, DM 12 CC 247–48; JDS interview with Capt. John Wilson, 1855, DM 17 CC 9.

39. JDS interview with Joseph Ficklin, ca. 1850s, DM 16 CC 257; JDS interview with [a Cincinnati woman], ca. 1840s, DM 13 CC 9. The phrase "culture of rank" comes from Blumin, *Emergence of the Middle Class*, 30.

40. Blair, "Dewees's Journal," 199–207. My reading of Mary Dewees's journal owes a great deal to Bushman, *Refinement of America.*

41. Blair, "Dewees's Journal," 205–15.

42. JDS interview with John Gass, [1843], DM 11 CC 12; Still, "Westward Migration," 321, 333; Oppel, "Paradise Lost," 204–6; JDS interview with Dr. A. Young, ca. 1850s, DM 11 CC 234. For an analysis of the changing taxonomy of the term "gentleman" in colonial and early national society, see Wood, *Radicalism,* 24–42, 194–95. On the triumph of gentility in frontier Lexington, see Friend, "Inheriting Eden," 180–223.

43. JDS interview with Mrs. Ephraim January, ca. 1840s, DM 11 CC 222.

44. Scribner, *Revolutionary Virginia,* 3:463, 4:176; JDS copy of Needham Parry's Diary, DM 14 CC 5–6; JDS interview with Joseph Ficklin, ca. 1850s, DM 16 CC 259; JDS interview with Col. Roger Quarles, ca. 1840s, DM 11 CC 148. Pennsylvania's slaveholding population was quite small in comparison to Virginia's; in 1790, only 2.5 percent of Pennsylvania families owned slaves, as opposed to 44.9 percent for Virginia and 17 percent for Kentucky. See U.S. Bureau of the Census, *Century of Population Growth,* 135. On the narrow limits of the Pennsylvania emancipation process, see Gary Nash and Jean Soderlund, *Freedom by Degrees.*

45. James Smith, "Tours," 401; Drake, *Pioneer Life,* 202–3; JDS interview with William Clinkenbeard, ca. 1840s, DM 11 CC 55; John Floyd to Joseph Martin, 19 May 1776, quoted in Hammon and Harris, "Dangerous Situation," 213; JDS interview with Joseph Ficklin, ca. 1850s, DM 16 CC 259.

46. JDS interview with Joseph Ficklin, ca. 1850s, DM 16 CC 259.

47. JDS interview with John Hedge, ca. 1840s, DM 11 CC 19–22; JDS interview with William Clinkenbeard, ca. 1840s, DM 11 CC 61; JDS interview with Benjamin Allen, ca. 1840s, DM 11 CC 76; JDS interview with Mrs. Sarah Graham, ca. 1840s, DM 12 CC 47. On regional distinctions in early Ohio, see Cayton, "Land, Power, and Reputation."

48. On food as a cultural medium, see Douglas and Isherwood, *World of Goods,* 66–67.

49. JDS interview with John Hanks, ca. 1840s, DM 12 CC 144; JDS interview with Josiah Collins, [1841], DM 12 CC 73; Drake, *Pioneer Life,* 10–11. On buttermilk as a poor man's dish, the *OED* quotes Swift, *State of Ireland* [1727]: "The families of farmers, who pay great rents, living in filth and nastiness upon buttermilk and potatoes." *The Compact Edition of the Oxford English Dictionary,* s.v. "buttermilk." On invented traditions, see Hobsbawm and Ranger, *The Invention of Tradition.*

50. JDS interview with Mrs. Phillips, [1854], DM 16 CC 291; Perkins, "Consumer Frontier," 496–97; Drake, *Pioneer Life,* 202. On tea and other British consumer goods, see Breen, " 'Baubles of Britain.' "

51. JDS interview with James Stevenson, ca. 1840s, DM 11 CC 250; JDS interview with Samuel Gibson, ca. 1840s, DM 12 CC 121; Drake, *Pioneer Life,* 202; Michaux, "Instructions," 169.

52. JDS interview with Hugh Garret, ca. 1840s, DM 11 CC 246; JDS interview

with Joseph Ficklin, ca. 1850s, DM 16 CC 269–71. After Virginia established Kentucky County in 1776, Kentuckians served in the Virginia legislature until statehood in 1792.

53. JDS interview with James Stevenson, ca. 1840s, DM 11 CC 250. Presumably, this was the first loaf of wheat bread that Stevenson had seen; cornbread was usually cooked in an iron skillet. On taverns catering to genteel customers, see Conroy, *In Public Houses*, 89–95, 257–58.

54. JDS interview with Benjamin Allen, ca. 1840s, DM 11 CC 72; JDS interview with William Clinkenbeard, ca. 1840s, DM 11 CC 66.

55. Banta, "Daniel Ketcham," 176–77; Janney, "Narrative," 471–72.

56. JDS interview with Joshua McQueen, ca. 1840s, DM 13 CC 126–27; JDS interview with [a Woodford County informant], ca. 1840s, DM 11 CC 282; Cronon, *Changes in the Land*, 131.

57. LCD interview with Mrs. Elizabeth Thomas, 1844, DM 12 C 26–27; John Jennings, "Journal," 146; Francis Jennings, *Invasion of America*, 149; Klett, *Journals of Charles Beatty*, 58–59.

58. JDS interview with Benjamin Allen, ca. 1840s, DM 11 CC 71; Jones, *Journal*, 42, 53, 54. On chocolate drinking, Mintz, *Sweetness and Power*, 108–10.

59. Jordan, "Journal of James Kenny," 22; Edgar, *Ten Years*, 355.

60. Richard White, *Middle Ground*, 390.

61. Vogt and Albert, *People of Rimrock*, 61. One historian who has consistently paid attention to kinship relations is John Mack Faragher, who has recently called for a closer examination of "the role of shared communal sentiment in cementing social relations," in "Americans, Mexicans, Métis," 94.

62. JDS interview with Caleb Williams, 1855, DM 11 CC 191. For a detailed examination of the kin network surrounding one frontier station, see Eslinger, "Migration and Kinship," 52–66.

63. JDS interview with James Stevenson, ca. 1840s, DM 11 CC 248–49.

64. JDS interview with William McClelland, ca. 1850s, DM 11 CC 183. Ginseng root, *Panax quinquefolius*, was an early cash crop in the Appalachian uplands, harvested by back settlers and hunters and shipped from Philadelphia to China as a highly valued medicinal remedy. James Wade, for example, recalled, "I dug ginseng in Greenbriar. Trimble, of Hazel Green, paid a debt of $3000 with it in Maysville. . . . In Greenbriar, we got fifty cents a pound—could gather two pounds a day. It took two pounds of green to make one of dry. It was scarce in Greenbriar." See JDS interview with James Wade, ca. 1840s, DM 12 CC 28.

65. JDS interview with Mrs. John Arnold, ca. 1840s, DM 11 CC 241; Thomas Clark, *History of Kentucky*, 75.

66. JDS interview with Caleb Williams, 1855, DM 11 CC 191; JDS interview with Col. Thomas Jones, ca. 1840s, DM 12 CC 232; JDS interview with William Moseby, ca. 1840s, DM 11 CC 270; JDS interview with William Clinkenbeard, ca. 1840s, DM 11 CC 58.

67. JDS interview with James Morris, ca. 1840s, DM 13 CC 202–4. A newspaper advertisement in the 1789 *Kentucky Gazette* offered 100 pounds of flour for only 15 shillings. See Garcia, "Great Deal of Money," 193.

68. JDS interview with Joseph Ficklin, ca. 1850s, DM 16 CC 265–69.

69. JDS interview with Capt. Nathaniel Hart [Jr.], [ca. 1843], DM 17 CC 190–203.

CHAPTER FOUR

1. Crèvecoeur, *Letters*, 46–47; "A citizen of Pennsylvania" [Benjamin Rush], *Columbian Magazine* (November 1786), quoted in Onuf, "Liberty, Development, Union," 188; McCoy, *Elusive Republic*, 17–32. On Jefferson's "yeoman imperialism," see Wiebe, *Opening*, 131–38.

2. Coward, *Kentucky in the New Republic*, 12–13; Teute, "Land, Liberty, and Labor," 63; Watlington, *Partisan Spirit*, 112. Among the classic essays on early Kentucky political life are Marshall, *History of Kentucky*; Mann Butler, *History of the Commonwealth*; Abernethy, *Three Virginia Frontiers*; and Barnhart, *Valley of Democracy*.

3. Slaughter, *Whiskey Rebellion*, 117; Tachau, "Whiskey Rebellion"; James Wilkinson to Estaban Miro (1790), quoted in Watlington, *Partisan Spirit*, 113. On backcountry turmoil elsewhere, see Hoffman, Tate, and Albert, *Uncivil War*; Taylor, *Liberty Men*; Brooke, "To the Quiet of the People"; and Bellesiles, "Establishment of Legal Structures." After reviewing the primary sources available for Kentucky's formative period, one historian recently noted that even those Kentuckians who left written records (and were, thus, more likely to belong to the elite) "were much more concerned with Indian raids and land deals than with the political developments that ultimately led to statehood." See Harrison, *Kentucky's Road to Statehood*, 184.

4. Foucault, *History of Sexuality*, 93–94. For a general orientation to the social theory of power relations, I have also found of value: Foucault, *Power/Knowledge*, 142; Giddens, *Central Problems*, 88–95; Wrong, *Power*; Blau, *Exchange and Power*. On the rhetoric of power in eighteenth-century America, see Bailyn, *Ideological Origins*, 55–93.

5. The phrase "small politics" comes from Bailey, *Gifts and Poison*, 2. For a suggestive article on the "small politics" of gossip in early America, see Norton, "Gender and Defamation."

6. Fortes and Evans-Pritchard, *African Political Systems*; Cohen, "Political Anthropology."

7. Robertson, *Petitions*, 38–41; Henning, *Statutes*, 9:257–61. South Carolina's failure at provincial administration presents a striking contrast to Virginia's efforts. See Beeman, "Political Response," 233; Greene, "Independence, Improvement, and Authority," 20–30; and Klein, *Unification*.

8. Henning, *Statutes*, 9:258; 10:315; 11:85–90; U.S. Bureau of the Census, *Century of Population Growth*, 207.

9. Henning, *Statutes*, 9:355–56; 10:23–27, 35–50, 431–32; Watlington, *Partisan Spirit*, 14–18.

10. Henning, *Statutes*, 10:50–65; JDS copy of letter from John Floyd to William Preston, 5 May 1780, DM 17 CC 124–26.

11. On the large and contentious question of the decline of political and social deference in eighteenth-century America, see Wiebe, *Opening*, 3–22; Wood, *Radicalism*, 243–86; Wood, "Interests"; Fliegelman, *Prodigals*; Shalhope, *Roots of Democracy*; Kloppenberg, "Virtues of Liberalism"; and Bailyn, *Ideological Origins*, 230–319.

12. Wood, *Radicalism*, 179–89; George Nicholas to James Madison, 5 September 1792, quoted in Coward, *Kentucky in the New Republic*, 10; Beeman, *Old Dominion*, 28–41. For the classic statement on deferential politics in colonial Virginia, see Sydnor, *Gentlemen Freeholders*. See also Isaac, *Transformation of Virginia*, 131–35; and Kulikoff, *Tobacco and Slaves*, 153–61. On the limits of gentry dominance in backcountry areas, see Beeman, "Deference"; Beeman, *Evolution*, 88–96; and Tillson, *Gentry and Common Folk*, 20–44.

13. Harrison, "A Virginian Moves to Kentucky," 203–4. The classic statement on the engrossment of western lands by gentry speculators is Abernethy, *Western Lands*. Recent quantitative studies have discovered that settlers and the speculators were not mutually exclusive groups. See Hammon, "Settlers, Land Jobbers, and Outlyers," 256; and Aron, "Pioneers and Profiteers."

14. JDS interview with John Hedge, ca. 1840s, DM 11 CC 19–21; JDS interview with [Martin] Wymore, ca. 1840s, DM 11 CC 130.

15. JDS interview with William Moseby, ca. 1840s, DM 11 CC 270–71.

16. On Kentucky's militia, see Stone, *Brittle Sword*, 1–39; and Talbert, *Benjamin Logan*. On the disjuncture between "tidy" militia law and "military reality," see Shy, *People Numerous and Armed*, 23–33. In 1784 Virginia passed a new omnibus militia law, which raised the age for military service to eighteen. Both the 1777 and 1784 laws provided exemptions to clergymen, state officers, etc. See Henning, *Statutes*, 11:476. On rates of pay for military service, see Cannon, "Kentucky's Active Militia"; and Harding, *Clark and His Men*.

17. Malone, *Skulking Way of War*, 117; Francis Jennings, *Invasion of America*, 146–70; William Whitley's Narrative, DM 9 CC 26; Henning, *Statutes*, 9:267.

18. JDS interview with John Hanks, ca. 1840s, DM 12 CC 141–42; Carmony, "Records' Memoir," 347–48; Francis Jennings, "Indians' Revolution," 343.

19. For differing explanations of political empowerment in the early Republic, see Nobles, *Divisions Throughout the Whole*; Shalhope, "Republicanism"; Appleby, "Liberalism"; Fischer, *Albion's Seed*, 772–74; and Elkins and McKitrick, "Meaning for Turner's Frontier."

20. Wade Hall, "Along the Wilderness Trail," 292; JDS copy of Levi Todd's Narrative, DM 15 CC 161; JDS interview with James Morris, ca. 1840s, DM 13 CC 202; JDS interview with Capt. Marcus Richardson, ca. 1840s, DM 12 CC 154–55.

21. JDS interview with John Hedge, ca. 1840s, DM 11 CC 23; JDS interview with William Niblick, ca. 1840s, DM 11 CC 85; JDS interview with William Moseby, ca. 1840s, DM 11 CC 270.

22. John Floyd to Joseph Martin, 19 May 1776, in Hammon and Harris, " 'In a

Dangerous Situation,'" 213–14; JDS interview with Richard French, ca. 1840s, DM 12 CC 210.

23. Keller, "What Is Distinctive," 78; JDS interview with Capt. George Stocton, ca. 1840s, DM 12 CC 231; JDS interview with Isaac Clinkenbeard, ca. 1840s, DM 11 CC 1.

24. JDS interview with Mrs. [Joice] Falconer, ca. 1840s, DM 11 CC 136; JDS interview with [a Woodford County informant], ca. 1840s, DM 11 CC 281.

25. JDS interview with [Martin] Wymore, ca. 1840s, DM 11 CC 131; JDS interview with William Risk, ca. 1840s, DM 11 CC 87. Testimony on the fluidity of land acquisition suggests that many of Kentucky's landless residents were either young men or new arrivals. Although it is beyond the scope of the present study, a sample of taxpayers followed through time would possibly reveal that the majority of early migrants either obtained property or moved on. Edward Pessen and Robert E. Gallman debated a similar issue on the effect of age on wealth distribution in the antebellum United States. See Gallman, "Professor Pessen"; and Pessen, "On a Recent Cliometric Attempt."

26. JDS interview with James Wade, ca. 1840s, DM 12 CC 14.

27. JDS interview with John Hanks, ca. 1840s, DM 12 CC 142–43. See also JDS interview with Col. Thomas Jones, ca. 1840s, DM 12 CC 232–34. On the pace and geographical settlement of eastern Kentucky, see Salstrom, "Agricultural Origins," 266.

28. JDS interview with John Hanks, ca. 1840s, DM 12 CC 142–43.

29. JDS interview with John Hanks, ca. 1840s, DM 12 CC 142–43; JDS interview with Col. Thomas Jones, ca. 1840s, DM 12 CC 234.

30. Lexington *Kentucky Gazette*, 15 March 1790; JDS interview with John Hanks, ca. 1840s, DM 12 CC 144.

31. JDS interview with John Rupard, [1843], DM 11 CC 101.

32. JDS interview with William Clinkenbeard, ca. 1840s, DM 11 CC 62; JDS interview with Col. John Graves, [ca. 1845], DM 11 CC 124; Wayne to Knox, 20 June 1793, quoted in Nelson, " 'Mad' Anthony Wayne," 4–6.

33. JDS interview with Josiah Collins, [1841], DM 12 CC 66; JDS interview with Joshua McQueen, ca. 1840s, DM 13 CC 117; JDS copy of "A Sketch of the Life of William Sudduth," November 1840, DM 12 CC 87; JDS interview with John Rupard, [1843], DM 11 CC 104; JDS interview with Maj. Herman Bowmar, ca. 1840s, DM 13 CC 171.

34. JDS interview with John Rupard, [1843], DM 11 CC 100–103.

35. On structures of rank and status in colonial Virginia and the meaning of "interest," see Isaac, *Transformation of Virginia*, 88–114, esp. 113.

36. Young, *Westward into Kentucky*, 70–71.

37. Ibid.

38. Ibid., 71–72.

39. JDS interview with Mrs. Gough, [1843], DM 11 CC 98; Collins, *Historical Sketches*, 244. On slave trickster tales, see Levine, *Black Culture*, 121–33.

40. JDS interview with Elijah Foley, ca. 1840s, DM 11 CC 134.

41. JDS interview with William Risk, ca. 1840s, DM 11 CC 87; JDS interview

with Maj. Jesse Daniel, [ca. 1843], DM 11 CC 93; JDS interview with William Risk, DM 11 CC 87. On Boone's land problems, see Bakeless, *Daniel Boone*, 340–50; and Faragher, "They May Say What They Please."

42. JDS interview with Cuthbert Combs, ca. 1840s, DM 11 CC 80.

43. Quoted by Eslinger, "Great Revival," 37; JDS interview with William Clinkenbeard, ca. 1840s, DM 11 CC 57–58; JDS interview with William Niblick, ca. 1840s, DM 11 CC 85. On terror of the wild, see Roderick Nash, *Wilderness and the American Mind*, 8–15.

44. Tuan, *Landscapes of Fear*, 6–19; JDS interview with Benjamin Allen, ca. 1840s, DM 11 CC 70, 77.

45. JDS interview with David Crouch, [ca. 1843], DM 12 CC 229; JDS interview with Mrs. Sarah Graham, ca. 1840s, DM 12 CC 48; JDS interview with Jacob Stevens, ca. 1840s, DM 12 CC 136; JDS interview with William Boyd, 1841, DM 12 CC 61.

46. On Indian hating and border warfare, see Horsman, *Race and Manifest Destiny*, 110–15.

47. JDS interview with [Martin] Wymore, ca. 1840s, DM 11 CC 130; JDS interview with Mrs. John Arnold, ca. 1840s, DM 11 CC 243; JDS interview with Benjamin Stites, 1842, DM 13 CC 61; JDS interview with Gen. [Thomas] Metcalfe, ca. 1850s, DM 11 CC 185; JDS interview with Benjamin Allen, ca. 1840s, DM 11 CC 78.

48. JDS interview with John Rankins, ca. 1840s, DM 11 CC 83.

49. JDS copy of a letter from John Floyd to [William Preston], 28 March 1783, DM 17 CC 144–45, 147.

50. Young, *Westward into Kentucky*, 136–37; JDS interview with Maj. Herman Bowmar, ca. 1840s, DM 13 CC 173. By 1789 Stucker was a captain in the Fayette County militia.

51. Collins, *Historical Sketches*, 551; William Whitley's Narrative, DM 9 CC 17–60; LCD interview with Mrs. Levisa McKinney, DM 9 CC 9; LCD interview with Solomon Clark, DM 9 CC 2; JDS interview with John Rupard, [1843], DM 11 CC 102.

52. Sahlins, "Poor Man, Rich Man," 289.

53. Howard, *Shawnee!*, 106–8; Calloway, *American Revolution in Indian Country*, 59–60.

54. JDS interview with William McBride, ca. 1840s, DM 11 CC 262. For a recent sketch of frontier slavery conditions, see Eslinger, "Shape of Slavery."

55. Levine, *Black Culture*, 300; Young, *Westward into Kentucky*, 136.

56. JDS interview with Benjamin Allen, ca. 1840s, DM 11 CC 77; JDS interview with —— Stevenson, ca. 1840s, DM 11 CC 51.

57. JDS interview with William Clinkenbeard, ca. 1840s, DM 11 CC 58; JDS interview with Capt. George Stocton, ca. 1840s, DM 12 CC 231; JDS interview with John Gass, [1843], DM 11 CC 13; JDS copy of the Record Book of New Providence Church, DM 14 CC 120.

58. JDS interview with Mrs. Samuel Scott, ca. 1840s, DM 11 CC 225–26.

59. On assertive western women, see Faragher, "History from the Inside-Out,"

555–56; Limerick, *Legacy of Conquest*, 48–54; Deutsch, *No Separate Refuge*; Jensen and Miller, "Gentle Tamers Revisited"; and Faragher, *Women and Men on the Overland Trail*. On the sanction of moral coercion, see Radcliffe-Brown, "Preface," xv–xvi.

60. Carmony, "Records' Memoir," 357; JDS interview with Capt. Nathaniel Hart [Jr.], [ca. 1843], DM 17 CC 207.

61. JDS interview with Mrs. Sarah Graham, ca. 1840s, DM 12 CC 51–52; JDS interview with [Martin] Wymore, ca. 1840s, DM 11 CC 130; William Whitley's Narrative, DM 9 CC 36.

62. JDS interview with William McBride, ca. 1840s, DM 11 CC 262; LCD interview with Levisa McKinney, DM 9 CC 11–12. On gender and ritual power in Indian culture, see Dowd, *Spirited Resistance*, 4–10.

63. The phrase "notorious prostitute" comes from JDS interview with Capt. Nathaniel Hart [Jr.], [ca. 1843], DM 17 CC 195. In the 1940s, a published transcription of this interview omitted without comment Hart's derogatory reference to Boone's daughter. See [Shane], "Henderson Company Ledger," 30.

64. JDS interview with Jeptha Kemper, ca. 1840s, DM 12 CC 132; JDS interview with Col. Thomas Hart, ca. 1840s, DM 11 CC 79; Ireland, *County Courts*, 14; JDS interview with William McClelland, ca. 1850s, DM 11 CC 184; Abernethy, *Three Virginia Frontiers*, 90.

65. Soltow, "Kentucky Wealth," 633; JDS interview with Joshua McQueen, ca. 1840s, DM 13 CC 119; JDS interview with John Hedge, ca. 1840s, DM 11 CC 19.

66. JDS interview with —— Hardesty, ca. 1840s, DM 11 CC 171; Drake, *Pioneer Life*, 179–81, 206. U.S. Bureau of the Census, *Seventh Census: 1850*, xxxvi.

67. Coward, *Kentucky in the New Republic*, 14–26; Eslinger, "The Great Revival," 165–67; Marshall, *History of Kentucky*, 1:197–98.

68. Logan actually lost two elections for governor, the first time in 1796 when he lost in the electoral college on the second ballot to James Garrard. Garrard, a Baptist minister, had come to Kentucky later than Logan and was better educated. Logan prospered economically in Kentucky, owning 6,000 acres at the time of the election; yet Garrard had done much better—acquiring 38,000 acres. See Talbert, *Benjamin Logan*, 284–98.

69. Collins, *Historical Sketches*, 485.

70. Mallory, *Life and Speeches of Clay*, 1:18–19.

71. Ibid., 1:255. On militancy and personal honor in Kentucky and the South, see Klotter, "Feuds in Appalachia"; Gorn, " 'Gouge and Bite' "; Franklin, *Militant South*; and Wyatt-Brown, *Southern Honor*.

CHAPTER FIVE

1. *Louisville News-Letter*, 23 May 1840, JDS scrapbook, DM 26 CC 72–74.

2. *Louisville Journal*, 2 May 1841, JDS scrapbook, DM 26 CC 20; Morehead, *Address*, 29; unattributed newspaper clipping, 26 May 1841, JDS scrapbook, DM 26 CC 14.

3. *Louisville News-Letter*, 23 May 1840, JDS scrapbook, DM 26 CC 72; JDS interview with Septimus Schull, c. 1841, DM 11 CC 53.

4. Hayden White, *Metahistory*, 51; JDS interview with Richard French, ca. 1840s, DM 12 CC 201, 204, 206. Draper is mistaken on one point: French's mother, Keziah, was the younger sister of the two captured Callaway girls. The phrase "what actually happened" comes from the "father" of modern objective history, Leopold von Ranke in *History of the Latin and Germanic Nations from 1494 to 1514* (1824), quoted in Wilcox, *Measure of Times Past*, 18. Historical works cited in Draper's letter include: Marshall, *History of Kentucky*; Flint, *Indian Wars*; Mann Butler, *History of the Commonwealth*; and McClung, *Sketches of Western Adventure*.

5. On concepts of time, see Whitrow, *Time in History*; Fraser, *Time, the Familiar Stranger*; Wilcox, *Measure of Times Past*; Carr, *Time, Narrative, and History*; and Glassie, *Passing the Time in Ballymenone*.

6. Whitrow, *Time in History*, 128–29; Wilcox, *Measure of Times Past*, 22–23.

7. Staples, *History of Pioneer Lexington*, 97; Watlington, *Partisan Spirit*, 69; Rohrbough, *Trans-Appalachian Frontier*, 399.

8. In the margin of Richard French's interview, for example, Shane wrote: "Calloway & Boon girls." Draper added: "July 1776." See DM 12 CC 204.

9. Whitrow, *Time in History*, 21–24.

10. JDS interview with Mrs. John Arnold, ca. 1840s, DM 11 CC 242; JDS interview with Col. Thomas Jones, ca. 1840s, DM 12 CC 232; JDS interview with Mrs. Shanklin, ca. 1840s, DM 11 CC 219.

11. JDS interview with [a Fayette County woman], ca. 1840s, DM 11 CC 177; JDS interview with Jane Stevenson, ca. 1840s, DM 13 CC 137; JDS interview with John Rankins, ca. 1840s, DM 11 CC 83.

12. JDS interview with Benjamin Allen, ca. 1840s, DM 11 CC 68; JDS interview with Samuel Potts Pointer, ca. 1840s, DM 12 CC 247; JDS interview with Mrs. Shanklin, ca. 1840s, DM 11 CC 217. New Year's, of course, was not a "holy day" in the traditional sense. Scottish Puritans, who regarded Christmas as a pagan rite, continued to celebrate New Year's Day after Charles II restored Christmas festivities in 1660. On shifting beliefs associated with this season, see Nissenbaum, *Battle for Christmas*.

13. *Virginia Gazette, and Petersburg Intelligencer*, 21 June 1796; JDS interview with Isaac Clinkenbeard, ca. 1840s, DM 11 CC 1; JDS interview with David Crouch, [ca. 1843], DM 12 CC 229; JDS interview with James McConnell, ca. 1840s, DM 11 CC 146.

14. Wallace, *Death and Rebirth of the Seneca*, 50–51; JDS interview with James Wade, ca. 1840s, DM 12 CC 21; JDS interview with Major Black, ca. 1840s, DM 12 CC 151; JDS interview with Benjamin Allen, ca. 1840s, DM 11 CC 76; JDS interview with John Rankins, ca. 1840s, DM 11 CC 83; JDS interview with [a Woodford County informant], ca. 1840s, DM 11 CC 281; JDS interview with Col. Thomas Jones, ca. 1840s, DM 13 CC 177; JDS interview with Josiah Collins, [1841], DM 12 CC 68.

15. JDS interview with John Gass, [1843], DM 11 CC 15; JDS interview with George Fearis, ca. 1840s, DM 13 CC 238–39; JDS interview with Levi Buck-

ingham, ca. 1840s, DM 13 CC 90; JDS interview with William Tyler, ca. 1840s, DM 11 CC 128; JDS interview with John Rupard, [1843], DM 11 CC 104.

16. JDS interview with John Gass, [1843], DM 11 CC 14; JDS interview with Daniel Kain, ca. 1850s, DM 14 CC 10; JDS interview with Mrs. Hinds, ca. 1840s, DM 11 CC 5; JDS interview with William Clinkenbeard, ca. 1840s, DM 11 CC 57; JDS interview with Jane Stevenson, ca. 1840s, DM 13 CC 139.

17. JDS interview with Mrs. John Arnold, ca. 1840s, DM 11 CC 241; JDS interview with Jane Stevenson, ca. 1840s, DM 13 CC 139; JDS interview with William Tyler, ca. 1840s, DM 11 CC 128. Tyler probably means here that he did not receive pay for guard duty, although other settlers reported receiving tax certificates for similar service; regular militia service, including participation in expeditionary forces, was paid.

18. Tanner, *Atlas*, 71–73; William Whitley's Narrative, DM 9 CC 34–35.

19. On the origins of linear time, see Wilcox, *Measure of Times Past*, 83–118; Whitrow, *Time in History*, 29–51.

20. Evarts Greene and Virginia Harrington, *American Population*, 192; JDS interview with John Hanks, ca. 1840s, DM 12 CC 138.

21. JDS interview with John Gass, [1843], DM 11 CC 11; JDS interview with Jane Stevenson, ca. 1840s, DM 13 CC 137; JDS interview with Joshua McQueen, ca. 1840s, DM 13 CC 115; JDS interview with William Niblick, ca. 1840s, DM 11 CC 84; JDS interview with John Dyal, ca. 1840s, DM 13 CC 226; JDS interview with William Moseby, ca. 1840s, DM 11 CC 270; JDS interview with Daniel Deron, ca. 1840s, DM 12 CC 239; JDS interview with Robert Jones, ca. 1840s, DM 13 CC 165; JDS interview with Samuel Graham, ca. 1840s, DM 11 CC 297.
At the Battle of Point Pleasant, October 1774, about 900 Shawnee and Indian allies attacked 1,200 Virginia militiamen fortified at the mouth of the Kanawha River. The "sham treaty at Boonesborough" refers to negotiations during the siege of Boonesborough, September 1778.

22. JDS interview with Mrs. Sarah Graham, ca. 1840s, DM 12 CC 47; JDS interview with [a Woodford County informant], ca. 1840s, DM 11 CC 280; JDS interview with Robert Gwynn, [1842], DM 11 CC 216; JDS interview with Mr. and Mrs. Darnaby, ca. 1840s, DM 11 CC 166; JDS interview with John Rankins, ca. 1840s, DM 11 CC 81; JDS interview with William Clinkenbeard, ca. 1840s, DM 11 CC 59; JDS interview with Isaac Clinkenbeard, ca. 1840s, DM 11 CC 3. Under Virginia law, a man who had settled (i.e., made some improvement such as building a cabin or raising a crop of corn) in Kentucky before 1 January 1778 could claim the 400 acres on which he lived, often called a "corn-right" farm. Isaac Clinkenbeard, who arrived in the fall of 1779, was too late for this offer; he purchased his claim from Benjamin Dunnoway.

23. JDS interview with Samuel Potts Pointer, ca. 1840s, DM 12 CC 247; JDS interview with Capt. John Wilson, 1855, DM 17 CC 7–10, 19.

24. JDS interview with —— Spence, ca. 1840s, DM 13 CC 188.

25. Drake, *Pioneer Life*, 174–75.

26. Henning, *Statutes*, 10:40; JDS interview with Major Bean, ca. 1840s, DM 11 CC 105; JDS interview with James Hedge, ca. 1840s, DM 12 CC 117–18.

27. Staples, *History of Pioneer Lexington*, 26, 77; Benjamin Wood to Joseph Lawrence, 27 June 1792, photocopy, 69M6, Wood Family Collection.

28. JDS interview with Major Bean, ca. 1840s, DM 11 CC 105; JDS interview with [a Woodford County informant], ca. 1840s, DM 11 CC 283; JDS interview with Elijah Foley, ca. 1840s, DM 11 CC 135; JDS interview with James Stevenson, ca. 1840s, DM 11 CC 250–51.

29. JDS interview with James Hedge, ca. 1840s, DM 12 CC 118; JDS interview with Jesse Graddy, ca. 1840s, DM 13 CC 130–31.

30. JDS interview with Col. William Sudduth, [ca. 1841], DM 12 CC 62; Staples, *History of Pioneer Lexington*, 80; JDS interview with Caleb Williams, 1855, DM 11 CC 194; JDS interview with Jeptha Kemper, ca. 1840s, DM 12 CC 130; JDS interview with Mrs. Sarah Graham, ca. 1840s, DM 12 CC 47.

31. For a provocative exploration of how members of another American community came to understand their place in time, see Breen, *Imagining the Past*.

32. JDS copy of letter from John Floyd to [William Preston], 19 January 1780, DM 17 CC 120.

33. JDS interview with Mrs. [Joice] Falconer, ca. 1840s, DM 11 CC 136; JDS interview with William Clinkenbeard, ca. 1840s, DM 11 CC 60; Bentley, "Letter from Harrodsburg," 370–71.

34. Collins, *Historical Sketches*, 456. This account is a good example of the paraphrasing (or even outright plagiarism) that characterized history writing at this time. For his account of the "hard winter," Collins is quoting Davidson's *History of the Presbyterian Church in Kentucky*. Davidson, in turn, is quoting (with his own rhetorical flourishes) Robert McAfee's transcription of the Record Book of the New Providence Church. See JDS copy of the same, DM 14 CC 115–16.

35. On the attack at Strode's, see JDS interview with Daniel Spohr, ca. 1840s, DM 11 CC 107–10. On Scott's death, see JDS interview with William Moseby, ca. 1840s, DM 11 CC 270–74; JDS interview with William Tillery, ca. 1840s, DM 11 CC 274–75.

36. JDS interview with Mrs. Ephraim January, ca. 1840s, DM 11 CC 223.

37. JDS interview with Chilton Allen, ca. 1840s, DM 11 CC 53; JDS interview with Mrs. Sarah Graham, ca. 1840s, DM 12 CC 45; JDS interview with Maj. Jesse Daniel, [ca. 1843], DM 11 CC 92; JDS interview with Jeptha Kemper, ca. 1840s, DM 12 CC 133; JDS interview with John Hedge, ca. 1840s, DM 11 CC 22; JDS interview with Caleb Williams, 1855, DM 11 CC 192.

38. McClung, *Sketches of Western Adventure*, viii. For the first complete reprinting of Bradford's "Notes," see Thomas Clark, *Voice of the Frontier*.

39. Carmony, "Records' Memoir," 325.

40. JDS copy of the Frankfort *Commonwealth*, June 20, 1835, DM 17 CC 176; Drake, *Pioneer Life*, 23, 209–12.

41. JDS interview with Ephraim Sowdusky, ca. 1840s, DM 11 CC 141–45.

42. JDS interview with James McIlvaine, ca. 1840s, DM 12 CC 58; JDS interview with [a Woodford County informant], ca. 1840s, DM 11 CC 284; JDS interview with Richard French, ca. 1840s, DM 12 CC 203.

43. JDS interview with Marcus Richardson, ca. 1840s, DM 12 CC 127; JDS interview with Richard French, ca. 1840s, DM 12 CC 203–5.

44. JDS interview with Alexander Hamilton, ca. 1840s, DM 11 CC 293. On Kentuckians as Indian haters, see Horsman, *Race and Manifest Destiny*, 110–11.

45. Linenthal, *Sacred Ground*; JDS interview with William Risk, ca. 1840s, DM 11 CC 88; JDS interview with Fielding Belt, ca. 1840s, DM 12 CC 245.

46. JDS interview with Cuthbert Combs, ca. 1840s, DM 11 CC 80; JDS interview with Maj. Jesse Daniel, [ca. 1843], DM 11 CC 92.

47. On the imperatives of national history, see Appleby, Hunt, and Jacob, *Telling the Truth about History*, 91–125.

48. JDS memorandum, n.d., DM 12 CC 194; JDS memorandum, n.d., DM 11 CC 53.

49. JDS memorandum, n.d., DM 11 CC 233–34; JDS memorandum, n.d., DM 11 CC 119–20; JDS memorandum, n.d., DM 12 CC 191–92.

50. JDS memorandum, n.d., DM 12 CC 194–95.

51. See, for example, Davis, "Who Owns History?"; Appleby, Hunt, and Jacob, *Telling the Truth about History*; and Englehart and Linenthal, *History Wars*.

APPENDIX A

1. For further information on Draper's purchase of Shane's materials, see Hesseltine and Gara, "Draper and the Shane Papers."

2. On their discovery, see Foley, "More Notes on the West," 111–13.

3. Hall, *Shane Manuscript Collection*, 99–100. Researchers using the microfilm edition of the PHS Shane Collection (filmed by the Genealogical Society of Utah several decades ago) should note that the collection has been reprocessed, and thus carries a new citation system. With the exception of volume 17, my references are to the paper archives as currently arranged at the PHS.

4. For chronological and descriptive guides to the Shane Papers housed within the Draper Manuscripts, see Weaks, *Calendar of the Kentucky Papers*; and Harper, *Guide to the Draper Manuscripts*.

Bibliography

MANUSCRIPT COLLECTIONS

Chicago, Illinois
University of Chicago Library, Department of Special Collections
   Reuben T. Durrett Collection
      J. Hector St. John Crèvecoeur, "Sketch of the River Ohio," Codex 52
      Pictures, Maps, and Sketches

Cincinnati, Ohio
Cincinnati Historical Society
   John Day Caldwell Papers

Frankfort, Kentucky
Kentucky Historical Society
   Map Collection
   Shane Biographical File

Lexington, Kentucky
University of Kentucky, Margaret I. King Library
   Division of Special Collections and Archives
      Wood Family Collection

Louisville, Kentucky
The Filson Club Historical Society
   Enoch Smith Survey Book

Madison, Wisconsin
State Historical Society of Wisconsin
   Lyman C. Draper Manuscript Collection (microfilm edition, 1980)
      Kentucky Papers
      Miscellaneous Draper Correspondence

Philadelphia, Pennsylvania
Presbyterian Historical Society

Biographical Files
John Dabney Shane Collection

Washington, D.C.
Library of Congress
Geography and Maps Division

OTHER WORKS

Abernethy, Thomas Perkins. *Western Lands and the American Revolution.* New York: D. Appleton-Century Co., 1937.

——. *Three Virginia Frontiers.* Baton Rouge: Louisiana State University Press, 1940.

Akenson, Donald H. "Why the Accepted Estimates of the Ethnicity of the American People, 1790, Are Unacceptable." *William and Mary Quarterly* 41 (January 1984): 102–19.

Allen, David Grayson. *In English Ways: The Movement of Societies and the Transferal of English Local Law and Custom to Massachusetts Bay in the Seventeenth Century.* Chapel Hill: University of North Carolina Press, 1981.

Anderson, Virginia DeJohn. "King Philip's Herds: Indians, Colonists, and the Problem of Livestock in Early New England." *William and Mary Quarterly* 51 (October 1994): 601–24.

Appleby, Joyce. "Liberalism and the American Revolution." *New England Quarterly* 49 (March 1976): 3–26.

Appleby, Joyce, Lynn Hunt, and Margaret Jacob. *Telling the Truth about History.* New York: W. W. Norton, 1994.

Aron, Stephen. "Pioneers and Profiteers: Land Speculators and the Homestead Ethic in Frontier Kentucky." *Western Historical Quarterly* 23 (May 1992): 179–98.

——. "The Significance of the Kentucky Frontier." *Register of the Kentucky Historical Society* 91 (Summer 1993): 298–323.

——. *How the West Was Lost: The Transformation of Kentucky from Daniel Boone to Henry Clay.* Baltimore, Md.: Johns Hopkins University Press, 1996.

Austin, Moses. " 'A Memorandum of M. Austin's Journey from the Lead Mines in the County of Wythe in the State of Virginia to the Lead Mines in the Province of Louisiana West of the Mississippi,' 1796–1797." *American Historical Review* 5 (April 1900): 518–42.

Bailey, F. G., ed. *Gifts and Poison: The Politics of Reputation.* Oxford: Oxford University Press, 1971.

Bailyn, Bernard. *The Ideological Origins of the American Revolution.* Cambridge: Harvard University Press, 1967.

——. *The Peopling of British North America: An Introduction.* New York: Vintage Books, 1986.

Bakeless, John. *Daniel Boone: Master of the Wilderness.* 1939. Reprint. Lincoln: University of Nebraska Press, 1989.

Banta, Richard E. "Daniel Ketcham with the Tawas: A Kentucky Captivity." *Filson Club History Quarterly* 22 (July 1948): 173–79.

Barnhart, John D. *Valley of Democracy: The Frontier versus the Plantation in the Ohio Valley, 1775–1818.* Lincoln: University of Nebraska Press, 1953.

Barsalou, Lawrence W. "The Content and Organization of Autobiographical Memories." In *Remembering Reconsidered: Ecological and Traditional Approaches to the Study of Memory,* edited by Ulric Neisser and Eugene Winograd, 193–243. Cambridge: Cambridge University Press, 1988.

Barth, Fredrik, ed. *Ethnic Groups and Boundaries: The Social Organization of Culture Difference.* London: George Allen and Unwin, 1969.

Beeman, Richard R. *The Old Dominion and the New Nation, 1788–1801.* Lexington: University Press of Kentucky, 1972.

——. *The Evolution of the Southern Backcountry: A Case Study of Lunenberg County, Virginia, 1746–1832.* Philadelphia: University of Pennsylvania Press, 1984.

——. "The Political Response to Social Conflict in the Southern Backcountry: A Comparative View of Virginia and the Carolinas during the Revolution." In *An Uncivil War: The Southern Backcountry during the American Revolution,* edited by Ronald Hoffman, Thad W. Tate, and Peter J. Albert, 213–39. Charlottesville: University Press of Virginia, 1985.

——. "Deference, Republicanism, and the Emergence of Popular Politics in Eighteenth-Century America." *William and Mary Quarterly* 49 (July 1992): 401–30.

Bellesiles, Michael A. "The Establishment of Legal Structures on the Frontier: The Case of Revolutionary Vermont." *Journal of American History* 73 (March 1987): 895–915.

Bentley, James R., ed. "Letters of Thomas Perkins to Gen. Joseph Palmer, Lincoln County, Kentucky, 1785." *Filson Club History Quarterly* 49 (April 1975): 141–51.

——, ed. "A Letter from Harrodsburg, 1780." *Filson Club History Quarterly* 50 (October 1976): 369–71.

Blair, John L. "Mrs. Mary Dewees's Journal from Philadelphia to Kentucky." *Register of the Kentucky Historical Society* 63 (July 1965): 195–217.

Blau, Peter M. *Exchange and Power in Social Life.* New Brunswick, N.J.: Transaction Publishers, 1989.

Bliss, Willard F. "The Tuckahoe in New Virginia." *Virginia Magazine of History and Biography* 59 (October 1951): 387–96.

Blumin, Stuart M. *The Emergence of the Middle Class: Social Experience in the American City, 1760–1900.* Cambridge: Cambridge University Press, 1989.

Boisvert, Richard A. *Kentucky Salt Licks: A Preservation Planning Perspective.* Lexington, Ky.: Office of State Archaeology, 1984.

Boles, John B. *Religion in Antebellum Kentucky.* Lexington: University Press of Kentucky, 1976.

Breen, T. H. "Persistent Localism: English Social Change and the Shaping of New England Institutions." *William and Mary Quarterly* 32 (January 1975): 3–28.

———. "Creative Adaptations: Peoples and Cultures." In *Colonial British America: Essays in the New History of the Early Modern Era*, edited by Jack P. Greene and J. R. Pole, 195–232. Baltimore, Md.: Johns Hopkins University Press, 1984.

———. *Tobacco Culture: The Mentality of the Great Planters on the Eve of Revolution.* Princeton, N.J.: Princeton University Press, 1985.

———. " 'Baubles of Britain': The American and Consumer Revolutions of the Eighteenth Century." *Past and Present* 119 (May 1988): 73–104.

———. *Imagining the Past: East Hampton Histories.* Reading, Mass.: Addison-Wesley Publishing Co., 1989.

Brewer, William F. "Memory for Randomly Sampled Autobiographical Events." In *Remembering Reconsidered: Ecological and Traditional Approaches to the Study of Memory*, edited by Ulric Neisser and Eugene Winograd, 21–90. Cambridge: Cambridge University Press, 1988.

Brooke, John L. "To the Quiet of the People: Revolutionary Settlements and Civil Unrest in Western Massachusetts, 1774–1789." *William and Mary Quarterly* 46 (July 1989): 425–62.

Brown, Richard D. *Knowledge Is Power: The Diffusion of Information in Early America, 1700–1865.* New York: Oxford University Press, 1989.

Bushman, Richard L. *The Refinement of America: Persons, Houses, Cities.* New York: Alfred A. Knopf, 1992.

Butler, Lawrence. "Letters from Lawrence Butler, of Westmoreland County, Virginia, to Mrs. Anna F. Craddock, Cumley House, Near Harborough, Leicestershire, England." *Virginia Magazine of History and Biography* 40 (October 1932): 362–70.

Butler, Mann. *A History of the Commonwealth of Kentucky.* Louisville, Ky.: Wilcox, Dickerman, and Co., 1834.

Calloway, Colin G. *The World Turned Upside Down: Indian Voices from Early America.* Boston: St. Martin's Press, 1994.

———. *The American Revolution in Indian Country: Crisis and Diversity in Native American Communities.* New York: Cambridge University Press, 1995.

Campbell, Julian James Noel. "Present and Presettlement Forest Conditions in the Inner Bluegrass of Kentucky." Ph.D. diss., University of Kentucky, 1980.

Cannon, Mrs. Jouett Taylor, ed. "Kentucky's Active Militia—1786." *Register of the Kentucky Historical Society* 32 (July 1934): 224–43.

Carmony, Donald F., ed. "Spencer Records' Memoir of the Ohio Valley Frontier, 1766–1795." *Indiana Magazine of History* 55 (December 1959): 323–77.

Carr, David. *Time, Narrative, and History.* Bloomington: Indiana University Press, 1986.

Carter, Paul. *The Road to Botany Bay: An Exploration of Landscape and History.* Chicago: University of Chicago Press, 1987.

Cayton, Andrew R. L. *The Frontier Republic: Ideology and Politics in the Ohio Country, 1780–1825.* Kent, Oh.: Kent State University Press, 1986.

———. "Land, Power, and Reputation: The Cultural Dimension of Politics in the Ohio Country." *William and Mary Quarterly* 47 (April 1990): 266–86.

———. "Marietta and the Ohio Company." In *Appalachian Frontiers: Settlement,*

Society, and Development in the Preindustrial Era, edited by Robert D. Mitchell, 187–200. Lexington: University Press of Kentucky, 1991.

——. " 'Separate Interests' and the Nation-State: The Washington Administration and the Origins of Regionalism in the Trans-Appalachian West." *Journal of American History* 79 (June 1992): 39–67.

Channing, Steven A. *Kentucky: A Bicentennial History*. New York: W. W. Norton, 1977.

Clark, Jerry E. *The Shawnee*. Lexington: University Press of Kentucky, 1977.

Clark, Thomas D. *A History of Kentucky*. Lexington, Ky.: John Bradford Press, 1960.

——. *Historic Maps of Kentucky*. Lexington: University Press of Kentucky, 1979.

——, ed. *The Voice of the Frontier: John Bradford's Notes on Kentucky*. Lexington: University Press of Kentucky, 1993.

Clifford, James. *The Predicament of Culture: Twentieth-Century Ethnography, Literature, and Art*. Cambridge: Harvard University Press, 1988.

Clifford, James, and George E. Marcus, eds. *Writing Culture: The Poetics and Politics of Ethnography*. Berkeley: University of California Press, 1986.

Clift, G. Glenn. *"Second Census" of Kentucky: 1800*. Baltimore, Md.: Genealogical Publishing Company, 1970.

Cohen, Abner. "Political Anthropology: The Analysis of the Symbolism of Power Relations." *Man* 4 (June 1969): 215–35.

Cohen, Anthony P. *The Symbolic Construction of Community*. New York: Tavistock Publishers, 1985.

Coleman, J. Winston, Jr. *A Bibliography of Kentucky History*. Lexington: University Press of Kentucky, 1949.

Collins, Lewis. *Historical Sketches of Kentucky*. 1847. Reprint. Lexington: Henry Clay Press, 1968.

Conkin, Paul K. *Cane Ridge: America's Pentecost*. Madison: University of Wisconsin Press, 1990.

Conroy, David W. *In Public Houses: Drink & the Revolution of Authority in Colonial Massachusetts*. Chapel Hill: University of North Carolina Press, 1995.

Coward, Joan Wells. *Kentucky in the New Republic: The Process of Constitution Making*. Lexington: University Press of Kentucky, 1979.

Creswell, Nicholas. *The Journal of Nicholas Cresswell, 1774–1777*. London: Jonathan Cape, 1925.

Crèvecoeur, J. Hector St. John. *Letters from an American Farmer*. 1782. Reprint. London: J. M. Dent and Sons, 1971.

Cronon, William. *Changes in the Land: Indians, Colonists, and the Ecology of New England*. New York: Hill and Wang, 1983.

Cronon, William, George Miles, and Jay Gitlin, eds., *Under an Open Sky: Rethinking America's Western Past*. New York: W. W. Norton, 1992.

Crosby, Alfred W. *Ecological Imperialism: The Biological Expansion of Europe, 900–1900*. Cambridge: Cambridge University Press, 1986.

Davidson, Robert. *History of the Presbyterian Church in the State of Kentucky....* New York: Robert Carter, 1847.

Davis, Charles T., and Henry Louis Gates, Jr. *The Slave's Narrative*. Oxford: Oxford University Press, 1985.

Davis, Natalie Zemon. *Fiction in the Archives: Pardon Tales and Their Tellers in Sixteenth-Century France*. Stanford, Calif.: Stanford University Press, 1987.

———. "Who Owns History? History in the Profession." *Perspectives* 34 (November 1996): 1–6.

Demos, John. *The Unredeemed Captive: A Family Story from Early America*. New York: Alfred A. Knopf, 1994.

Deutsch, Sarah. *No Separate Refuge: Culture, Class, and Gender on an Anglo-Hispanic Frontier in the American Southwest, 1880–1940*. New York: Oxford University Press, 1987.

Dicken-Garcia, Hazel. *To Western Woods: The Breckinridge Family Moves to Kentucky in 1793*. Rutherford, N.J.: Fairleigh Dickinson University Press, 1991.

Doddridge, Joseph. *Notes on the Settlement and Indian Wars of the Western Parts of Virginia and Pennsylvania, from the Year 1763 until the Year 1783 Inclusive*. Wellsburgh, Va.: Office of the Gazette, 1824.

Douglas, Mary, and Baron Isherwood. *The World of Goods: Towards an Anthropology of Consumption*. New York: W. W. Norton, 1979.

Dowd, Gregory Evans. *A Spirited Resistance: The North American Indian Struggle for Unity, 1745–1815*. Baltimore, Md.: Johns Hopkins University Press, 1992.

Downes, Randolph C. "Dunmore's War: An Interpretation." *Mississippi Valley Historical Review* 21 (December 1934): 311–30.

Downs, Roger M. "Cognitive Mapping: A Thematic Analysis." In *Behavioral Problems in Geography Revisited*, edited by Kevin R. Cox and Reginald G. Golledge, 95–122. New York: Meuthen and Co., 1981.

Drake, Daniel. *Pioneer Life in Kentucky*. Cincinnati: Robert Clarke, 1870.

Durrett, Reuben T. *John Filson: The First Historian of Kentucky*. Louisville, Ky.: John P. Morton, 1884.

———. *Traditions of the Earliest Visits of Foreigners to North America: The First Formed and First Inhabited of the Continents*. Louisville, Ky.: John P. Morton, 1908.

Edgar, Matilda, ed. *Ten Years of Upper Canada in Peace and War, 1805–1815: Being the Ridout Letters*. Toronto: William Briggs, 1890.

Edmunds, R. David. "Native Americans, New Voices: American Indian History, 1895–1995." *American Historical Review* 100 (June 1995): 717–40.

Elkins, Stanley, and Eric McKitrick. "A Meaning for Turner's Frontier." *Political Science Quarterly* 69 (September–December 1954): 321–53, 565–602.

Escott, Paul D. *Slavery Remembered: A Record of Twentieth-Century Slave Narratives*. Chapel Hill: University of North Carolina Press, 1979.

Eslinger, Ellen T. "The Great Revival in Bourbon County, Kentucky." Ph.D. diss., University of Chicago, 1988.

———. "Migration and Kinship on the Trans-Appalachian Frontier: Strode's Station, Kentucky." *Filson Club History Quarterly* 62 (January 1988): 52–66.

———. "The Shape of Slavery on the Kentucky Frontier, 1775–1800." *Register of the Kentucky Historical Society* 92 (Winter 1994): 1–23.

Faragher, John Mack. *Women and Men on the Overland Trail.* New Haven, Conn.: Yale University Press, 1979.

———. "History from the Inside-Out: Writing the History of Women in Rural America." *American Quarterly* 33 (Winter 1981): 537–57.

———. *Sugar Creek: Life on the Illinois Prairie.* New Haven, Conn.: Yale University Press, 1986.

———. "They May Say What They Please: Daniel Boone and the Evidence." *Register of the Kentucky Historical Society* 88 (Autumn 1990): 373–93.

———. "Americans, Mexicans, Métis: A Community Approach to the Comparative Study of North American Frontiers." In *Under an Open Sky: Rethinking America's Western Past,* edited by William Cronon, George Miles, and Jay Gitlin, 90–109. New York: W. W. Norton, 1992.

———. *Daniel Boone: The Life and Legend of an American Pioneer.* New York: Henry Holt, 1992.

Ferling, John E. *A Wilderness of Miseries: War and Warriors in Early America.* Westport, Conn.: Greenwood Press, 1980.

Fields, Barbara J. "Ideology and Race in American History." In *Region, Race, and Reconstruction: Essays in Honor of C. Vann Woodward,* edited by J. Morgan Kousser and James McPherson, 143–77. New York: Oxford University Press, 1982.

Filson, John. *The Discovery, Settlement, and Present State of Kentucke. . . .* Wilmington, Del.: James Adams, 1784.

Fischer, David Hackett. *Albion's Seed: Four British Folkways in America.* New York: Oxford University Press, 1989.

Fliegelman, Jay. *Prodigals and Pilgrims: The American Revolution against Patriarchal Authority, 1750–1800.* Cambridge: Cambridge University Press, 1982.

Flint, Timothy. *Indian Wars of the West: Containing Biographical Sketches of Those Pioneers Who Headed the Western Settlers in Repelling the Attacks of the Savages.* Cincinnati: E. H. Flint, 1833.

Foley, Mary Peers. "More Notes on the West by the Rev. Shane." *Register of the Kentucky Historical Society* 52 (April 1954): 111–13.

Fortes, M., and E. E. Evans-Pritchard. *African Political Systems.* London: Oxford University Press, 1969.

Foucault, Michel. *The History of Sexuality: An Introduction.* New York: Vintage Books, 1978.

———. *Power/Knowledge: Selected Interviews and Other Writings, 1972–1977.* New York: Pantheon Books, 1980.

Franklin, John Hope. *The Militant South, 1800–1861.* Cambridge: Harvard University Press, 1956.

Fraser, J. T. *Time, the Familiar Stranger.* Amherst: University of Massachusetts Press, 1987.

Friend, Craig Thompson. "Inheriting Eden: The Creation of Society and Community in Early Kentucky, 1792–1812." Ph.D. diss., University of Kentucky, 1995.

Frish, Michael. *A Shared Authority: Essays on the Craft and Meaning of Oral and Public History.* Albany: State University of New York Press, 1990.

Gallman, Robert E. "Professor Pessen on the 'Egalitarian Myth.'" *Social Science History* 2 (Winter 1978): 194–207.

Garcia, Hazel Dicken. "'A Great Deal of Money . . .': Notes on Kentucky Costs, 1786–1792." *Register of the Kentucky Historical Society* 77 (Summer 1979): 186–200.

Garcia, Hazel Faye. "Communication in the Migration to Kentucky, 1769–1792." Ph.D. diss., University of Wisconsin-Madison, 1977.

Geertz, Clifford. *Local Knowledge: Further Essays in Interpretive Anthropology.* New York: Basic Books, 1983.

Giddens, Anthony. *Central Problems in Social Theory: Action, Structure, and Contradictions in Social Analysis.* Berkeley: University of California Press, 1979.

Gilmore, William J. *Reading Becomes a Necessity of Life: Material and Cultural Life in Rural New England, 1780–1835.* Knoxville: University of Tennessee Press, 1989.

Ginzburg, Carlo. *Clues, Myths, and the Historical Method.* Baltimore, Md.: Johns Hopkins University Press, 1986.

Glassie, Henry. *Pattern in the Material Folk Culture of the Eastern United States.* Philadelphia: University of Pennsylvania Press, 1968.

——. *Passing the Time in Ballymenone: Culture and History of an Ulster Community.* Philadelphia: University of Pennsylvania Press, 1982.

Gorn, Elliot J. "'Gouge and Bite, Pull Hair and Scratch': The Social Significance of Fighting in the Southern Backcountry." *American Historical Review* 90 (February 1985): 18–43.

Gould, Peter, and Rodney White. *Mental Maps.* Boston: Allen and Unwin, 1986.

Green, Lewis Warner. *Inaugural Address Delivered before the Board of Trustees of Hampden-Sydney College, January 10th, 1849.* Pittsburgh: Johnston and Stockton, 1849.

Greene, Evarts B., and Virginia D. Harrington. *American Population before the Federal Census of 1790.* New York: Columbia University Press, 1932.

Greene, Jack P. "Independence, Improvement, and Authority: Toward a Framework for Understanding the Histories of the Southern Backcountry during the Era of the American Revolution." In *An Uncivil War: The Southern Backcountry during the American Revolution,* edited by Ronald Hoffman, Thad W. Tate, and Peter J. Albert, 3–36. Charlottesville: University Press of Virginia, 1985.

Greene, Jack P., et al. "*Albion's Seed: Four British Folkways in America*—A Symposium." *William and Mary Quarterly* 48 (April 1991): 223–308.

Grele, Ronald J. "On Using Oral History Collections: An Introduction." *Journal of American History* 74 (September 1987): 570–78.

Hahn, Steven, and Jonathan Prude, eds. *The Countryside in the Age of Capitalist Transformation: Essays in the Social History of Rural America.* Chapel Hill: University of North Carolina Press, 1986.

Hall, Wade, ed. "Along the Wilderness Trail: A Young Lawyer's 1785 Letter from

Danville, Kentucky, to Massachusetts." *Filson Club History Quarterly* 61 (July 1987): 283–94.

Hall, William K. *The Shane Manuscript Collection.* Galveston, Tex.: Frontier Press, 1990.

Halttunen, Karen. *Confidence Men and Painted Women: A Study of Middle-Class Culture in America, 1830–1870.* New Haven, Conn.: Yale University Press, 1982.

Hammon, Neal O. "Settlers, Land Jobbers, and Outlyers: A Quantitative Analysis of Land Acquisition on the Kentucky Frontier." *Register of the Kentucky Historical Society* 84 (Summer 1986): 241–62.

——, ed. "The Journal of James Nourse, Jr., 1779–1780." *Filson Club History Quarterly* 47 (July 1973): 258–66.

Hammon, Neal O., and James Russell Harris, eds. " 'In a Dangerous Situation': Letters of Col. John Floyd, 1774–1783." *Register of the Kentucky Historical Society* 83 (Summer 1985): 202–36.

Harding, Margery Heberling. *George Rogers Clark and His Men: Military Records, 1778–1784.* Frankfort: Kentucky Historical Society, 1981.

Harley, J. B. "Maps, Knowledge, and Power." In *The Iconography of Landscape: Essays on the Symbolic Representation, Design, and Use of Past Environments,* edited by Denis Cosgrove and Stephen Daniels, 277–312. Cambridge: Cambridge University Press, 1988.

Harper, Josephine. *Guide to the Draper Manuscripts.* Madison: State Historical Society of Wisconsin, 1983.

Harrison, Lowell H. "A Virginian Moves to Kentucky, 1793." *William and Mary Quarterly* 15 (April 1958): 201–13.

——. *Kentucky's Road to Statehood.* Lexington: University Press of Kentucky, 1992.

Hatch, Nathan O. *The Democratization of American Christianity.* New Haven, Conn.: Yale University Press, 1989.

Henderson, A. Gwyn, Cynthia E. Jobe, and Christopher A. Turnbow. *Indian Occupation and Use in Northern and Eastern Kentucky during the Contact Period (1540–1795): An Initial Investigation.* Lexington: University of Kentucky, [1986].

——. "Dispelling the Myth: Seventeenth- and Eighteenth-Century Indian Life in Kentucky." *Register of the Kentucky Historical Society* 90 (Winter 1992): 1–25.

Henning, William Waller, ed. *The Statutes at Large: Being a Collection of All the Laws of Virginia, from the First Session of the Legislature, in the Year 1619.* 13 vols. Richmond, Va.: Samuel Pleasants, Jr., 1819–23.

Henretta, James A. "Social History as Lived and Written." *American Historical Review* 84 (December 1979): 1293–1322.

Hesseltine, William B., and Larry Gara. "Lyman C. Draper and the Shane Papers." *Filson Club History Quarterly* 27 (October 1953): 327–33.

Hinderaker, Eric. *Elusive Empires: Constructing Colonialism in the Ohio Valley, 1673–1800.* Cambridge: Cambridge University Press, 1997.

Hobsbawm, Eric, and Terence Ranger, eds. *The Invention of Tradition.* Cambridge: Cambridge University Press, 1983.

Hoffman, Ronald, Thad W. Tate, and Peter J. Albert, eds. *An Uncivil War: The Southern Backcountry during the American Revolution.* Charlottesville: University Press of Virginia, 1985.

Horsman, Reginald. *Race and Manifest Destiny: The Origins of American Racial Anglo-Saxonism.* Cambridge: Harvard University Press, 1981.

Howard, James H. *Shawnee! The Ceremonialism of a Native American Tribe and Its Cultural Background.* Athens: Ohio University Press, 1981.

Hubbard, S. G. *Catalogue of an Extensive Collection of Books, In Various Departments of Literature and Science: Being the Library of the Late Rev. John D. Shane....* Cincinnati: Cincinnati Gazette Printer, 1864.

Hunter, William A. "History of the Ohio Valley." In *Northeast*, edited by Bruce G. Trigger, 588–93. Vol. 15 of *Handbook of North American Indians.* Washington: Smithsonian Institution, 1978.

Imlay, Gilbert. *A Topographical Description of the Western Territory of North America.* 1792. Reprint. New York: Johnson Reprint Corporation, 1968.

Ireland, Robert M. *The County Courts in Antebellum Kentucky.* Lexington: University Press of Kentucky, 1972.

Isaac, Rhys. *The Transformation of Virginia, 1740–1790.* Chapel Hill: University of North Carolina Press, 1982.

Jackson, Peter. *Maps of Meaning: An Introduction to Cultural Geography.* London: Unwin Hyman, 1989.

Jakle, John A. *Images of the Ohio Valley: A Historical Geography of Travel, 1740–1860.* New York: Oxford University Press, 1977.

Janney, Abel. "Narrative of the Capture of Abel Janney by the Indians in 1782." *Ohio Archaeological and Historical Society Publications* 8 (1899–1900): 465–73.

Jennings, Francis. *The Invasion of America: Indians, Colonialism, and the Cant of Conquest.* New York: W. W. Norton, 1975.

———. "The Indians' Revolution." In *The American Revolution: Explorations in the History of American Radicalism*, edited by Alfred F. Young, 319–48. DeKalb: Northern Illinois University Press, 1976.

———. *The Ambiguous Iroquois Empire: The Covenant Chain Confederation of Indian Tribes with English Colonies from Its Beginnings to the Lancaster Treaty of 1744.* New York: W. W. Norton, 1984.

———. *Empire of Fortune: Crowns, Colonies, and Tribes in the Seven Years War in America.* New York: W. W. Norton, 1988.

Jennings, John. " 'Journal from Fort Pitt to Fort Chartres in the Illinois Country,' March–April, 1766." *Pennsylvania Magazine of History and Biography* 31 (1907): 145–56.

Jensen, Joan M., and Darlis A. Miller. "The Gentle Tamers Revisted: New Approaches to the History of Women in the American West." *Pacific Historical Review* 49 (May 1980): 173–213.

Jillson, Willard Rouse. *Filson's Kentucke.* Louisville, Ky.: John P. Morton, 1929.

———. *Pioneer Kentucky.* Frankfort, Ky.: State Journal Company, 1934.

Jones, David. *A Journal of Two Visits Made to Some Nations of Indians on the West*

Side of the River Ohio, in the Years 1772 and 1773. 1774. Reprint. New York: Joseph Sabin, 1865.

Jones, Maldwyn A. "The Scotch-Irish in British America." In *Strangers within the Realm: Cultural Margins of the First British Empire,* edited by Bernard Bailyn and Philip D. Morgan, 284–313. Chapel Hill: University of North Carolina Press, 1991.

Jordan, John W., ed. "Journal of James Kenny, 1761–1763." *Pennsylvania Magazine of History and Biography* 37 (1913): 1–47.

Keller, Kenneth W. "What Is Distinctive about the Scotch-Irish?" In *Appalachian Frontiers: Settlement, Society, and Development in the Preindustrial Era,* edited by Robert D. Mitchell, 69–86. Lexington: University Press of Kentucky, 1991.

Kett, Joseph F., and Patricia A. McClung. "Book Culture in Post-Revolutionary Virginia." *Proceedings of the American Antiquarian Society* 94 (April 1984): 97–105.

Klein, Rachel N. *Unification of a Slave State: The Rise of the Planter Class in the South Carolina Backcountry, 1760–1808.* Chapel Hill: University of North Carolina Press, 1990.

Klett, Guy Soulliard, ed., *Journals of Charles Beatty, 1762–1769.* University Park: Pennsylvania State University Press, 1962.

Kloppenberg, James T. "The Virtues of Liberalism: Christianity, Republicanism, and Ethics in Early American Political Discourse." *Journal of American History* 74 (June 1987): 9–33.

Klotter, James C. "Feuds In Appalachia: An Overview." *Filson Club History Quarterly* 56 (July 1982): 290–317.

———. *The Breckinridges of Kentucky, 1760–1981.* Lexington: University Press of Kentucky, 1986.

Knobel, Dale T. *Paddy and the Republic: Ethnicity and Nationality in Antebellum America.* Middletown, Conn.: Wesleyan University Press, 1986.

Kulikoff, Allan. *Tobacco and Slaves: The Development of Southern Cultures in the Chesapeake, 1680–1800.* Chapel Hill: University of North Carolina Press, 1986.

Lakoff, George, and Mark Johnson. *Metaphors We Live By.* Chicago: University of Chicago Press, 1980.

Landsman, Ned. *Scotland and Its First American Colony, 1683–1765.* Princeton, N.J.: Princeton University Press, 1985.

Lemon, James T. *The Best Poor Man's Country: A Geographical Study of Early Southeastern Pennsylvania.* New York: W. W. Norton, 1972.

Le Roy Ladurie, Emmanuel. *Montaillou: The Promised Land of Error.* New York: Random House, 1979.

Levine, Lawrence W. *Black Culture and Black Consciousness: Afro-American Folk Thought from Slavery to Freedom.* New York: Oxford University Press, 1977.

Limerick, Patricia Nelson. *The Legacy of Conquest: The Unbroken Past of the American West.* New York: W. W. Norton, 1987.

Linenthal, Edward Tabor. *Sacred Ground: Americans and Their Battlefields.* Urbana: University of Illinois Press, 1993.

Linenthal, Edward T., and Tom Engelhardt, eds. *History Wars: The Enola Gay and Other Battles for the American Past*. New York: Henry Holt, 1996.

Lofland, Lyn. *A World of Strangers: Order and Action in Urban Public Space*. New York: Basic Books, 1973.

Lowenthal, David. *The Past Is a Foreign Country*. Cambridge: Cambridge University Press, 1985.

Lowenthal, David, and Martyn J. Bowden, eds. *Geographies of the Mind: Essays in Historical Geosophy in Honor of John Kirtland Wright*. New York: Oxford University Press, 1976.

Lucas, Marion B. *From Slavery to Segregation, 1760–1891*. Vol. 1 of *A History of Blacks in Kentucky*. Frankfort: Kentucky Historical Society, 1992.

McClung, John A. *Sketches of Western Adventure Containing an Account of the Most Interesting Incidents Connected with the West, from 1755 to 1794*. Dayton, Ohio: Ells and Claflin, 1847.

McConnell, Michael. *A Country Between: The Upper Ohio Valley and Its Peoples, 1724–1774*. Lincoln: University of Nebraska Press, 1992.

McCoy, Drew. *The Elusive Republic: Political Economy in Jeffersonian America*. New York: W. W. Norton, 1982.

McDonald, Forrest, and Grady McWhiney. "The Antebellum Southern Herdsman: A Reinterpretation." *Journal of Southern History* 41 (May 1975): 147–66.

McHargue, J. S. "Canebrakes in Prehistoric and Pioneer Times in Kentucky." *Annals of Kentucky Natural History* 1 (September 1941): 1–13.

Macmaster, Richard K. "The Cattle Trade in Western Virginia, 1760–1830." In *Appalachian Frontiers: Settlement, Society, and Development in the Preindustrial Era*, edited by Robert D. Mitchell, 127–49. Lexington: University Press of Kentucky, 1991.

McNeil, Donald R., ed. *The American Collector*. Madison: State Historical Society of Wisconsin, 1955.

Malinowski, Bronislaw. *Argonauts of the Western Pacific: An Account of Native Enterprise and Adventure in the Archipelagoes of Melanesian New Guinea*. 1922. Reprint. Prospect Heights, Ill.: Waveland Press, 1984.

Mallory, Daniel. *The Life and Speeches of the Hon. Henry Clay*. Vol. 1. New York: Robert P. Bixby, 1843.

Malone, Patrick M. *The Skulking Way of War: Technology and Tactics among the New England Indians*. Baltimore, Md.: Johns Hopkins University Press, 1991.

Marcus, George E., and Michael M. J. Fischer. *Anthropology as Cultural Critique: An Experimental Moment in the Human Sciences*. Chicago: University of Chicago Press, 1986.

Marshall, H[umphrey]. *The History of Kentucky*. 2 vols. Frankfort, Ky.: George S. Robinson, 1824.

May, Henry F. *The Enlightenment in America*. New York: Oxford University Press, 1976.

Meek, Ronald L. *Social Science and the Ignoble Savage*. Cambridge: Cambridge University Press, 1976.

Meinig, D. W., *Atlantic America, 1492–1800*. Vol. 1 of *The Shaping of America: A Geographical Perspective on 500 Years of History*. New Haven, Conn.: Yale University Press, 1986.

———, ed. *The Interpretation of Ordinary Landscapes*. New York: Oxford University Press, 1979.

Merrell, James H. *The Indians' New World: Catawbas and Their Neighbors from European Contact through the Era of Removal*. Chapel Hill: University of North Carolina Press, 1989.

———. "Some Thoughts on Colonial Historians and American Indians." *William and Mary Quarterly* 66 (January 1989): 94–119.

———. " 'The Customes of Our Countrey': Indians and Colonists in Early America." In *Strangers within the Realm: Cultural Margins of the First British Empire*, edited by Bernard Bailyn and Philip D. Morgan, 117–56. Chapel Hill: University of North Carolina Press, 1991.

Michaux, Phyllis, ed. "Instructions from the Ohio Valley to French Emigrants." *Indiana Magazine of History* 84 (June 1988): 161–75.

Miller, Howard. *The Revolutionary College: American Presbyterian Higher Education, 1707–1837*. New York: New York University Press, 1976.

Milner, Clyde A. "The View from Wisdom: Four Layers of History and Regional Identity." In *Under an Open Sky: Rethinking America's Western Past*, edited by William Cronon, George Miles, and Jay Gitlin, 203–22. New York: W. W. Norton, 1992.

Mintz, Sidney W. *Sweetness and Power: The Place of Sugar in Modern History*. New York: Viking Penguin, 1985.

Mitchell, Robert D. *Commercialism and Frontier: Perspectives on the Early Shenandoah Valley*. Charlottesville: University Press of Virginia, 1977.

Monmonier, Mark. *How to Lie with Maps*. Chicago: University of Chicago Press, 1991.

Moore, Arthur K. *The Frontier Mind: A Cultural Analysis of the Kentucky Frontiersman*. Lexington: University Press of Kentucky, 1957.

Moore, Henrietta L. *Space, Text, and Gender: An Anthropological Study of the Marakwet of Kenya*. Cambridge: Cambridge University Press, 1986.

Morehead, James T. *An Address in Commemoration of the First Settlement of Kentucky: Delivered at Boonesborough the 25th of May, 1840*. Frankfort, Ky.: A. G. Hodges, 1840.

Morgan, Prys. "From a Death to a View: The Hunt for the Welsh Past in the Romantic Period." In *The Invention of Tradition*, edited by Eric Hobsbawm and Terence Ranger, 43–100. Cambridge: Cambridge University Press, 1983.

Nash, Gary B. "The Hidden History of Mestizo America." *Journal of American History* 82 (December 1995): 941–62.

Nash, Gary B., and Jean R. Soderlund. *Freedom by Degrees: Emancipation in Pennsylvania and Its Aftermath*. New York: Oxford University Press, 1991.

Nash, Roderick. *Wilderness and the American Mind*. New Haven, Conn.: Yale University Press, 1982.

Nelson, Paul David. "'Mad' Anthony Wayne and the Kentuckians of the 1790s." *Register of the Kentucky Historical Society* 84 (Winter 1986): 1–17.

Nissenbaum, Stephen. *The Battle for Christmas*. New York: Alfred A. Knopf, 1996.

Nobles, Gregory H. *Divisions throughout the Whole: Politics and Society in Hampshire County, Massachusetts, 1740–1775*. Cambridge: Cambridge University Press, 1983.

———. "Breaking into the Backcountry: New Approaches to the Early American Frontier." *William and Mary Quarterly* 46 (October 1989): 641–70.

———. "Straight Lines and Stability: Mapping the Political Order of the Anglo-American Frontier." *Journal of American History* 80 (June 1993): 9–35.

Norton, Mary Beth. "Gender and Defamation In Seventeenth-Century Maryland." *William and Mary Quarterly* 44 (January 1987): 3–39.

O'Malley, Nancy. *"Stockading Up": A Study of Pioneer Stations in the Inner Bluegrass Region of Kentucky*. Lexington, Ky.: Program for Cultural Resource Assessment, 1987.

Onuf, Peter S. *The Origins of the Federal Republic*. Philadelphia: University of Pennsylvania Press, 1983.

———. "Liberty, Development, and Union: Visions of the West in the 1780s." *William and Mary Quarterly* 43 (April 1986): 179–213.

Oppel, Mary Cronon. "Paradise Lost: The Story of Chaumiere Des Praries." *Filson Club History Quarterly* 56 (April 1982): 201–10.

Palmer, William P., et al., eds. *Calendar of Virginia State Papers and Other Manuscripts*. Richmond, Va.: Public Printer, 1875–93.

Perkins, Elizabeth A. "The Consumer Frontier: Household Consumption in Early Kentucky." *Journal of American History* 78 (September 1991): 486–510.

Pessen, Edward. "On a Recent Cliometric Attempt to Resurrect the Myth of Antebellum Egalitarianism." *Social Science History* 3 (Winter 1979): 208–27.

Polenberg, Richard. *One Nation Divisible: Class, Race, and Ethnicity in the United States since 1938*. New York: Penguin Books, 1980.

Portelli, Alessandro. *The Death of Luigi Trastulli and Other Stories: Form and Meaning in Oral History*. Albany: State University of New York Press, 1991.

Purvis, Thomas L. "The Ethnic Descent of Kentucky's Early Population: A Statistical Investigation of European and American Sources of Emigration, 1790–1820." *Register of the Kentucky Historical Society* 80 (Summer 1982): 253–66.

Pusey, William Allen. *The Wilderness Road to Kentucky: Its Location and Features*. New York: George H. Doran, 1921.

Radcliffe-Brown, A. R. "Preface." In *African Political Systems*, edited by M. Fortes and E. E. Evans-Pritchard, xi–xxiii. London: Oxford University Press, 1969.

Redd, John. "Reminiscences of Western Virginia." *Virginia Magazine of History and Biography* 6 (April 1899): 337–46.

Robertson, James Rood. *Petitions of the Early Inhabitants of Kentucky to the General Assembly of Virginia, 1769 to 1792*. Louisville, Ky.: John P. Morgan, 1914.

Roeber, A. G. "In German Ways? Problems and Potentials of Eighteenth-

Century German Social and Emigration History." *William and Mary Quarterly* 44 (October 1987): 750–74.

———. " 'The Origin of Whatever Is Not English among Us': The Dutch-Speaking and the German-Speaking Peoples of Colonial British America." In *Strangers within the Realm: Cultural Margins of the First British Empire,* edited by Bernard Bailyn and Philip D. Morgan, 220–83. Chapel Hill: University of North Carolina Press, 1991.

Rohrbough, Malcolm J. *The Trans-Appalachian Frontier: People, Societies, and Institutions, 1775–1850.* New York: Oxford University Press, 1978.

Roosevelt, Theodore. *The Winning of the West.* 6 vols. New York: Current Literature Publishing Co., 1905.

Rosaldo, Renato. "From the Door of His Tent: The Fieldworker and the Inquisitor." In *Writing Culture: The Poetics and Politics of Ethnography,* edited by James Clifford and George E. Marcus, 77–97. Berkeley: University of California Press, 1986.

Ross, Dorothy. "Grand Narrative in American Historical Writing: From Romance to Uncertainty." *American Historical Review* 100 (June 1995): 651–77.

Rothert, Otto A. "Shane, the Western Collector." *Filson Club History Quarterly* 4 (January 1930): 1–16.

Sahlins, Marshall D. "Poor Man, Rich Man, Big-Man, Chief: Political Types in Melanesia and Polynesia." *Comparative Studies in Society and History* 5 (April 1963): 285–303.

Sahlins, Peter. *Boundaries: The Making of France and Spain in the Pyrenees.* Berkeley: University of California Press, 1989.

Salstrom, Paul. "The Agricultural Origins of Economic Dependency, 1840–1880." In *Appalachian Frontiers: Settlement, Society, and Development in the Preindustrial Era,* edited by Robert D. Mitchell, 261–83. Lexington: University Press of Kentucky, 1991.

Schwartz, Douglas W. *Conceptions of Kentucky Prehistory: A Case Study in the History of Archaeology.* Lexington: University Press of Kentucky, 1967.

Scribner, Robert L., ed. *Revolutionary Virginia, the Road to Independence: A Documentary Record.* 7 vols. Charlottesville: University Press of Virginia, 1973–83.

Secor, Robert. "Ethnic Humor in Early American Jest Books." In *A Mixed Race: Ethnicity in Early America,* edited by Frank Shuffelton, 163–93. New York: Oxford University Press, 1993.

Shalhope, Robert E. "Republicanism and Early American Historiography." *William and Mary Quarterly* 39 (April 1982): 334–56.

———. *The Roots of Democracy: American Thought and Culture, 1760–1800.* Boston: G. K. Hall, 1990.

Shane, J. D. *The Bush in the Flame: A Sketch of the Immigrant Church.* Cincinnati: John D. Thorpe, 1858.

[———]. "The Henderson Company Ledger." *Filson Club History Quarterly* 21 (January 1947): 22–48.

Shy, John. *A People Numerous and Armed: Reflections on the Military Struggle for American Independence*. New York: Oxford University Press, 1976.

Slaughter, Thomas P. *The Whiskey Rebellion: Frontier Epilogue to the American Revolution*. New York: Oxford University Press, 1986.

Smith, Alice E. "The Draper Manuscripts." In *The American Collector*, edited by Donald R. McNeil, 45–61. Madison: State Historical Society of Wisconsin, 1955.

Smith, Bonnie G. "Gender and the Practices of Scientific History: The Seminar and Archival Research in the Nineteenth Century." *American Historical Review* 100 (October 1995): 1150–76.

Smith, James. "Tours into Kentucky and the Northwest Territory." *Ohio Archaeological and Historical Society Publications* 16 (1907): 349–401.

Sollors, Werner, ed. *The Invention of Ethnicity*. New York: Oxford University Press, 1989.

Soltow, Lee. "Kentucky Wealth at the End of the Eighteenth Century." *Journal of Economic History* 43 (September 1983): 617–33.

Speed, Thomas. *The Wilderness Road*. Louisville, Ky.: John P. Morton, 1886.

Staples, Charles R. *History of Pioneer Lexington, 1779–1806*. Lexington, Ky.: Transylvania Press, 1939.

Still, Bayrd, ed. "The Westward Migration of a Planter Pioneer in 1796." *William and Mary Quarterly* 21 (October 1941): 318–43.

Stone, Richard G., Jr. *A Brittle Sword: The Kentucky Militia, 1776–1912*. Lexington, Ky.: University Press of Kentucky, 1977.

Sydnor, Charles S. *Gentlemen Freeholders: Political Practices in Washington's Virginia*. Chapel Hill: University of North Carolina Press, 1952.

Tachau, Mary K. Bonsteel. "The Whiskey Rebellion in Kentucky: A Forgotten Episode of Civil Disobedience." *Journal of the Early Republic* 2 (Fall 1982): 239–59.

Talbert, Charles Gano. *Benjamin Logan: Kentucky Frontiersman*. Lexington: University Press of Kentucky, 1962.

Tanner, Helen Hornbeck, ed. *Atlas of Great Lakes Indian History*. Norman: University of Oklahoma Press, 1987.

——. "The Land and Water Communication Systems of the Southeastern Indians." In *Powhatan's Mantle: Indians in the Colonial Southeast*, edited by Peter H. Wood, Gregory A. Waselkov, and M. Thomas Hatley, 6–20. Lincoln: University of Nebraska Press, 1989.

Taylor, Alan. *Liberty Men and Great Proprietors: The Revolutionary Settlement on the Maine Frontier, 1760–1820*. Chapel Hill: University of North Carolina Press, 1990.

Teute, Fredrika Johanna. "Land, Liberty, and Labor in the Post-Revolutionary Era: Kentucky as the Promised Land." Ph.D. diss., Johns Hopkins University, 1988.

Thelen, David. "Memory and American History." *Journal of American History* 75 (March 1989): 1117–29.

Tillson, Albert H., Jr. "The Southern Backcountry: A Survey of Current Research." *Virginia Magazine of History and Biography* 98 (July 1990): 387–422.

——. *Gentry and Common Folk: Political Culture on a Virginia Frontier, 1740–1789.* Lexington: University Press of Kentucky, 1991.

Tivers, Jacqueline. "How the Other Half Lives: The Geographical Study of Women." *Area* 10 (1978): 302–6.

Tolzman, Don Heinrich, ed. *The First Description of Cincinnati and Other Ohio Settlements: The Travel Report of Johann Heckewelder (1792).* Lanham, Md.: University Press of America, 1988.

Tuan, Yi-Fu. *Topophilia: A Study of Environmental Perception, Attitudes, and Values.* Englewood Cliffs, N.J.: Prentice-Hall, 1974.

——. *Landscapes of Fear.* New York: Pantheon Books, 1979.

——. "Thought and Landscape: The Eye and the Mind's Eye." In *The Interpretation of Ordinary Landscapes,* edited by D. W. Meinig, 89–102. New York: Oxford University Press, 1979.

Turner, Frederick Jackson. *The Frontier in American History.* 1920. Reprint. Tuscon: University of Arizona Press, 1986.

Tuttle, William M., Jr. *"Daddy's Gone to War": The Second World War in the Lives of America's Children.* New York: Oxford University Press, 1993.

Union Theological Seminary. *Plan of the Union Theological Seminary of the General Assembly, under the Care of the Synods of Virginia and North-Carolina; With a Brief Sketch of Its History.* Richmond, Va.: J. Macfarlan, 1831.

——. *Catalogue of the Officers and Students of the Union Theological Seminary in Prince Edward Co., Virginia from 1824 to 1848.* New York: Joseph H. Jennings, 1848.

U.S. Bureau of the Census. *A Century of Population Growth from the First Census of the United States to the Twelfth, 1790–1900.* Washington: Government Printing Office, 1909.

——. *Seventh Census: 1850.* Washington: Robert Armstrong, 1853.

Usner, Daniel H. *Indians, Settlers, and Slaves in a Frontier Exchange Economy: The Lower Mississippi Valley before 1783.* Chapel Hill: University of North Carolina Press, 1992.

Vansina, Jan. *Oral Tradition as History.* Madison: University of Wisconsin Press, 1985.

Vogt, Evon Z., and Ethel M. Albert, eds. *People of Rimrock: A Study of Values in Five Cultures.* Cambridge: Harvard University Press, 1967.

Wallace, Anthony F. C. *The Death and Rebirth of the Seneca.* New York: Random House, 1972.

Watlington, Patricia. *The Partisan Spirit: Kentucky Politics, 1779–1792.* Chapel Hill: University of North Carolina Press, 1972.

Watson, Harry L. *Liberty and Power: The Politics of Jacksonian America.* New York: Noonday Press, 1990.

Weaks, Mabel Claire. *Calendar of the Kentucky Papers of the Draper Collection of Manuscripts.* Madison: State Historical Society of Wisconsin, 1925.

Weeks, Louis B. *Kentucky Presbyterians*. Atlanta: John Knox Press, 1983.

Weissbach, Lee Shai. "The Peopling of Lexington, Kentucky: Growth and Mobility in a Frontier Town." *Register of the Kentucky Historical Society* 81 (Spring 1983): 115–33.

Whitaker, Arthur Preston. *The Spanish-American Frontier: 1783–1795*. 1927. Reprint. Lincoln: University of Nebraska Press, 1969.

White, Hayden. *Metahistory: The Historical Imagination in Nineteenth-Century Europe*. Baltimore, Md.: Johns Hopkins University Press, 1973.

White, Richard. *The Middle Ground: Indians, Empires, and Republics in the Great Lakes Region, 1650–1815*. Cambridge: Cambridge University Press, 1991.

Whitrow, G. J. *Time in History: Views of Time from Prehistory to the Present Day*. Oxford: Oxford University Press, 1988.

Wiebe, Robert H. *The Segmented Society: An Introduction to the Meaning of America*. New York: Oxford University Press, 1975.

——. *The Opening of American Society: From the Adoption of the Constitution to the Eve of Disunion*. New York: Alfred A. Knopf, 1984.

Wilcox, Donald J. *The Measure of Times Past: Pre-Newtonian Chronologies and the Rhetoric of Relative Time*. Chicago: University of Chicago Press, 1987.

Wood, Gordon. "Interests and Disinterestedness in the Making of the Constitution." In *Beyond Confederation: Origins of the Constitution and American National Identity*, edited by Richard Beeman, Stephen Botein, and Edward C. Carter II, 69–109. Chapel Hill: University of North Carolina Press, 1987.

——. *The Radicalism of the American Revolution*. New York: Alfred A. Knopf, 1992.

Worster, Donald. "Transformations of the Earth: Toward an Agroecological Perspective in History." *Journal of American History* 76 (March 1990): 1087–1106.

Wrong, Dennis H. *Power: Its Forms, Bases, and Uses*. Chicago: University of Chicago Press, 1988.

Wyatt-Brown, Bertram. *Southern Honor: Ethics and Behavior in the Old South*. New York: Oxford University Press, 1982.

Young, Chester Raymond, ed. *Westward into Kentucky: The Narrative of Daniel Trabue*. Lexington: University Press of Kentucky, 1981.

Zelinsky, Wilbur. "Where the South Begins: The Northern Limit of the Cis-Appalachian South in Terms of Settlement Landscape." *Social Forces* 30 (December 1951): 172–78.

Index

Boone, Susan (Susannah, Suzy), 26, 145, 220 (n. 63)
Boone and Callaway kidnapping, 38, 69, 93, 153
Boonesborough, Ky.: construction of fortifications, 63, 64; Indian siege of, 88, 97, 142–43, 158; housing in, 101; ethnic population, 114–15; claimed as first settlement in state, 151, 152; fear of Indians in, 161
Border war (1774–94), 14, 123–24, 167–68; and construction of stations, 62–63; and militia companies, 124; violence of, 136–37; seasonality of, 158–59; Northwest Ordinance and, 162
Bouquet's Campaign, 196
Bourbon County, Ky., 101, 168
Bowman, John, 64, 71, 164
Bowman's expedition, 131
Boyd, William, 62
Boyle, Stephen, 137
Braddock's Campaign, 123
Bradford, John, 169
Breckinridge, John, 55, 71, 122
Brissot de Warville, Jacques-Pierre, 160
Brock, Tice, 97, 142–43
Brookey, John, 198
Brooks, Abijah, 104
Brown, John, 196
Bryan's (Bryant's) Station, 68, 147; roads to, 74–75; residents of, 114; siege of, 114, 137
Buck, Colonel, 60
Buckingham, Levi, 65
Buffalo hunting, 77, 95, 99, 167
Buffalo traces, 75, 76
Bullit's Lick, 81
Burke, Richard, 97
Butler, Mrs., 101
Buttermilk, 105, 214 (n. 49)

Callaway, Betsy, 69
Callaway, Jack, 171

Callaway, Mrs., 142–43
Callaway, Richard, 153
Campbell, Billy, 199
Campbell, Daniel, 198
Campbell, Hugh, 200
Canada, 149
Canebrakes, 74, 77
Cane Ridge, Ky., 22
"Cappo," 89
Carolina emigrants, 103
Carr's Creek Massacres, 196, 197
Cassidy (Cassiday), Michael (captain), 146, 172–73
Cattle raising, 109
Census of 1790, 54, 83, 84, 120
Census of 1850, 148
Charles II (king of England), 221 (n. 12)
Cherokee Indians, 11–12, 69, 109, 144–45; land cessions, 13; Chickamauga, 139
Chickasaw Indians, 11–12
Children, 31; and Indian attacks, 68, 69–70, 90, 137
Chillicothe expedition, 131
Chocolate drinking, 110
Choctaw Indians, 93
Cincinnati, Ohio, 66, 169
Cincinnati Historical Society, 177
Civil disobedience, 118
Clark, George Rogers, 65, 91
Clark County, Ky., 168; courthouse, 142
Clark's Campaign (1782), 92
Clark's expedition (1780), 159
Clark's Vincennes expedition (1779), 131
Clay, Green, 134
Clay, Henry, 148–50
Cleveland, Eli, 99–100
Clinkenbeard, Isaac, 127, 157, 161, 167, 222 (n. 22)
Clinkenbeard, William, 113; Shane's interview with, 25; settlement in Kentucky, 35, 76, 161, 167; on In-

dian attacks, 73, 76, 94, 158; on native vegetation, 74; on buffalo hunting, 77; on Indian clothing, 89, 92; as militiaman, 92, 130; on ethnic differences, 96, 104, 213 (n. 33); on Tory settlers, 103; on Indian food, 107; on wolf baiting, 135

Clothing, 87–92, 94

"Cohees," 84–85, 106

Collins, Josiah, 96–97, 105, 158; on Boone's children, 26; Shane's interview with, 26–27, 28; on salt licks, 75; as militiaman, 131

Collins, Lewis: *Historical Sketches of Kentucky*, 134, 167, 168, 223 (n. 34)

Columbia, Ohio, 66

Combs, Cuthbert, 135, 173

"Coming out," 60

Communal ties, 113–14

Conservatism, cultural, 95, 212–13 (n. 28)

Constant's Station, 72, 78, 93

Corn cultivation, 157–58

"Corn-right" farms, 222 (n. 22)

Cornwallis, Charles, first marquis, 160

Cosby, Zacharias, 15

County governments, 120

Courthouses, 164–65

Courts, 120

Covalt, Abraham, 158

Covalt's Station, 65

Crab Orchard, 62

Craig, John, 70, 127, 197

Craig, Lewis, 107, 113, 127

Craig's Station, 161, 167

Crawford, Alexander, 97

Crawford, John, 34, 54, 76

Cresswell, Nicholas, 87–88, 90, 94

Crèvecoeur, Hector St. John de: on backcountry settlers, 1, 82, 117, 122; on Ohio River, 10, 46; travels through Ohio Valley, 41–42, 43, 52, 79; on Louisville, 42, 56

Crockett, Davy, 145

Crouch, David, 53, 61, 70, 73, 136, 157

Crouch, Mrs. David, 52–53

Crouch, Jonathan, 136

Cultural differences, 82–83, 85–86, 87, 95

Cunningham, Hugh, 96

Dale, Abraham, 124

Daniel, Jesse, 169, 173

Darnaby, Ned, 61

Davidson, Robert: *History of the Presbyterian Church in Kentucky*, 223 (n. 34)

Delaware Indians, 11–12, 29, 102; land cessions, 13; militia attacks on, 14

Deron, Daniel, 62

Dewees, Mary, 87, 100–101, 105

Dickerson, William, 93

Downing's Station, 161

Drake, Daniel, 162–63, 170; on Indian attacks, 32–33, 69–70, 73; on Maryland emigrants, 103; on food and drink, 105, 106; on white population decline, 147–48

Draper, Lyman Copeland, 18; antiquarian research, 8, 28, 38, 153, 154–55, 169; acquisition of Shane's manuscripts, 15, 19, 177; Shane and, 36; annotation of Shane's notebooks, 154–55, 195–96

Draper Collection, 2

Dunmore's War, 13, 14

Dunnoway, Benjamin, 222 (n. 22)

Dutch immigrants, 97–98, 99, 213 (n. 33)

Dutch Station, 41

Dyal, John, 41–42, 43, 58, 63, 68, 78

Economic standing, 34–36; inequality of wealth, 83, 147, 207–8 (n. 29)

Edmiston, Robert, 198

Education, 16, 17

Edward's Campaign, 131–32

Elections, 148–49; presidential, of 1840, 20

Elliott, Colonel, 90

McConnell, Alexander, 96–97, 199–200

McConnell, Frances, 198

McConnell, James, 33–34

McConnell, William (captain), 200

McConnell, William (of McConnell's Station), 198, 199

McConnell's Station, 198

McCutchen, Rachel, 68

McCutchen, William, 158

McDowell, Colonel, 132

McDowell, Samuel, 35

McElwaine, Moses, 199

McGary, Hugh, 136, 168

McIlvaine, James, 171

McKinney, John ("Wildcat"), 36, 197

McKinney, Levisa Whitley, 139, 144

McMullen, James, 94

McMullin (legislator), 146

McQueen, Joshua, 77, 91, 108–9, 131, 147

Madison, James, 121

Madoc legend, 72

Malinowski, Bronislaw, 23

"Manifest destiny," 12, 166

Maps, 47–50

Marietta, Ohio, 66

Marshall, Humphrey, 148; *History of Kentucky*, 169

Maryland emigrants, 29, 103

Mason and Dixon Line, 46

Massie's Station, 66

Masterson's Station, 68, 137, 161

Mayslick, Ky., 104, 114, 125, 147

Meade, David, 93, 101–2, 105

Memoirs, 169–70

Metcalfe, Thomas, 74, 137, 148

Metes and bounds surveys, 50, 120

Métis, 93

Metsigemewa (Shawnee), 110

Miami Indians, 11–12, 14, 29

Migrants, 54–55; cultural diversity of, 3, 82–83, 95; origins in eastern states, 12, 29, 104; information on western lands, 55, 56–60; and

"promised land" myth, 55–56, 59; militiamen, 58; and Indian attacks, 58–59, 60–61, 104, 160–61; "coming out," 60; routes of travel, 60, 61–62; construction of stations, 62–64; cultural conservatism of, 95, 212–13 (n. 28); family units, 112–13; and land claims, 122–23; seasonal variations, 156–57; Revolutionary War and, 160. *See also* Settlers, backcountry

Militia companies: service in, and western settlement, 58; clothing, 88; universal service in, 99, 124, 217 (n. 16); guerrilla warfare tactics, 124, 131; officers and leadership, 130–32, 138–40, 148

Milligan, Jim, 196

Milner, Clyde A., II, 205 (n. 41)

Mingo Bottom, 79

Mingo Indians, 11–12, 29

Missionaries, 109

Mississippi River, 10, 72

Monongahela River, 10, 46, 60

Montgomery County, Ky., 168

Moore, William, 36

Moore's Station, 143

Moravian Indians, 96

Morehead, James T., 152

Morgan, Abel, 35

Morgan, David, 136

Morgan, Ralph, 127–28

Morgan's Station, 154, 168

Morris, James, 113–14

Morrison, Mrs., 73, 86

Moseby, Nicholas, 113, 126

Moseby, William, 69, 123

Mound building, 71–72

Mountain laurel, 207 (n. 23)

Mountain ranges, 44, 50

Munsee Indians, 29

Mush, 106–7

Myers, Jacob, 134

Natchez, Miss., 91

Nationalism, 4, 5, 173

Rankins, John, 25–26, 75, 156, 161
"Ready Money Jack," 38, 104
Records, Spencer, 63, 89–90, 96, 98, 132–33, 169
Redd, John, 93
"Redstone country," 46, 54
Regional stereotypes, 103, 104
Religious beliefs, 33, 107
Revolutionary War, 3–4; and war against Indians, 14, 102, 160, 168; nostalgia for heroes of, 20, 22, 23; and political organizations, 121; and westward migration, 160. *See also* American Revolution
Rice, David, 23–24
Richardson, Marcus, 60, 171
Ridout, Thomas, 110
Risk, William, 127, 134–35, 172
Rivers, 46, 47, 50–51
Rodgers, John, 147
Roeber, A. G., 213 (n. 33)
Roosevelt, Theodore, 202 (n. 3)
Ross, Angus, 105
Runnells, Captain, 60, 100
Rupard, John, 92, 129–30, 131–32
Rush, Benjamin, 117

Sahlins, Marshall, 140
St. Clair's Shame, 124, 160–61
"Salt licks," 75
Salt packing, 34–35, 81
Sandusky (Wyandot town), 90
Scalping, 136
Scearcy, Dick, 68
Schoolteachers, 36
Schull (Scholl), Septimus, 28, 152
Scioto River, 11
Scotch-Irish immigrants, 29, 100, 126, 213 (n. 30)
Scott, Charles, 21, 123, 139, 146
Scott, Daniel, 69
Scott, Patrick, 54, 59
Scott County, Ky., 161
Scottish Enlightenment, 16, 28, 117
Scottish immigrants, 29, 83, 96, 174; Puritans, 221 (n. 12)

Seneca Indians, 11–12
Serviceberries, 53, 207 (n. 22)
"Settlements, interior," 52, 60
Settlers, backcountry: stereotypes of, 1, 5, 8, 117; Shane's interviews with, 2, 7–9, 14, 22; demographics, 28–34; economic standing, 34–36; construction of stations, 62–64. *See also* Migrants
"Settling out," 67–68, 78, 161
Seven Years' War, 13
Shane, Charles Grandison, 15
Shane, Henry, 15
Shane, John, 15
Shane, Rev. John Dabney: upbringing and education, 15–16; sermons and missionary activities, 17; and historical interpretation, 17, 27, 28, 166, 174–75; library, 17–18, 19; *illus.*, 18; death of, 19; historical scrapbooks, 19, 20–22; elected to Wisconsin Historical Society, 36
—interviews with westerners, 2, 14, 44; and Indians, 3, 29, 174; collection process, 7, 8–10, 22–28, 36–38; "Historical Collections," 22, 24, 33, 177; "Collections in Church History," 22, 177; and oral history, 24, 27, 170; demographics of informants, 28–31, 32–34; and dates, 38, 154–55; and migrants' information sources, 57; and language use, 96; and "small" politics, 118, 132; and border warfare, 167–68
Shane, Mary Cosby, 15
Shanklin, Mrs., 27, 89, 156
Shanklin, Robert, 156
Shawnee Indians, 11–12, 29, 70, 102; land cessions, 13; warfare with white settlers, 13–14, 107, 131, 136, 159; white captives of, 69, 76, 91, 92; hospitality to whites, 92, 109; ethnic identity, 92–93; war chiefs, 140–41
Shawnee Run, 76, 79
Shelby (Shelbyville), Ky., 56

Trails, 74–75
Transylvania Company, 119, 151
Travelers' accounts, 3, 43, 45–46, 51–52, 57
Treasury warrants, 120–21
Trickster tales, 133–34
Trumbo, George, 76–77
Tuan, Yi-Fu, 43
"Tuckahoes," 84, 85, 106
Turner, Frederick Jackson: and Shane's interviews, 15; frontier thesis, 79, 83, 146–47, 174, 202 (n. 3)
Tygart's Valley, 53
Tyler, William, 159, 222 (n. 17)

Union Theological Seminary, 16

Van Buren, Martin, 20
Vancouver, Charles, 128–29
Vanmetre, Jacob, 113
Vincennes expedition, 131
Virginia: Indian commissioners, 13–14, 102; emigrants from, 29, 84–85, 102–3, 122; western land claims, 46, 58; administration of Kentucky country, 58, 119–20; gentlemen in, 100; separation of Kentucky from, 118, 119; and western land sales, 119, 120–21, 122; militia law, 124, 217 (n. 16); slaveholding in, 214 (n. 44)
Virginia General Assembly, 119, 120
Virgin soil epidemics, 12
Voting rights, 148

Wade, James, 75, 215 (n. 64); and religion, 33; birth of, 52; westward migration, 54, 62, 128; on Indians, 71, 76, 77, 88; on white colonization, 77; and hunting, 132–33
Watkins, Captain, 142
Wayne, Anthony, 130–31, 161, 168–69
Wea Indians, 14, 29
Western country, 10; white settlement

of, 14, 55; travelers' accounts of, 43, 44, 45, 57; boundaries of, 44, 45–46, 50; Indian-white border, 47; "promised land" mythology, 55–56, 59; "in and out" metaphors, 78
Wheeling, W.Va., 7
Whig Party, 20
Whiskey tax, 118
White, Mrs., 98
Whitesides, John, 137
Whitley, Esther, 139, 144–45, 146
Whitley, Levisa, 139, 144
Whitley, William, 90, 124, 139–40, 144–45, 159, 169
Wickersham's Station, 158
Wilderness, 45–46, 61–62
Wilderness Road, 34
Wilderness trace, 61, 62
Wiley, Jenny, 129
Wilkinson, James, 107
Williams, Caleb, 112, 169
Williams, Samuel, 113
Wilson, John, 100, 161–62
Wilson Station, 121
Winchester, Ky., 164, 165
Wisconsin State Historical Society, 2, 15, 36, 177
Wolf baiting, 135–36
Wolf Creek, 66
Women, 91, 141, 142–46; Shane's interviews with, 29; and Indian attacks, 68–69
Wood, Benjamin, 163–64
Wood, Joseph, 163
Woodford County, Ky., 164–65, 168, 195
Woods, Hannah, 144
Woods, Jimmy, 197
Works Progress Administration, 31–32
Wyandot Indians, 69, 75, 126
Wymore, Martin, 36, 73, 127

Yocum, George, 34–35, 52, 91–92
Young, Joe, 171